T0313733

Dangerous Opportunities

DANGEROUS OPPORTUNITIES

THE FUTURE OF FINANCIAL INSTITUTIONS, HOUSING POLICY, AND GOVERNANCE

EDITED BY STEPHANIE BEN-ISHAI

UNIVERSITY OF TORONTO PRESS
Toronto Buffalo London

Rotman-UTP Publishing
An imprint of University of Toronto Press
Toronto Buffalo London
utorontopress.com

Library and Archives Canada Cataloguing in Publication

Title: Dangerous opportunities : the future of financial institutions, housing
    policy, and governance / edited by Stephanie Ben-Ishai
Names: Ben-Ishai, Stephanie, editor.
Description: Includes bibliographical references and index.
Identifiers: Canadiana (print) 20210162554 | Canadiana (ebook) 20210162821 |
    ISBN 9781487506087 (cloth) | ISBN 9781487533267 (PDF) | ISBN
    9781487533274 (EPUB)
Subjects: LCSH: Financial institutions – Canada. | LCSH: Financial
    institutions – Law and legislation – Canada. | LCSH: Housing policy –
    Canada. | LCSH: Corporate governance – Canada.
Classification: LCC HG185.C2 D36 2021 | DDC 332.10971 – dc23

ISBN 978-1-4875-0608-7 (cloth)   ISBN 978-1-4875-3327-4 (EPUB)
                                     ISBN 978-1-4875-3326-7 (PDF)

We acknowledge the financial support of the Government of Canada, the
Canada Council for the Arts, and the Ontario Arts Council, an agency of the
Government of Ontario, for our publishing activities.

Canada Council Conseil des Arts
for the Arts   du Canada

ONTARIO ARTS COUNCIL
CONSEIL DES ARTS DE L'ONTARIO
an Ontario government agency
un organisme du gouvernement de l'Ontario

Funded by the   Financé par le
Government   gouvernement
of Canada   du Canada

Contents

Acknowledgments

This book and "surviving" this pandemic would not have been possible without the support of a small number of friends and family. I am especially grateful to Poonam, a contributor to this book, for our daily calls, full of ideas, laughs, and energy to push ahead. My mother, Ilana, has found some way to help me with almost everything I have ever done and imbued in me a way of looking at the world that allows me to carry on through crises. I appreciate her now more than ever, as I struggle to parent through a tough year, with no end in sight. My son, Larry, is my true joy. He gives me meaning, light, and encouragement, and I am so delighted that he shares my passion for the written word.

I am grateful to my students, past and present, for their questions, warmth, and excitement for areas that sometimes feel "old" to me. I've learned from and appreciated them so much more through this year than ever before. In particular, I am indebted to Mandy Bedford, who is now a lawyer but had a significant role in helping at the early stages of this book. More recently, I am grateful to Erin Bertens who has helped with the final stages of this book project. Both Mandy and Erin are brilliant women who I hope will play significant roles in helping shape our post-pandemic economic recovery.

Stephanie Ben-Ishai

The Shaky Foundations of the Home Capital Crisis

*Stephanie Ben-Ishai**

Home Capital was never supposed to be the source of a potential financial crisis.

The savings and lending company had been in operation since 1986, and reached $1 billion in assets only in 2001.[1] This relatively minor player in the mortgage market is far removed from the big five financial institutions, which together control 80% of the Canadian banking sector and have been in business in various forms since before Confederation.[2] In 2017, Home Capital held less than $20 billion in mortgages, where the biggest banks held more than $1.1 trillion.[3] Why was it, then, that by April 2017, policy-makers, market analysts, academics, and commentators alike were convinced that this relatively small lender would trigger the next recession in Canada?

The story became even more improbable when the source of Home Capital's troubles was revealed. A few years earlier, Home Capital learned that several of its mortgage brokers had been falsifying income information on mortgage applications.[4] After launching an internal investigation, nicknamed Project Trillium, Home Capital fired forty-five brokers and stepped up its internal controls over underwriting.[5] Problems arose, however, when Home Capital

---

* Professor and Distinguished Research Professor at Osgoode Hall Law School

failed to notify the Ontario Securities Commission (OSC), the primary regulator, about this investigation and misrepresented the causes of the decline in its new mortgage originations in its quarterly filings.[6] All companies that trade shares on Canadian stock exchanges must make timely disclosure of all "material facts."[7] Essentially, this means that if information about the corporation could significantly affect the trading price of the security, it must be made public.[8] The investigation was not included in Home Capital's disclosures to the OSC, nor was it disclosed to its investors.[9]

The OSC eventually learned of the investigation through a whistleblower memo prepared by a Home Capital employee in mid-2015.[10] By the time the OSC issued enforcement notices related to the non-disclosure in March 2017, Home Capital had already updated its corporate governance framework,[11] completed an audit of any mortgages linked to those brokers who engaged in misconduct, and had undergone staffing changes, including the replacement of the chief executive officer.[12] Despite the audit revealing that the mortgages arising from the falsified applications were low risk and were being serviced by the borrowers, the OSC's announcement triggered a collapse of Home Capital's share price.[13] For example, Home Capital's shares lost 65% of their value in a single day in April 2017.[14]

More concerningly for Home Capital was its stark drop in deposits. After the OSC's allegations were made public, 95%, or $600 million, of the deposits in high-interest savings accounts were pulled from the company.[15] Home Capital, like all banks and lending institutions, keeps a small portion of deposits on hand, and lends out the rest to other customers. With a smaller capital base, Home Capital was unable to offer new mortgages, which further damaged its share price.[16] "An ordinary compliance action [had] morphed into a full-scale liquidity crisis."[17]

Home Capital's challenges quickly spread throughout the alternative mortgage market. Its competitor, Equitable Bank, saw its share price drop more than 25% over fears that it would be the next institution to run into trouble.[18] Genworth and Street Capital also saw declines in their share prices.[19] Suddenly, a regulatory enforcement action against a relatively well-performing company, in a sector with a low rate of default, was threatening to take down the Canadian economy.[20] Experts raised concerns over the potential for economy-wide contagion effects and the risk that turbulence in the financial system could lead to a significant reduction in real economic activity, much like what was experienced during the global financial crisis years earlier.

This book arose from conversations between internationally recognized legal experts that began during the height of the crisis. Our expertise has a very wide ambit, encompassing topics such as bankruptcy, corporate governance, pensions, securities regulation, and tax. While Home Capital's story ultimately had a "happy ending," we quickly realized that the problems highlighted by this episode are likely to persist into the next financial crisis. Furthermore, the resolution of this affair raised additional questions about the context surrounding the mortgage lending industry and corporate governance, which merited further exploration. This book is our response to these questions.

At the time of drafting, the authors could not have predicted that this book would near completion in the context of one of the worst global economic outlooks in generations. The virus that triggered a localized shock in China is now truly global, directly affecting almost every country in the world. Presently, the duration, scope, and consequences of the pandemic are largely unknown. There is a palpable threat that the liquidity problems currently experienced by households and businesses will lead to a chain reaction of non-performing loans, insolvencies, and bankruptcies, sending the global economy into a tailspin of financial and economic crises. As the economic damage stemming from the COVID-19 pandemic continues to evolve and escalate in countries throughout the world, it is unlikely that financial institutions or mortgage markets will be spared. It is important that academics, practitioners, and governments carefully consider and discuss the best ways to weather this economic storm. This discussion must be informed by the hard-earned lessons from past crises such as the Home Capital saga if we are to achieve a more successful and resilient recovery. This book is our contribution to this conversation.

Using Home Capital as the starting point, the chapters of this book will highlight often-overlooked perspectives at the intersection of the law and business scholarship. It will question the compartmentalization of financial regulators, compare our regime to the American framework, explore the enhanced role in corporate governance played by pension funds, examine the continuous disclosure regime and board independence, and provide an integrated approach to tax and housing policy. While each chapter addresses an element of the Home Capital story, the diverse topics covered mean that chapters can be read in conjunction or on their own.

The book begins with an exploration of the central contributor to Home Capital's troubles: the company's failure to disclose Project Trillium and its responses to it. What emerged from the OSC's Statement of Allegations was the apparent choice by the company's management to hide or obfuscate the investigation through vague language.[21] Home Capital, as a publicly traded company, was required to disclose the investigation to its investors and the market since it was a "material fact." Poonam Puri puts the disclosure regime in the context of the principles-based system of regulation adopted by Canada's securities regulators and explores how this system intersects with private actions such as class action suits. To ensure the good governance of publicly traded companies, she argues that independent directors are essential, but not sufficient. As Home Capital's experience illustrates, even a more diverse than average board of directors following industry best practices can still ignore red flags. Puri takes this example to call for more diversity on corporate boards, and more robust standards of independence for directors.

The book then moves on to examine the role that the Healthcare Pension Plan of Ontario (HOOPP) played in supporting Home

Capital. HOOPP was the first player to aid Home Capital by offering a $2 billion line of credit.[22] Though the line of credit was an important element in re-stabilizing Home Capital, questions were raised about why its competitor, Equitable Group, was able to receive a similar loan on "significantly [less] onerous" terms than Home Capital's.[23] One explanation, both for the availability of the loan and for its terms, could be the overlap in board membership. In 2017, the chief executive officer of HOOPP sat on Home Capital's board of directors, and the chair of Home Capital's board also served on the board of HOOPP.[24] Simon Archer argues that these overlapping relationships, rather than acting as a source of conflict, served as an informal mechanism to manage the wider systemic effects that would be caused by the mortgage lender failing. Through tracing the "Canadian model" of pension fund governance and investment, he finds that HOOPP's intervention in Home Capital was consistent with earlier actions taken to ensure good governance of publicly traded corporations. Even HOOPP's seemingly novel role as a promoter of wider market integrity appears less so when other examples of pension fund intercession in a crisis are considered.

Home Capital's main source of business is non-prime mortgages, also known as the much-maligned subprime mortgage. The traditional narrative is that these financial instruments were lent to borrowers with an incomplete understanding of the terms of their new loans, leading to an unexpectedly high number of defaults, and triggering a global financial crisis.[25] One response to the recession was to create or improve upon financial literacy and investor education programs.[26] In Canada, this has led to a national strategy on financial literacy, and increased efforts by the provincial securities regulators.[27] Gail Henderson lays out the programs put in place by the regulators, before questioning if they fall within the regulators' mandates and if such efforts merely "responsibilize" or shift the regulatory burden to investors. She also examines the efficacy of the investor protection efforts as they apply to Home Capital, finding that the securities regulators are most successful when they focus on discouraging the major players in a sector from engaging in practices that are likely to mislead consumers.[28] It remains unclear at the time of writing whether the new national securities regulator, the Cooperative Capital Markets Regulatory Authority, will assume responsibility for investor education, and what form future investor education initiatives will take.

Next, the book will discuss one of the most concerning aspects of the Home Capital story – that of regulatory fragmentation for non-bank lenders. Unlike banking institutions, credit unions and non-banks do not have a single regulatory regime. Rather, the regulations that they are subject to depends on a variety of factors, including if they operate in one province or throughout the country, and if their size leads to a designation as "domestically systemically important." Behind the big five banks, credit unions are the largest source of residential mortgages, holding 13% of the total market.[29] Stephanie Ben-Ishai details both the Canadian and American frameworks for regulating mortgages and the reforms that have been made since the global financial crisis, including the new B-20 guidelines. Home Capital illustrated that the distressed institution does not need to be a major player in order to cause a systemic risk to financial markets. Ben-Ishai's contribution to this book leaves us with a troubling question that speaks to the risk posed by regulatory fragmentation: if Canadian financial regulators were unable to anticipate the challenges with a federally regulated institution such as Home Capital, how would the system fare if the trouble originated with a provincially regulated lender?

The final chapter of the book implores us to not view Home Capital's troubles in isolation from the mortgage industry as a whole and its normative underpinnings. The desire to own one's own home or "get on the property ladder" is a strong one in Canada. Two-thirds of Canadian households own their own home, giving Canada one of the highest rates of homeownership among developed nations.[30] Even for average Canadians, their dwelling serves the dual purpose of being their home and an investment to help their retirement.

These pressures make it attractive for intervention by all levels of government that are either seeking to increase their support or help encourage economic growth. The housing sector also raises a variety of social issues, including those of inter-generational income and wealth inequality. Jinyan Li surveys the range of tax policies designed to encourage homeownership and argues that this important mechanism should be utilized by Canada's National Housing Strategy (NHS). She argues that tax policy should be part of the solution to runaway housing prices, particularly in major metropolitan areas, and that such reforms might reduce some of the system-level risks exposed by the Home Capital saga. By focusing only on the bottom segment of the housing market, affordable housing, she posits that the NHS misses an opportunity to address housing pressures faced by renters and owners.

These chapters provide an important contribution to the scholarship on Home Capital – which has largely failed to develop since 2017. We believe that this episode in recent Canadian financial history represents an illustrative preview into the character and potential responses of the current global economic crisis and any future crises that might arise. Shocks are often notable for the surprising places that they originate from, a reality that we are all acutely aware of in the pandemic context. In 2006, few people would have expected that the world would be plunged into recession as a result of the American mortgage market. Similarly, the source of Home Capital's challenges was wholly unexpected. Home Capital, as an analytical lens into our financial institutions, mortgage markets, and economy, gives us the invaluable opportunity to learn from our mistakes. By gaining a greater awareness of how the market has evolved, and the gaps in regulatory responses, we can be better prepared to anticipate, respond to, and recover from current and future financial crises.

CHAPTER ONE

Governance Challenges in Times of Crisis

*Poonam Puri**

Introduction

During times of crisis, business as usual is not a viable option. Company decisions that in normal times might take months, if not years, to plan and implement may need to be made in a matter of days or hours. Compounding the scarcity of time during a crisis are potential limitations in access to capital, disrupted supply chains, operational interruptions, increased public scrutiny and pressure, and conflicting stakeholder demands. As the current pandemic has revealed, decisions made by boards during times of crisis have a significant impact on the company's survival and continued success. During the unprecedented economic and social fallout caused by COVID-19, some companies that strategically pivoted their businesses were able to survive, while others did not fare as well.

Good governance means preparing for crises before they occur. Board directors and management of companies must develop internal control systems to identify, monitor, and mitigate risks that are both internal and external to the organization. They must also

---

* Professor at Osgoode Hall Law School and Co-founder and Director of the Osgoode Investor Protection Clinic

develop comprehensive strategies to respond to crises when they do occur. Successfully managing risks during a crisis also requires companies to be prepared to provide timely communication to their shareholders, stakeholders, regulators, and the public. COVID-19 has shown that in the face of uncertainty, companies must nevertheless keep their shareholders and other stakeholders informed on key strategic and business issues, including the impact of the pandemic on their liquidity and financial position, operations, and workforce, as well as their anticipated expenditures in response to the pandemic.

During a crisis, companies may need to focus on long-term growth and survival, often at the expense of more immediate profit and gains. This may mean shifting the focus from shareholders alone to incorporate the interests of other stakeholders, including employees and customers, into their decision-making processes. While this stakeholder governance model has already been steadily gaining traction in recent years, the COVID-19 pandemic may accelerate this change. In fact, some of the largest employers in the world are responding to the crisis by supporting their stakeholders with measures that include remote work and modified work schedules, community relief, and customer accommodations. As the world slowly transitions from crisis management to recovery, the move from shareholder primacy to stakeholder governance may very well become the new normal.

This chapter examines some of the fundamental tools and principles of good governance that can make or break the future of a company during a crisis. One tool, central to the regulation of the public capital markets and investor protection, is mandatory disclosure. Companies must make full, true, and plain disclosure of all material information when they go public. They are also mandated to make continuous disclosure on an annual and quarterly basis, as well as, in the Canadian context, in response to material changes.

What constitutes material information, and what changes are significant enough to qualify as material, has been the subject of intense debate among academics, senior management teams of public companies, and boards of directors. Complicating this already contentious issue is the fact that what is considered a material change may shift during a crisis, and there may be less time available to determine whether, and to what extent, to disclose.

Another consideration is whether the crisis originates internally or if it is caused by external events, such as the COVID-19 pandemic. Generally speaking, companies should be well prepared to handle internal or external crises if they have a robust enterprise risk management plan in place. This risk management plan should include any relevant risks that materialized during the crisis or that can be pointed to as a cause. Companies should have a good understanding of the causes and impacts of the range of risks, as well as planned responses based on scenario planning. Disclosure requirements may differ for an internal risk that has materialized, as compared to an external risk that has surfaced, as a company should have more access to information and be in a better position to make a timely and full disclosure in relation to internal events. However, this was not the case in the Home Capital crisis, where the company failed to properly make public disclosure of the results of an internal investigation that had revealed fraudulent practices by the company's independent brokers.

This chapter uses Home Capital as a case study to critically analyze the concept of disclosure of material information through three frameworks: the rules versus principles debate, the regulatory enforcement process for continuous disclosure violations used by Canadian securities regulators, and the relationship between public and private enforcement in this context. It explores what went wrong during the Home Capital crisis in 2018 when the company failed to make timely and accurate public disclosure of its internal crisis, and the resulting enforcement actions and private proceedings brought against the company. In addition, this chapter touches on other principles fundamental to good governance, including the debate on short-termism versus long-termism, and the tension between and move from shareholder primacy to stakeholder governance.

In addition to mandated disclosure, another tool at the heart of good public company governance in Canada is the concept of independent directors. Public companies are required to have independent directors on the audit committee, and they must disclose if, and why, they deviate from the best practice of having a majority of independent directors on their board. The concept is simple: independent directors will bring their independent judgment to bear in overseeing the management and affairs of the company. Independence is defined by the regulator as the principle that the director has no relationship with the corporation that could, in the view of the board, be reasonably expected to interfere with the exercise of that director's independent judgment.[1] Canadian regulators have also provided a laundry list of best practices for board composition, recruitment, orientation, and diversity, among other items. By examining Home Capital's board governance at the time of the crisis, this chapter explores why independence is necessary but not sufficient, and why a strong governance framework for boards requires that its board members avoid groupthink and steward effectively.

I. The Home Capital Crisis

Home Capital Group Inc. (Home Capital) is an alternative lender headquartered in Toronto that provided mortgage lending services and other credit products targeted primarily at those who did not satisfy the criteria of traditional banks.[2] The company was founded by Gerald Soloway, who held the roles of CEO and board director for nearly thirty years and, as discussed below, stepped down from both roles as a result of fallout from the crisis.[3]

Home Capital went public in 1986 by listing its shares on the Toronto Stock Exchange (TSX).[4] At its peak in August 2014, Home Capital's share price was nearly $55. In the same month, however, Home Capital initiated an internal investigation into irregularities with mortgage applications received through certain brokers.[5]

The internal investigation, which Home Capital dubbed Project Trillium, revealed practices of fraudulent income documentation in some broker channels. As a result, Home Capital terminated relationships with those mortgage brokers and also made significant changes to its internal controls structure and underwriting processes. The changes included separating its origination and underwriting functions, improving underwriter verification of applicant income, and examining underwriter compensation practices to emphasize risk mitigation.[6] The brokers who had been terminated generated approximately 10% of Home Capital's total 2014 originations, leading to an immediate drop in originations and a significant effect upon the financial statements after their termination.[7] As well, Home Capital's efforts to remediate the systemic issues internally led to lower than expected mortgage originations in the first half of 2015 because of longer processing times.[8]

Home Capital's internal investigation and its results were not disclosed to investors until July 2015.[9] When the company did make the public disclosure, its share price fell by nearly 20%.[10] In its public disclosures before July 2015, the company attributed the fall in new mortgages to macroeconomic and seasonal factors, among others. For example, the 2014 public disclosure did not reference Project Trillium, the termination of the brokers, the corrective efforts that had been undertaken, or the impact that these changes would have on existing and new mortgage business. Instead, Home Capital added three sentences to the Operational Risk section of its 2014 Annual Management Discussion and Analysis (MD&A) statement:

> In addition to cyber-crime, the Company is *continuously exposed to other various types of fraud* stemming from the nature of the Company's business. For example, the Company *must often rely on information provided by customers* and other third parties in its decisions to enter into transactions such as extending credit. [Emphasis added][11]

However, two days before filing the 2014 annual disclosure, Home Capital's then-CFO sent an internal email saying that the additional disclosure about the internal investigation was "buried pretty deep within existing wording on cyber risk. I would be impressed if someone even asked about it."[12]

Similarly, when Home Capital filed its first quarter 2015 interim financial statements in May 2015, it stated,

> The first quarter was characterized by a traditionally slow real estate market, exacerbated by very harsh winter conditions. The Company has remained cautious in light of continued macroeconomic conditions and continues to perform ongoing reviews of its business partners ensuring that quality is within the Company's risk appetite.[13]

Meanwhile, Home Capital's internal President's Report on the first quarter clearly stated that the corrective actions taken as a result of the internal investigation were the primary reason for the fall in both originations and the company's share of broker channel mortgage business.[14] Additionally, just days before the first-quarter 2015 results were disclosed, the CFO sent a memo to the audit committee members stating that the reduction in originations was not solely due to weather.[15] The CFO raised the fact that it might need to be disclosed that certain brokers had been terminated, and that the company might not be able to meet its 2015 annual financial targets.[16] He also told the Audit Committee that Home Capital would add a statement about the effect of the broker firings in its 2015 annual disclosure.[17] Presumably, this was the reference to "ongoing reviews of its business partners" referenced above and the additional commentary tucked in under cybersecurity risks in the Operational Risk section of the MD&A.

The CEO, president, and CFO all participated in an earnings call with analysts to discuss first-quarter 2015 results. One analyst asked about the lower originations:

> The first question I have is going back to originations, I totally get how, given what was going on with macro, well, you guys would be more kind

of cautious on originations in the traditional business. I'm just trying to understand, I guess, from the prime insured side, are you guys saying you were also kind of a bit careful there too, this being an insured product? Is that part of the reason why the originations kind of were where they were?[18]

The CEO responded with a "yes," and the president added, "As Gerry pointed out earlier, just with the technology change, there were some bumps there. Just given the smaller size of the accelerator product, it was probably a little bit more noticeable there."[19]

The analyst followed up, "But were you guys being a little bit more cautious on underwriting?" To which the CEO replied, "None of that has changed. I think it's very similar to what it was last year. There isn't a dramatic one quarter change. There's been no new competitor. There's been no new change in brokers. Brokers are exactly the same in my estimate."[20]

Home Capital faced both public enforcement action by staff of the Ontario Securities Commission (OSC) for continuous disclosure violations, and private proceedings through a secondary market securities class action.[21] OSC staff alleged that Home Capital did not satisfy its continuous disclosure obligations in its 2014 annual filing and its first-quarter 2015 filing. The OSC charged that the statements were materially misleading or untrue and that they did not state a fact that was required to be stated or that was necessary to make a statement not misleading in the light of the circumstances in which it was made.

Rather than going to a contested hearing, Home Capital settled with the OSC. The settlement agreed that the termination of brokers and changes to the internal controls constituted a material change that Home Capital had knowledge of by February 2015.[22] Home Capital and OSC staff agreed that Home Capital had failed to fulfil its continuous disclosure obligations by not publicizing the material change within the requisite ten days from the date on which the change occurred. They also agreed that the disclosure that Home Capital did make in July 2015 was effectively hidden because it was insufficient for investors to grasp the nature, significance, and impact of the material change.[23]

In what appears to be the first of its kind, the OSC settlement was explicitly interlinked with the private class action. Specifically, the OSC panel approved a $12 million settlement contingent on $11 million being allocated to the investors in the private action.[24] The class action was settled for $29.5 million.[25]

The Home Capital case study demonstrates the competing pressures that management face from different stakeholders and how their weight can compound during times of crisis. At the forefront is the Project Trillium internal investigation and the need for immediate action. While the company terminated brokers internally, they failed to act externally: they neglected to properly carry out their continuous disclosure obligations.

The decision to postpone disclosure and obscure it with boilerplate language is indicative of the board grappling with the need to meet annual financial targets. This focus on short-term targets and financial metrics highlights the governance theme of short-termism versus long-termism, which is discussed further below.

Finally, despite the Audit Committee's access to the CFO's memorandum and the opportunity to review the Annual Statements, the disclosure that was ultimately made was inadequate. This highlights another key element of good governance: board and subcommittee decision-making in a time of crisis. The section on the role of the board below discusses how board independence and composition can improve decision-making rigor and help prevent groupthink.

II. Regulatory Mechanisms to Mandate Disclosure of Material Information

Continuous disclosure has been a part of the Canadian securities regulatory regime for almost seventy-five years. Its inception can be traced back to the *Ontario Securities Act of 1945*,[26] the 1965 Kimber

Report,[27] and the *Securities Act, 1966*,[28] which included modifications to the continuous disclosure regime. While the Kimber Report focused on the disclosure of financial information, it also emphasized the importance of adequate disclosure for investors to make informed investment decisions.[29] A 1997 report by the TSX Committee on Corporate Disclosure (also known as the Allen Report) propelled the addition of a statutory civil liability framework for secondary market misrepresentations and highlighted the rising number of disclosure violations in the Canadian capital markets.[30]

Today, the principle of continuous disclosure is a pillar of the Canadian securities regulators' mandates to protect investors, encourage fair and efficient capital markets, promote confidence in the secondary capital markets, and contribute to the stability of the financial system and the reduction of risk.[31] Fundamental to achieving these purposes are requirements for timely, accurate, and efficient disclosure of information, among other things.[32]

Canada's continuous disclosure regime consists of two equally important prongs: periodic disclosure and timely disclosure. Periodic disclosure requires public companies to file financial statements, an MD&A, and information forms on a quarterly and/or annual basis.[33] By contrast, timely disclosure requires public companies to publicize material changes in a timely and accurate manner.[34] Specifically, the Ontario *Securities Act* provides that "where a material change occurs in the affairs of a reporting issuer," it must issue a news release immediately and file a material change report within ten days.[35] Timely and full disclosure of material information ensures a level playing field for all investors, providing them with equal access to material information and allowing them to make informed investment decisions.[36] In Canada, timely disclosure turns on whether a material change has occurred.[37] Thus, it is critical for Canadian companies to be able to determine what constitutes a material change. The Ontario *Securities Act* defines a "material change" as "a change in the business, operations, or capital of the issuer that would reasonably be expected to have a significant effect on the market price or value of any of the securities of the issuer."[38]

Various aspects of Canada's mandatory timely disclosure regime illustrate attempts by legislators, policy-makers, and courts to add nuance to the application of the regime. In particular, the timely disclosure requirements are designed to balance the need to provide investors with sufficient information to level the playing field, and to protect issuers from making premature disclosure of changes that have a low likelihood of actually occurring. For example, proposals made by senior management or a subset of the board to implement a material change must be disclosed only to the extent that approval of the entire board is likely.[39]

A. Regulators Take Action by Transforming Principles to Rules

While securities legislation sets out overarching principles, securities regulators routinely provide interpretive guidance through rules, instruments, and policies. The regulator's interpretation of its legislative provisions is important for market participants, particularly when the regulator has the last word on what constitutes adequate disclosure in the context of an enforcement action.

In some instances, Canadian regulators have made efforts to provide detailed industry-specific disclosure requirements or guidance, such as for mining and oil and gas companies, or more recently, for the nascent cannabis industry.[40] For example, *National Instrument 43-101*, which came into effect in 2011, requires that mining companies ensure that all technical information about material property is based on information prepared by or under the supervision of a qualified person.[41] Similarly, the Canadian Securities Administrators (CSA) has advised issuers in the cannabis industry that they should disclose the accounting policies applied to their biological assets and their method of measuring the fair value of those assets.[42]

As well, securities regulators issue guidance from time to time through notices that would be generally applicable across all issuers. For example, the CSA recently issued *Notice 51-354*, which pertains to climate change–related disclosure requirements, including climate change–related risks, risk management, and oversight.[43] However, such notices are not "hard" law; they are CSA staff's interpretation of the legislation, which issuers can choose to accept or challenge.

B. Courts Step In

Courts are an important institution in resolving disagreements between regulators and market participants. The courts become involved when issuers disagree with the regulator's interpretation of the law, the application of the law to the facts, or when the parties are unable to reach a settlement agreement with the regulator, unlike Home Capital. For example, in *Cornish v Ontario Securities Commission* (*Coventree*),[44] the issuer and the regulator disagreed about whether Coventree Inc. failed to make a timely disclosure about the impact of the asset-based commercial paper market on Coventree's business. Ultimately, the Ontario Divisional Court dismissed Coventree's appeal, concluding that the OSC applied the correct materiality threshold, and that the OSC's finding that Coventree breached its disclosure obligations was reasonable.[45]

Ultimately, the final call on whether a change constitutes a material change warranting timely disclosure lies with the regulator. Historically, courts have tended to show deference to the OSC when the necessity and materiality of the disclosure is contested. In *Coventree*, the court held that the OSC did not need to bring forward any expert evidence because "the determination of whether a material change has occurred is an issue which goes to the heart of the regulatory expertise and mandate of the Commission."[46] The Supreme Court has also ruled that the business judgment rule does not apply to the corporate disclosures required by securities regulators.[47] In Home Capital, the fact that the Home Capital board and management received external advice on their disclosure decisions was not good enough. In the regulator's view, the advice was wrong and, unlike in corporate law, this fact could not save the company from liability.

Importantly, Canadian courts have also expressly rejected the proposition that management's hopes and optimistic subjective views of a turnaround relieve a company from its disclosure obligations.[48] In Home Capital's case, the OSC emphasized this point, stating that management is not entitled to delay disclosure that has "caused or can reasonably be expected to cause a deterioration in financial results ... in the hope that it can manage itself out of a hole."[49] Therefore, once Home Capital's internal investigation led to material changes, such as the termination of brokers and significant changes to its internal controls, it needed to disclose it.[50] By pushing disclosure off until July in the hope that more new mortgages would be issued, Home Capital had violated its continuous disclosure obligations.

C. Disclosure Must Be Clear from the Perspective of a Reasonable Investor

When it comes to disclosure, there has always been a sharp focus on the principle of presenting information in a manner that is easy for the public to understand. The 1965 Kimber Report emphasized this point, stating that disclosure requirements cannot be effective "unless the resulting information is presented in a clear and understandable manner."[51] This principle is relevant to companies using the blanket, forward-looking language often found in periodic disclosures of risk factors.

The OSC clarified its stance on this approach in Home Capital. The OSC panel noted that Home Capital elaborated on its operational risks by stating that it "may encounter a financial loss as a result of an event with a third party service provider" and that it "may change relationships as appropriate."[52] However, the OSC found this disclosure was inadequate because Home Capital failed to specifically mention the impact of the 2014 terminations and subsequent remedial actions.[53] The OSC's message through the Home Capital case is loud and clear: companies should be vigilant in monitoring identified risks that could result in a material change warranting timely disclosure. It is also important for companies to pay attention to the language used in disclosures, because if investors do not understand the message, disclosure effectively has not been made. Public disclosure should make sense to the investors who read it without commentary or explanation.

D. From Compliance to Enforcement

It is important to note that Canadian regulators did not engage in an organized review of continuous disclosure filings until 1999, when the OSC formed a continuous disclosure team.[54] Since then, a number of reviews have been conducted by the OSC, including industry-specific ones.[55] The creation of a harmonized continuous disclosure review program by the CSA in 2004 has further standardized the review process.[56] With the dual goals of educating issuers about their continuous disclosure obligations and ensuring compliance, the CSA publishes its findings every two years, highlighting common deficiencies in disclosure practices.[57] For example, in its last disclosure review, the CSA noted that 51% of its review outcomes "required issuers to take action to improve and/or amend their disclosure or resulted in the issuer being referred to enforcement, cease traded or placed on the default list."[58]

The effectiveness of securities enforcement is a hotly debated topic in Canada. Robust enforcement paves the way for stronger capital markets, which in turn reduces the cost of capital and increases liquidity.[59] Concerns cited about public securities enforcement in Canada include inefficient resource allocation, the frequency and degree of monetary penalties, the lack of adequate enforcement in high-profile matters, and the delays between detection of misconduct and action.[60] Many of these concerns are raised in comparison to the Securities and Exchange Commission (SEC) in the United States. However, it is important to highlight the SEC's different philosophical approach to securities enforcement relative to its Canadian counterparts, which prioritize compliance.[61] Companies in the United States are not subject to timely disclosure requirements outside of quarterly disclosures. Therefore, it is almost necessary for the SEC to adopt a more hard-line enforcement posture to ensure adequate investor protection.

In Canada, regulatory enforcement activity rarely focuses on continuous disclosure violations in the capital markets. Over the last decade, disclosure violations constituted less than 10% of total respondents.[62] In fact, in certain years, this percentage dropped to nearly zero. Even by value of financial penalties, disclosure violations have generally constituted less than 5% of total penalties imposed by regulators.[63] While this may raise questions about the effectiveness of the continuous disclosure requirements under the Canadian securities regulatory regime, it is important to understand that not every case of misconduct progresses to enforcement at the securities commissions. For example, as part of the OSC's priority to protect investors and promote confidence in Ontario's capital markets, the OSC focuses on "cases that pose the greatest risks to Ontario capital markets and investors."[64] In 2018, only thirty-seven cases, or 9%, assessed by the OSC Enforcement Branch at the intake level were transferred to the investigation stage.[65] In addition, the OSC's compliance reviews use risk-based criteria to select companies. A periodic risk-assessment questionnaire is sent to companies to collect information about their business operations to develop the criteria, allowing the OSC to focus its limited resources on firms posing a higher risk to the capital markets.[66]

The OSC has adopted a number of new enforcement tools in the last decade or so, signaling an effort to ramp up enforcement. One such tool is the Credit for Cooperation Program, which has been in place since 2002.[67] Companies that self-report securities violations and cooperate with OSC staff receive credit that could result in a narrower scope of allegations, a reduction in sanctions, settlement agreements including no-contest settlements, or no enforcement action at all.[68] In 2014, the OSC added to its enforcement toolkit by introducing no-enforcement action agreements and no-contest settlements.[69] The former allows OSC staff to provide explicit confirmation to self-reporting companies that no enforcement action will be taken by the OSC.[70] Under the latter, companies can enter into settlement agreements with the OSC without admitting facts or liability.[71]

The impetus for no-enforcement action agreements and no-contest settlements was that companies were less willing to cooperate during investigations and make admissions in settlements as the result of concerns about concurrent civil litigation.[72] Once the parties agree on a settlement, it requires approval by an OSC adjudication panel. The panel "must be satisfied that the settlement is fair and reasonable and the approval of the settlement is in the public interest, based on the facts and sanctions agreed to by the parties, in light of applicable regulatory principles, prior Commission sanctions and the regulatory settlement process."[73] However, no-contest settlements in particular have been criticized as being potentially contrary to the public interest. Critics argue that they can diminish the deterrence effect of enforcement, resulting in fewer precedents for investors and other parties to rely upon in enforcing the law, and that they can shield companies from negative media attention if they do not comply with their obligations.[74]

The OSC has also recently started relying on whistle-blower tips to streamline its enforcement activity. In May 2016, the Ontario government amended the *Securities Act* to prohibit companies from punishing employees who engage in whistleblowing.[75] Later that year, the OSC also launched a whistle-blower program to encourage individuals to report securities law violations that may otherwise be difficult to detect using financial incentives.[76] A 2018 review by the OSC showed that 10% of tips received by the OSC were referred to the enforcement team, and 7% were connected with active investigations.[77]

Settlement is a powerful enforcement tool. Typically, if OSC staff and the respondent company have reached an agreed statement of facts, they can enter into a settlement agreement without the OSC issuing a public statement of allegations. Both parties have incentives to settle: the OSC is driven to successfully resolve cases, while a settlement saves time and money for the company. In the case of Home Capital, a statement of allegations preceded the settlement agreement. This indicated that the company did not reach a settlement with OSC staff in the earlier stages of the investigation, despite the incentives to do so.

Does increasing the frequency and severity of public enforcement lead to more effective deterrence of disclosure violations? Public deterrence plays an important role, particularly in disciplining smaller companies, which are seldom the target of private enforcement.[78] Apart from imposing harsher financial penalties, initiatives such as the OSC's recent whistle-blower program may be critical to improving enforcement effectiveness.[79] In Home Capital's case, a whistle-blower's memorandum sent to the Audit Committee chair about the failure to comply with continuous disclosure obligations predated the company's eventual disclosure to the public by only about a month.[80]

Private enforcement effectiveness is equally important for investor protection and efficient capital markets.[81] Private enforcement typically follows some indication of public enforcement action by a securities regulator. Public enforcement action signals potential disclosure violations (along with disclosure of admissions and evidence) to plaintiff-side law firms, setting the stage for a potential class action.[82] Apart from this initial intersection, it is difficult to predict the trajectory of private enforcement versus public enforcement action. However, enhancing the interrelationship between public and private enforcement could help securities regulators facilitate investor compensation.[83]

In this regard, the Home Capital settlement was striking, since it was the first time that an OSC settlement was interlinked explicitly with a private class action. In that settlement, the OSC panel approved a $12 million settlement contingent on at least $11 million being allocated to the investors comprising the class in the private action.[84] Overall, the class action was settled for $29.5 million.[85] If the settlements had not been linked, the class action plaintiff would have been able to rely on any admissions made by Home Capital in the enforcement action, giving Home Capital an incentive to agree to an interlinked settlement. From the OSC's perspective, perhaps ensuring that nearly one-third of the class action settlement was paid as part of the OSC settlement gave the panel comfort in signing off. The OSC settlement not only brought the public enforcement action to a close, but also ensured significant certainty for investor compensation in the private action, potentially saving considerable time and legal fees for Home Capital.

Structurally, Canadian regulators have taken a compliance-based approach to securities regulation in the past. However, this appears to be changing. The OSC has introduced a number of new enforcement tools, signaling its efforts to strengthen enforcement. While public enforcement effectiveness is critical, private enforcement plays a vital role as well. The OSC can play a part in developing the relationship between public and private enforcement, helping to strike the right balance between securities regulation and investor compensation. It is too early to say whether Home Capital was an isolated case or a sign that the securities regulator is willing to facilitate private enforcement through public actions.

III. The Role of the Board

A primary objective of corporate governance is to create accountability mechanisms to ensure that corporate managers are acting in the best interests of the corporation.[86] However, there is no uniform way to implement good governance mechanisms. The consequences of poorly implemented mechanisms can make the difference between averting a crisis and fueling one, as was the case with Home Capital.

Continuous disclosure, for one, plays a key role in Canadian securities regulation by protecting investors, encouraging fair and efficient capital markets, promoting confidence in secondary markets, and reducing systemic risk. However, an unintended consequence of continuous disclosure is the pressure that public companies face to report growth and profitability quarter-over-quarter, which facilitates short-termism. Similarly, while an independent corporate board can serve as a check on corporate mismanagement, a lack of truly independent, diverse directors can result in influenced decision-making and groupthink.

This section considers several aspects of board governance that contribute to effective governance: the movement from short-termism to long-termism, the consideration of shareholder versus stakeholder interests, and board composition matters, including the role of independent directors and the push for greater leadership diversity on boards.

A. Short-Termism versus Long-Termism and Shareholder versus Stakeholder Interests

The debate between short-termism and long-termism, and the related debate between shareholder primacy and stakeholder primacy, have long been areas of discussion among corporate governance practitioners and academics. Short-termism is a focus on immediate profit, gains, and interests, often at the expense of long-term growth and interests. By contrast, long-termism imposes longer time horizons on decision-making, often at the expense of more immediate gains. The shareholder primacy theory holds that shareholder interests should receive priority relative to all other corporate stakeholders, including employees, suppliers, creditors, consumers, and the broader community. Stakeholder primacy takes a more holistic view, arguing that the interests of all affected corporate stakeholders should be considered when making decisions.

It is critical that the terms "shareholder primacy" and "short-termism" not be equated. While it is true that a shareholder primacy view may lead companies to focus on short-term financial gains, as arguably happened in the case of Home Capital, shareholders may also have interests other than immediate financial gain and may endorse a long-term view. Similarly, it would be incorrect to equate stakeholder primacy with long-termism, and to assume that all corporate stakeholders focus on long-term gains.

In Canada, corporate statutes have tended to focus on directors, officers, and shareholders. Directors and officers have two statutory duties: a fiduciary duty to act honestly and in good faith with a view to the best interests of the corporation, and a duty to exercise the care, diligence, and skill that a reasonably prudent person would exercise in comparable circumstances.[87] Shareholders can elect directors, appoint auditors, receive financial statements, and, where directors and officers breach their two statutory duties, apply for statutory remedies.[88] Canadian corporate law statutes make few references to other stakeholders including employees, customers, suppliers, creditors, or the broader community and environment. Canadian corporate law has historically supported a shareholder primacy view.

However, the stakeholder primacy view has been gaining traction with recent amendments to the *Canada Business Corporations Act (CBCA)*,[89] changes that have their roots in *BCE Inc v 1976 Debentureholders (BCE)*.[90] In *BCE*, the Supreme Court of Canada, in interpreting the fiduciary duty of directors, generously interpreted the "best interests of the corporation" principle to mean the best interests of the *corporation*, not the shareholders alone (i.e., a stakeholder-interest view).[91] Moreover, the Supreme Court of Canada endorsed long-termism by expressly stating that this fiduciary duty of directors is a "broad, contextual concept" with an eye to the "long-term interests of the corporation."[92] The *CBCA*'s recent amendments codified this aspect of the *BCE* decision, by adding retirees and pensioners to the list of relevant stakeholders to be considered by directors discharging their fiduciary duty.[93]

This movement toward long-termism has garnered wide support in the business community. In August 2019, the Business Roundtable issued a new "Statement of Purpose of the Corporation" that endorsed the importance of corporations taking a long-term view to business.[94] For the first time since 1978, the business community departed from the principle of shareholder primacy in favor of a new modern standard for corporate responsibility, which realizes that "by taking a broader, more complete view of corporate purpose, boards can focus on creating long-term value, better serving everyone – investors, employees, communities, suppliers and customers."[95] The statement's signatories have committed to a range of stakeholder-centric goals as well as generating long-term value for shareholders, through transparent and effective engagement.[96]

In Home Capital's case, the company's executives appeared to be so focused on short-term stock prices, quarterly results, and earning guidance that they tried to delay or obfuscate its disclosures. At the same time, it would appear that they used vague language in their disclosures so that they had a possible defense if they were later questioned by a regulator. Instead, they should have made the disclosures earlier, as they ultimately agreed in their subsequent settlement. Arguably, Home Capital's short-term perspective was fueled, in some part, by their continuous disclosure reporting obligations.

Many regulators around the world have identified the role that quarterly continuous disclosure can play in fueling a short-term perspective and have moved toward biannual financial reporting. In 2013, a European Union directive made quarterly reporting optional for companies in its then twenty-eight, now twenty-seven, member countries.[97] Australia and New Zealand similarly do not require quarterly financial reports.[98] In August 2018, former U.S. President Donald Trump asked the SEC to study the impact of allowing companies to file reports with the securities regulator every six months instead of every quarter.[99] In December 2018, the SEC requested public comments on "the nature and timing of the disclosures that reporting companies are required to provide in their quarterly reports filed on Form 10-Q."[100] Notably, the SEC's Request for Comment stated,

> In addition, we are seeking comment on how the periodic reporting system, earnings released, and earnings guidance may affect corporate decision making and strategic thinking – positively or negatively – including whether it fosters an inefficient outlook among registrants and market participants by focusing on short-term results. For example, some market participants have urged companies to "move away from providing" earnings per share guidance that companies give and instead put more focus in Form 10-Qs on demonstrating progress made against the company's long-term strategic plans.[101]

Ultimately, while some commenters supported reducing the frequency of reporting, the majority of stakeholders – including investors, companies, and auditors – favored the existing system.[102] Accounting companies came out in strong support of quarterly reporting, while others had more moderate views. For instance, FedEx recommended that the SEC cut back on onerous disclosure requirements for quarterly reports rather than get rid of them entirely.[103]

In August 2020, the SEC announced that it voted to adopt several amendments to modernize its public disclosure rules for the first time in thirty years.[104] Although there were no changes to the quarterly reporting requirements, the amendments are intended to increase the efficiency and flexibility of the disclosure framework by eliciting improved disclosures that reflect the particular circumstances of each registrant, improve the readability of disclosure documents, and reduce repetition and the disclosure of non-material information.[105] The amendments are in line with the SEC's new principles-based approach to disclosure and notably have an increased focus on human capital disclosure, requiring registrants to describe their human capital resources and any human capital measures or objectives used to manage their business that are material to an understanding of the business.[106] Chairman Jay Clayton recognized that "human capital accounts for and drives long-term business value in many companies much more so than it did 30 years ago."[107] This is in line with the recent trends toward long-termism and stakeholder primacy.

Interestingly, the initiation of a quarterly reporting requirement in the United Kingdom in 2007, followed by the elimination of this requirement in 2014, did not have a material impact on the investment decisions made by UK public companies.[108] The quarterly reporting requirement did, however, result in more companies publishing qualitative rather than quantitative quarterly reports, and providing more managerial guidance about future earnings or sales. There was also an increase in analyst coverage of public companies and greater accuracy of analyst forecasts of company earnings.[109] A year after the elimination of the quarterly reporting requirement in 2014, only 10% of UK companies had stopped issuing quarterly reports.[110] These companies tended to have a small market capitalization and did not issue managerial guidance during the period of mandatory quarterly reporting.[111] This indicates that reducing the frequency of disclosure may not be the correct strategy to pursue a shift to long-termism.

In Canada, the issue of reducing quarterly reporting requirements has been discussed on a few occasions. Semiannual reporting considerations featured prominently in a CSA consultation paper on venture issue regulation in May 2010, and again in the CSA's 2017 consulting paper on how best to reduce regulatory burden for non-investment fund reporting issuers.[112] More recently, in November 2018,[113] the OSC and Ministry of Finance established a Burden Reduction Taskforce to consider and act on suggestions to "eliminate unnecessary rules and processes" while still protecting investors and the overall integrity of the market.[114] Notably, the taskforce considered the following questions, among others:

- Are there forms and filings that issuers, registrants or market participants are required to submit that should be streamlined or required less frequently?
- Are there particular filings with the OSC that are unnecessary or unduly burdensome?
- Are there requirements under OSC rules that are inconsistent with the rules of other jurisdictions and that could be harmonized?
- Are there specific requirements that no longer serve a valid purpose?[115]

The OSC received sixty-nine comment letters and 199 suggestions on how to enhance the competitiveness of Ontario's capital markets and reduce regulatory burden, which it used as a basis for 107 specific actions aimed at reducing burden for market participants.[116] During its last update in May 2020, the OSC indicated that 27% of these actions have been completed, 36% were on track, and 37% were delayed, with some delay resulting from COVID-19.[117]

More recently, in February 2020, the Ontario government established the Capital Markets Modernization Taskforce and appointed an independent expert panel to make regulatory proposals to modernize Ontario's capital markets.[118] The taskforce has consulted with over 110 stakeholders, including regulators, exchanges, financial institutions, industry associations, law firms, issuers, and investor advocacy groups.[119] It identified over seventy key issues, with one of the central themes still being the reduction of duplicative regulatory burden. This includes streamlining the timing of disclosure by changing the requirement for quarterly financial statements to allow for an option to file semiannual reporting.[120] Overall, the taskforce is attempting to balance the importance of maintaining effective investor protection with reducing regulatory burden. It is also focused on harmonizing Ontario's regulatory requirements with the recent modernization efforts that have taken place in the United States.

Short-term decision-making also comes from the market. Earnings guidance, which is expected by analysts and investors, fuels a "do better than last quarter" mentality. While most companies are unlikely to do away with earnings guidance, companies can place their earnings results in a broader context with other non-quantitative measures that are significant for the long-term success of their business.[121]

B. Long-Termism and Stakeholder Primacy at a Time of Crisis

The COVID-19 pandemic is an unprecedented crisis that has had devastating effects across regions and industries. Despite a temporary shift in focus to short-term economic survival, it has also triggered more long-term concerns, including the importance of business agility, strategic planning and changes to resource allocation, evaluation of environmental risks and impact, and the value of human capital. It has also altered the way that people view the role of companies in addressing social issues.

Survival and success during the COVID-19 pandemic and looming global recession challenges the past decades' infatuation with short-termism. Over the past year we have seen great uncertainty as a result of capital and resource shortages as well as unpredictable and volatile demand. While survival has required companies to be agile and responsive to this new reality, overwhelmingly, they must be prepared. A long-term view to business is necessary. Boards and management need to plan, not just for the next quarter, but for how they will proactively adjust to the pandemic-driven environment. Action that benefits a company in the early stages of the pandemic can be its downfall if leadership rests on short-term success.

In a similar vein, the effect of the pandemic on companies, consumers, and global markets is contributing to the continuing rise of stakeholder primacy. Maximization of shareholder value, achieved through short-term financial results, is a hollow metric in the post-COVID-19 environment. Stakeholder primacy is a more holistic form of governance that, during a global recession, better responds to the uncertainty faced by all stakeholders. It underscores the valuing of the interests of consumers, creditors, employees, and local communities, which are all affected by the pandemic. To recognize what these interests entail, and how they intersect with the business of the company, it is important to have an independent and diverse board that can turn a critical eye to these relationships.

IV. Board Composition: Independence and Diversity in Canadian Public Companies

The independence and diversity of the board of directors of an organization increase separation from management and enable forward-thinking decision-making. Independence promotes accountability by reducing management's influence on the board and allowing the board to properly evaluate whether management is responding effectively to a crisis. Diversity improves the rigor of decision-making by minimizing the board's susceptibility to bias-driven decision-making such as groupthink. An independent and diverse board is in a better position to evaluate whether management's current or planned course of action is sustainable and in the best interests of the company. Prioritizing these elements of board composition sets companies up for success, even in times of crisis.

The COVID-19 pandemic has presented a plethora of challenges for companies, demanding a higher standard of corporate governance. Demand for certain products and services has been unpredictable and the pandemic has affected supplier reliability, the availability and health of employees, and access to resources. The multifaceted uncertainty of COVID-19 demands immediate action. However, decision-making under conditions of time and information scarcity is especially vulnerable to mistakes and bias.

This section explores the benefits of independent boards and diversity in board composition. Neither guarantees success. For example, the Home Capital board did actually meet best practices in independence standards and was relatively diverse. That said, both independence and diversity are desirable features, as they improve the ability of the board to make difficult decisions. Indeed, an independent and diverse board is better equipped to overcome the challenges of this pandemic and future crises.

A. Board Independence

The board of directors is instrumental in setting the company's strategy, actively overseeing the corporation and its management, monitoring business performance, and ensuring compliance with legal obligations.[122] An effective and independent board of directors is an essential legal mechanism in the Canadian governance regime to act as a check on management's role in operating the business.[123] A truly independent board can ask hard questions of management, give objective and critical thought to important issues, and hold management accountable to keep directors apprised of key issues and developments facing the corporation.[124] In the event of a crisis, an independent board can also evaluate the robustness of contingent succession plans in case key C-suite members are unable to perform their duties, as well as continually evaluate and re-evaluate strategic direction and operational performance in light of the immediate, near-term, mid-term, and long-term objectives of the company.

Securities regulators and government alone do not set the expectations of independent directors.[125] Governance advisory firms, such as Institutional Shareholder Services Inc. (ISS) and Glass Lewis & Co., LLC (Glass Lewis), also play a key role through their influence on institutional investors. While regulators and governments have established certain bright line rules for board independence, governance expectations of board independence are largely structured as best practices. For example, under corporate law, one-third of the board of directors of an Ontario *Business Corporations Act*[126] corporation must not be "officers or employees of the corporation or any of its affiliates."[127] Similarly, distributing corporations governed by the *CBCA*, which are required to have three or more directors, need to have at least two directors who are not "officers or employees of the corporation or its affiliates."[128] In contrast, securities law does not establish any bright line rules. Instead, *National Policy 58-201* recommends that a majority of the board should be composed of independent directors and that the chair of the board should also be an independent director or, alternatively, an independent lead director should be appointed.[129] ISS and Glass Lewis similarly recommend that the board should be composed of a majority of independent directors.[130]

Both corporate and securities law take a bright line rule approach to the composition of audit committees of the board, but securities law takes a stricter approach. While corporate law requires corporations to establish and maintain an audit committee composed of a majority of non-management directors, securities law mandates that *every* audit committee member must be independent.[131] ISS and Glass Lewis go one step further by recommending that not only the audit committee, but also the compensation and nominating committees, be composed entirely of independent directors.[132]

Independence is defined differently across the various sources. Securities law sets a higher threshold for the definition of independence than corporate law. Corporate law considers directors to be independent if they are not officers or employees of the corporation, or any of its affiliates. In securities law, directors are considered to be independent only if they have no relationship with the corporation that could be reasonably expected to interfere with the exercise of their independent judgment.[133] ISS considers directors to be independent if they have no financial, personal, or other relationship to the company that a reasonable person might conclude could influence their objectivity in a way that could affect their ability to satisfy their fiduciary duty to shareholders.[134] Glass Lewis sets the bar slightly higher by considering directors to be independent if they have no direct or indirect material financial or familial connections with the company, its executives, its independent auditor, or other board members, except for service on the board and the standard fees paid for that service.[135]

Since securities regulation primarily uses a best practices and disclosure approach, companies may simply not make full disclosure in areas where they are not meeting best practices. In fact, a CSA compliance review five years before the Home Capital fiasco found an "unacceptable level of compliance" throughout the market with *National Instrument 58-101*.[136] The areas of deficient disclosure included the basis for determining independence and meetings of independent directors. Specifically, some issuers failed to explain why a particular director was considered not to be independent. The CSA stressed that vague and general statements on the non-independence of directors were not acceptable. In relation to meetings of independent directors, some issuers disclosed that they did not hold meetings with independent directors alone, but failed to specify what other practices the board engaged in to enable "open and candid discussion" among its independent directors.

A board can comply with bright line rules and best practices and still not be truly independent in practice. Consider the case of Home Capital. On paper, the Home Capital board had all the makings of a board independent of management: an independent chair and more than a majority of independent directors, as per the best practice.[137] Additionally, that board was fairly diverse in gender, comprising of 30% women.[138] Yet it still failed to fulfill its continuous disclosure obligations, despite the red flags and warning signs raised by the whistleblower's memo to the Audit Committee.[139] This demonstrates that while appointing independent directors to the board is necessary, it is not enough.

Directors are typically predisposed to the phenomenon of groupthink, which is "a mode of thinking that people engage in when they are deeply involved in a cohesive in-group, when the members' striving for unanimity overrides their motivation to realistically appraise alternative courses of actions."[140] Management directors, particularly CEOs, can play a critical role in influencing corporate culture as well as the boardroom tone and dynamics, which can influence decision-making.[141] A CEO who dominates the board reduces the rigor of the decision-making process as well as the board's ability to independently monitor the corporation and hold its management accountable to the best interests of its stakeholders.[142]

This problem is further exacerbated by the fact that independent directors often have to rely on insiders, such as the CEO, for information to exercise their oversight role. The 2019 guidelines of ISIS state specifically that to preserve

> the independent balance of power necessary for independent directors to fulfill their oversight mandate and make difficult decisions that may run counter to management's self-interests, executives, former executives and other related directors should not dominate the board or continue to be involved on key board committees charged with the audit, compensation, and nomination responsibilities.[143]

Home Capital's founder, Gerald Soloway, served as both the CEO and director of Home Capital for nearly thirty years. While he was not the chair of the board, his presence on the board may have led to a lack of objectivity across board decisions. Independent directors may see things objectively, while insiders may be reluctant to publicly disclose negative information. One non-independent director with the ability to disproportionately influence the board can undermine its overall independence.

Effective board independence requires directors to be able to give independent and critical thought to issues the board is dealing with. Directors should be able to exercise their independent judgment, even if it brings them into conflict with management, other directors, a party that nominated them to be a director, a majority of shareholders, or other key corporate stakeholders.[144]

Re-evaluating the independence of a board can play an integral role in the aftermath of a crisis. Home Capital shows us just this. The OSC panel that approved the settlement acknowledged that Home Capital acted appropriately after the disclosure issue was discovered. Among other things, Home Capital appointed an independent committee, as well as a third-party accounting firm to conduct an internal investigation into the irregularities, made subsequent remediation efforts, and reported the irregularities to the relevant regulatory bodies.[145]

However, good governance goes beyond responding appropriately in the wake of crisis. A top-down restructuring is essential to signal a company's commitment to avoiding a recurrence of the same circumstances, and to instill confidence in investors, the regulator, and the public. In fact, the OSC panel noted that a significant mitigating factor was Home Capital's substantial efforts to overhaul its governance and leadership.[146] This included its founder, CEO, and director stepping down from the board of directors, as well as other significant changes to the board composition, including the addition of new, independent directors and a new chair.[147]

A subset of directors, or even a single director, with too much influence can substantially alter the board's decision-making dynamic. Is it possible that the Home Capital crisis could have been averted if an insider had not been on the board? Simply appointing independent directors to the board is not enough; nominating committees should make better use of skills matrices to determine the behavioral predispositions of nominees and assess their tendency toward groupthink behavior.[148]

Another problematic aspect of director relationships is interlocking directorships. A board interlock exists when a director or executive at one firm simultaneously serves on the board of another firm.[149] Board interlocks are not prohibited under corporate or securities law; in fact, it is a decades-old practice that is the product of social relations, although some studies show that these interlocks have been on the decline.[150] Glass Lewis recommends against interlocking directorships because it "poses conflicts that should be avoided to ensure the promotion of shareholder interests above all else."[151] Too many board interlocks can facilitate the homogeneity problem at the board table because many of the board members may also have social relationships influencing their decisions. Rather, appointing directors with limited corporate social networks can help bring fresh perspectives into the boardroom. The Home Capital board seemed to be generally mindful of these issues at the time of its crisis. Though not an interlocking directorship issue, it is to be noted that Jim Keohane stepped down from the board in 2017 following Home Capital receiving a line of credit from the Healthcare of Ontario Pension Plan, where Keohane was the president and the CEO.[152]

B. Board Composition: Push for Diversity in Canadian Public Companies

Diversity on boards is an important safeguard for protecting strong decision-making during times of crisis. Boards navigating crises face the dilemma of balancing the need for quick action with the scarcity of time. Boards will need to make some of their most important decisions without the luxury of optimal decision-making structures. This breeds an environment that is prone to error and bias-driven decision-making, such as groupthink. It is crucial for boards to be prepared for uncertainty and crises by ensuring diversity in the boardroom and composition of key decision-makers.

A key factor that increases groupthink is the homogeneity of boards; boards tend to be composed of directors with similar social, cultural, and racial backgrounds.[153] While this can foster collegiality among board members, it can also make it difficult for independent directors to challenge management, resulting in too much like-mindedness across the board and decreasing directors' incentives to give independent and critical thought to issues the board is dealing with.[154]

Leadership diversity is becoming a leading governance issue for Canadian public companies. Diversity on boards, in gender, race, ethnicity, age, background, and expertise, among other things, can help avoid groupthink among directors by breaking up homogeneity on boards.[155] A number of empirical studies have found that increasing diversity on boards, particularly of women and visible minorities, has a positive impact on a corporation's long-term financial performance and prevents the tendency to groupthink.[156] Some have suggested that greater gender diversity on boards may result in better decision-making in the face of risk and uncertainty, which could ultimately lessen the negative impact of financial crises.[157] However, this hypothesis remains preliminary, with one study suggesting that this effect of gender diversity on boards may not be present outside the banking industry.[158]

Adequate leadership diversity at the board and senior management level is a core component of good governance and critical for advancing strong corporate sustainability. The synergy of diverse perspectives, experiences, insights, and skills in the boardroom facilitates a robust corporate decision-making process with consideration of a greater range of stakeholder interests, leading to more effective solutions.[159] A diverse boardroom that mirrors its stakeholders is more adept at identifying and mitigating risks while also capitalizing on opportunities.

Over the last decade, there has been extensive academic debate on whether gender diversity on boards improves business performance.[160] A pair of Canadian studies from 2009 and 2016 found that companies listed on the S&P/TSX Composite Index with one or more women directors generated 4% higher annual stock market returns when compared to companies with no women directors.[161] Companies with more women in decision-making roles have also been found to run more conservative balance sheets, show superior sales growth, demonstrate higher cash flow returns on investments, and have lower leverage.[162] However, in 2018, women held only

15% of total board seats for companies listed on the TSX, and nearly 35% of companies had no women on their boards.[163]

In light of such slow progress, many players in the Canadian landscape have been pushing for increased leadership diversity, including securities regulators, governments, proxy advisory firms, and institutional investors, with "diversity" focusing primarily on gender diversity. The Canadian debate has concentrated especially on two types of regulatory regimes: (1) a hardline approach of quotas similar to many European countries and Quebec in the case of public sector boards; and (2) a disclosure regime where companies are required to disclose their efforts to foster diversity on boards and in senior management. A disclosure regime has been the mechanism of choice in Canada. However, it has been largely ineffective in boosting leadership diversity, as the total board seats occupied by women has only increased by 4% in the last four years.[164]

Securities regulators have played a leading role in introducing regulation to boost leadership diversity. A decade ago, companies and the public may have questioned whether leadership diversity falls within the mandate of securities regulation. But in 2014, securities regulators in ten Canadian provinces and territories established a "comply or explain" disclosure model for gender diversity, requiring companies listed on the TSX to provide disclosure on the number of women on their board and in senior management and whether they have set targets, whether they have a written policy, and whether there are term limits or other mechanisms for board renewal.[165] Former OSC Chair Maureen Jensen explained that the rationale for this disclosure regime is that "diverse boards are good for Canadian companies and they're good for the Canadian economy, and we believe attention needs to be paid to this issue."[166]

The Canadian federal government has followed suit. In 2016, the federal government introduced Bill C-25, *An Act to Amend the Canada Business Corporations Act, the Canada Cooperatives Act, the Canada Not-for-profit Corporations Act, and the Competition Act*, which received royal assent on 1 May 2018.[167] As a result, *CBCA* corporations will be required to disclose information on the diversity of their boards and senior management teams at every annual shareholders' meeting, including the number and percentage of members of the board and of senior management who are women, Indigenous persons, members of visible minorities, and persons with disabilities. Both securities regulators and the government are using mandated disclosure as their legal instrument, as opposed to bright line mandated prohibitions.

While securities regulation has focused on gender diversity, corporate law has expanded the scope of "diversity" to other forms, including race and ethnicity. It is unclear whether this expanded scope of diversity disclosure will actually increase diversity on boards. Hardline quotas may be a better approach altogether. In fact, the OSC has recognized the slow progress, and stated that it "may be time [to] take a look at supplementing the ['comply or explain'] rule with guidelines … or maybe taking other regulatory action, such as disclosure enhancements, refilings, education or awareness."[168] The federal government's efforts through corporate law have generally followed the disclosure approach of securities regulators, as is evident from the latest amendments to the CBCA.[169]

It is questionable as to whether the government will introduce quotas in light of the historical context. In 2010, Senator Céline Hervieux-Payette introduced Bill S-206, *An Act to Establish Gender Parity on the Board of Directors of Certain Corporations, Financial Institutions and Parent Crown Corporations*, calling for a mandatory rule requiring at least 50% women on the boards of public companies, financial institutions, and Crown corporations within three years of the legislation being enacted. This came at a time when Canada did not have enough public or government support for quotas. Governance best practices, be it board independence or director orientation programs, focused on a "disclose what you do" approach. Debate was adjourned on the Bill in the Senate, and it did not pass before the 2011 federal election.[170]

Glass Lewis generally recommends voting against the chair of the nominating committee where there are no female directors on the board or if the board has not adopted a formal written diversity policy.[171] ISS takes a more lenient approach by recommending that investors withhold votes for the chair of the nominating committee if the company has not disclosed a formal written gender diversity policy and there are no female directors on the board.[172] The governance advisory firms do not yet explicitly incorporate other forms of diversity in their voting recommendations such as race and ethnicity, cultural and education background, professional experience, and age.

At this point, it seems that Canadian governments, regulators, advisory firms, and investors are taking a best practices and disclosure approach to boosting leadership diversity, focusing on the financial benefits of more balanced boards. These disclosure-based approaches may need to be complemented by mandatory quotas at some point to bring about substantial change in the Canadian corporate governance landscape. After all, it is appropriate for the law to set a floor or minimum standard where the market has tried and failed to change behavior or achieve desired outcomes.

Conclusion

The Home Capital crisis has many lessons for us about strong leadership and value-driven corporate governance. It would be ill-advised for the twenty-first century company to downplay disclosure obligations and fixate on the short-term interests of shareholders. Indeed, at the time of writing this chapter, the world has been engulfed by the COVID-19 pandemic. Exceptional conditions, experienced in times of crisis, have become the norm. Navigating troubled waters – and steady ones too – requires companies to undertake a thorough consideration and self-evaluation of the obligations and themes discussed above: continuous disclosure obligations, the relationship between public and private enforcement, short-termism versus long-termism, and the independence and diversity of the board of directors.

Continuous disclosure has been a cornerstone of the Canadian securities regulatory regime for almost three-quarters of a century; it is central to the regulation of the public capital markets. In addition to making full, true, and plain disclosure of all material information at the time that they go public, companies must also make mandated periodic disclosure as well as, in Canada, timely disclosure of material changes in between periodic reporting.

The principle of materiality is key to determining when timely disclosure is warranted. There are no bright line rules for determining materiality. The Canadian mandatory disclosure regime is based largely on principle, but with injections of rules and guidance from securities regulators and the courts in order to strike the right balance between ensuring adequate disclosure and preventing premature disclosure. Regulatory enforcement of continuous disclosure violations paves the way for securities regulators to constantly calibrate the disclosure regime by creating additional rules and providing guidance that is useful for companies based on the specific scenarios presented by the cases that are pursued by enforcement. Historically, the securities regulators have had the last word in assessing compliance with securities obligations, given the deference that has been accorded to them by the courts.

The effectiveness of securities enforcement is a hotly debated topic in Canada. Robust enforcement is critical to strong capital markets, which have a lower cost of capital and higher liquidity. For decades, Canadian securities regulators have been subject to criticism for taking a relatively lax approach to enforcement in the area of disclosure as compared to their counterparts in the United States and other countries. Structurally, Canadian securities regulators have taken a compliance-based approach to securities regulation in the past, but this is changing. The OSC has introduced a number of new enforcement tools, signaling its efforts to ramp up enforcement. Private enforcement and compensation to harmed investors is also critical. Securities regulators should further develop the relationship between public and private enforcement to assist with investor compensation. It is too early to say whether the OSC's interlinked settlement with the private class action in Home Capital is an isolated case, or a sign that the securities regulator is willing to facilitate private enforcement through public enforcement actions.

Finally, a diverse, independent, well-functioning board with long-term perspectives on decision-making can make the difference between averting a crisis and fueling one. A board that takes a long view on corporate purpose with stakeholder interests in mind can better create long-term value for shareholders and better serve the interests of other stakeholders, including employees, customers, and the local community. While a stakeholder governance model has already been steadily gaining traction in recent years, the COVID-19 pandemic may accelerate this change. A truly independent board can ask hard questions of management, give independent and critical thought to business and strategic issues, and help to avoid corporate mismanagement. But board independence alone will not suffice. A diverse board can enhance the independence of the board by reducing the risk of groupthink and have a positive impact on a corporation's long-term financial performance by introducing a confluence of diverse perspectives, experiences, insights, and skills in the boardroom.

CHAPTER TWO

HOOPP and Home Capital: Pension Funds as Good Governors and Crisis Managers

Simon Archer*

Introduction

In retrospect, the Home Capital affair materialized and then re-solved itself quickly. A quick resolution may have surprised some observers, as it appeared that the Home Capital saga had the poten-tial to trigger a more general crisis in Canadian subprime mortgage markets. Despite some serious problems with Home Capital's oper-ation and governance, that didn't happen. Why not?

Other chapters of this volume discuss the fraud and governance problems at Home Capital, the regulatory responses during the crisis, and the class proceedings that followed. This chapter will consider more closely the remarkable role of a pension plan – the Healthcare of Ontario Pension Plan (HOOPP) – in the Home Capital episode. HOOPP's experience is an example of the position pension funds may hold in promoting integrity in Canadian capital markets – one that has moved from a traditional role as passive investor to active defenders and promoters of good governance to, most recently, intervenors pro-moting wider market integrity and mediators of systemic risks.[1]

---

* Partner at Goldblatt Partners and Co-director of the Comparative Research in Law and Political Economy Forum at Osgoode Hall Law School

This chapter first discusses the role of HOOPP in the Home Capital events generally, noting its stabilizing effect on the crisis and the eventual repayment of the loaned capital. It then identifies the issues and question about Home Capital as an investment and identifies how HOOPP addressed those questions. Finally, the chapter takes a wider perspective and discusses the roles and position of large (typically public sector) occupational pension funds in Canadian capital markets and their relationships to regulation of those markets, suggesting an emerging role for these funds in mitigating or otherwise addressing systemic risk.

I. Canary in a Coal Mine or Tempest in a Teapot?

At first, the story seemed to contain the elements of an emerging financial crisis. In the background were regular reports of Canadian household debt reaching all-time highs,[2] the steady growth in subprime lending in Canada by non-bank lenders,[3] and, of course, the memory of subprime lending in the United States that sparked the global financial crisis of 2008.[4]

The Home Capital events have been summarized in the introduction to this volume.[5] The key role of this chapter is to examine the intervention in the form of emergency financing from, of all possible sources, a health care pension fund. The intervention came as a result of – and raised questions about – overlapping boards and the propriety of a pension fund investing retirement savings in a distressed subprime lender.[6] Some tense weeks ensued as markets reacted, until a white knight showed up in the form of Warren Buffett. Buffet bought a sizable share of equity in the lender – at a steep discount to pre-crisis trading value – and extended a line of credit on better terms than the pension fund did.[7]

The crisis – if it was a crisis – resolved itself quickly after that. The pension fund's line of credit was retired.[8] A shareholder class proceeding that was commenced over the lack of timely disclosure resolved relatively quickly for a modest recovery.[9] By August, the securities regulator had concluded its proceedings.[10]

At its nadir, Home Capital's shares traded at $5.85. They bounced up to about $16.00 when the Buffett deal was announced (Buffett bought in at $9.50 and by the end of 2018 had sold most of his shares at $16.50), and it trades around $22.00 at the time of writing.[11]

II. Crisis Delayed or Avoided?

Since 2015, we have seen a moderation in the rise in Canadian housing prices, at least in the hottest markets.[12] However, there has not been a significant test of subprime mortgagees' ability to pay, nor a market event that would test the ability of subprime lenders to continue operations.[13] After the spring of 2017, reporting on Home Capital itself fell off quickly, and commentators and market participants have returned to periodic fretting over the leverage of Canadian households[14] and generalized anxiety about asset valuations.[15]

The relatively limited impact of the whole Home Capital episode may explain the lack of reflective commentary on the episode after the flurry of initial reporting.[16] Currently, the only scholarly published paper on the subject is a case study for an executive MBA program.[17] The episode is referenced in passing in a paper that takes a critical look at the development of housing and mortgage policy in Canada over the past forty years, and by a British report on systemic risk management as an example of a stable business that was subject to irrational capital flight.[18]

The Brown and Veenstra case study offers competing theses as to the meaning of the Home Capital events. Are we to interpret them as demonstrating that Canadian subprime borrowing is less prone to default, and subject to legal and regulatory factors that adequately mitigate the risks inherent to this type of lending? Did Canadian regulators and market actors work well to prevent a run on Home Capital and permit it to conduct a governance restructuring in an orderly fashion? Are the risks in subprime markets still inherent, and just not yet manifest?[19]

The case study also provides a useful snapshot of the risk profile of subprime lending. According to that study, the Canadian housing market has several unique features that should reduce loan defaults. Only two provinces, Saskatchewan and Alberta, have non-recourse mortgage rules preventing lenders from garnishing a borrower's wages or seizing assets besides the one purchased with the mortgage. The Canadian mortgage industry is regulated by federal and provincial legislation limiting insured mortgage amortization terms. In 2010 and 2011, then Minister of Finance Jim Flaherty announced three amendments to the rules for government-backed insured mortgages to "support the long-term stability of Canada's housing market and continue to encourage home ownership for Canadians." These initiatives included a requirement for borrowers to meet qualifications for a five-year fixed rate mortgage using a bank's posted rates, regardless of whether lower interest rates and/or shorter terms are negotiated. It also included a reduction in the maximum amount that borrowers are able to withdraw during refinancing from 95% to 90% of their home value. Finally, it required a minimum 20% down payment for non-owner-occupied properties purchased for speculation and/or investment. Effective 15 February 2016, a minimum 10% down payment is required on the portion of the purchase price over $500,000 (5% for the first $500,000). In addition, borrowers making lower down payments are required to hold additional insurance.

The elements of the Home Capital story that loomed largest in the spring of 2017 were two problems of good corporate governance. First, Home Capital's executives failed to disclose the fraudulent mortgage originations when they were discovered by internal controls, and second, whether the emergency financing was truly given to Home Capital at arm's length. Discussing these elements in closer detail may help address many of the questions that the Home Capital saga brought to light.

III. From Corporate Governance to Systemic Risks

The problems at Home Capital did not suddenly spring up in 2017. They had, in fact, been known internally since June 2014, when an investigation identified several false mortgage applications and eventually led to the termination of the staff who had created them.[20] That internal process also ushered in the "retirement" of the co-founder of the company, who had failed to disclose these material events.[21] The Ontario Securities Commission (OSC), the primary regulator, knew of the problem since it was disclosed in 2015 but waited to take enforcement action until March 2017.[22]

Once the OSC commenced an enforcement action, resolution was relatively swift. By 7 August 2017 senior executives had been ordered to pay fines, $11 million had been ordered to be returned to investors, and promises were made to review and improve continuous disclosure practices.[23] The predictable shareholder class action that followed the announcement of the OSC investigation also settled quickly for $29 million by 22 June 2017.[24]

HOOPP was alleged to have had a role in the "problem" of the dual-serving directors. Jim Keohane, CEO of HOOPP, sat on Home Capital's board of directors.[25] Kevin Smith, the chair of Home Capital's board of directors, also sat as a board member of HOOPP.[26] Once the loan transaction negotiation commenced, Smith stepped down as chair of the Home Capital board and resigned from the HOOPP board, and Keohane resigned from Home Capital's board.[27] In a similar development, a provincial appointee to the OPTrust board (the Ontario Public Service Employees Union pension fund) also resigned from that position when he joined the Home Capital board. It appears this resignation was made in order to avoid perceptions of conflict of interest, even though there was no conflict found by the provincial conflict of interest commissioner.[28] These alleged conflicts were resolved in the normal manner – resignation or recusal from decisions where there was or could have been a conflict.

Keohane may have been perceived to have been in a conflict because his pension fund provided an emergency loan to a potentially risky borrower, although those risks were arguably very low when the terms of the loan are examined (they are discussed below).

However, from the perspective of Home Capital shareholders, another potential conflict arose concerning the HOOPP loan and whether Home Capital obtained the best possible terms for that loan, given the overlapping board members' connection to HOOPP. For comparison, when Equitable Group obtained a similar loan a week later on 1 May 2017 from consortium of Canadian banks, its terms were "significantly [less] onerous" than those of the HOOPP loan to Home Capital.[29]

It is very difficult to second guess these decisions in hindsight. Depositors had made a run on Home Capital and it needed to obtain liquidity quickly to continue its mortgage business. Competitors, suffering from incipient "contagion," scrambled to obtain financing at the same time (which they would ultimately not use).[30] Short of direct evidence from Keohane and Smith, it is difficult to assess the availability of credit at the speed with which it was needed.

The Canadian Coalition for Good Governance and the Shareholder Association for Research and Education – two leading organizations of institutional investors – emphasize informal engagement as a primary mode of using their shareholder voice, as opposed to simply exiting, using more formal proxy voting activities, or litigation. Mapping out the ways in which this engagement takes place would (it is hoped) provide insights into particular relationships and conditions among institutional investors, regulators, and issuers, particularly as responses to shocks or crisis events. This might also assist in explaining, for example, differences in Canadian and American capital market experiences of those shocks.

From a greater distance, the more interesting aspect is the informal way in which the risks of the failure of the lender and wider systemic effects were managed through overlapping board relationships, and the potential role of government and regulators in coordinating the response. These circumstances and relationships provide an opportunity to consider the effective use of informal forms of capital market regulation and responses to systemic risk events. Examples of similar work include Bill Carroll's Corporate Mapping Project, and John Coates's "Problem of 12," which focuses on the role of asset managers and their effects on corporate governance.[31] Detailed information on pension fund holdings, overlapping boards, and other ownership information can be pieced together where that information appears in public filings or is voluntarily disclosed by a pension fund (as it was in the HOOPP example). Generally speaking, however, it is difficult to find details of board positions and other ownership information on pension fund portfolios. This problem is exacerbated where firms are held privately, as is the case in an increasing percentage of large pension fund portfolios.

Accordingly, a useful method to study the informal networks of pension funds as they interact in Canadian capital markets would be an ethnography or series of interviews with key actors, as a complement to evidence of material culture documents and data analysis. Regulatory reports, statistical profiles, and survey research – some of which is quoted in the notes to this chapter – may not be practical or successfully illustrate the ways in which these networks operate to regulate affairs. Archives and publicly available data may be accessible, but rarely quickly enough to avert a crisis. More generally, ethnography will be better positioned to render the connections between perspectives on financial markets, globalization, risk management, and the negotiated encounters that are the bulk of quotidian activity of fund management and the nexus of decision-making in crises. We are lucky in the case of Home Capital that HOOPP, in order to be transparent and defend its decision-making, let the terms of its loan to Home Capital become public. Without this information, we would be unable to make any real assessment of value, costs, or prudence – a problem with the private equity components of these portfolios.

IV. Strange Bedfellows

It was perhaps surprising at the time to see a *pension fund* making a $2 billion loan to a distressed company under conditions that seemed to indicate a systemic problem. After all, the depositors of Home Capital had withdrawn half a billion dollars in fear of its inability to meet its obligations, the share price had dropped 66% from pre-crisis levels, and its nearest competitors in the market saw their share prices drop accordingly.[32] Canadian financial market observers have grown used to seeing Canadian pension funds in all sorts of transactions, but it is still strange to associate the staid and prudent management of retirement funds with such risky activities.

In the spring of 2017 when the loan was made, Keohane had to combat these perceptions for both the general public and HOOPP stakeholders, including participating employers, plan beneficiaries, and the Ontario government. Pension funds are essentially private investors. Despite their investment policies often being publicly available, they do not normally make the terms of individual investments public. However, given the circumstances surrounding Home Capital, HOOPP determined that it needed to err on the side of caution and make these terms public to avoid the appearance of mismanagement or impropriety.[33] As part of this strategy, HOOPP publicized the terms of the line of credit. The line of credit was subject to an immediate draw of $1 billion and required Home Capital to pay an upfront commitment fee of $100 million to HOOPP.[34] The interest rate on the outstanding amount borrowed was 10% and the "standby fee" for undrawn funds was 2.5%.[35] The line of credit translated to an effective interest rate of 22.5% on the first $1 billion drawn down. Keohane also explained the security for the loan as first call on mortgages up to 200% of loan value: for every $1 loaned, $2 of mortgages would be collateral.[36] At the time of the loan, it was believed that most of the loans that were originated through the fraudulent applications were already off the books.[37] Keohane estimated that home prices would have to fall by almost 65% for the fund to lose money.[38] Keohane's position was quickly vindicated when Warren Buffett later took a position in Home Capital.

V. Pension Funds in Canadian Capital Markets

Explaining HOOPP's role in the Home Capital story involves three related developments: the evolution of Canadian pension funds' investment practices, the increased position of pension funds in the Canadian financial markets, and their relation to formal and informal regulation in those markets. To those who follow Canadian pension funds' investment activities, the HOOPP loan to Home Capital and the overlapping boards may be less surprising than it sounds. Some would even argue it is consistent with the evolution of the "Canadian model" of pension fund governance and investment, and their evolving role in Canadian and global capital markets.[39] Canadian pension funds have sometimes been identified as "innovators" in capital markets, particularly when compared to more traditional models of passive pension fund investment. One specific area in which they have been characterized as innovators is in infrastructure investment.

The Canadian model is globally recognized and has been developed over the past forty years.[40] This model is epitomized in the large public service and broader public sector pension plans and funds in Canada.[41] These funds are typically governed by joint boards (meaning union- and management-appointed boards), feature diversified portfolios, which often lead the development of asset classes, and have internalized investment management teams with a global presence that rival and partner with other large investment funds.[42] In response to current conditions, and of note in the context of this book, this model has developed a new reliance on leverage (borrowing) in their search for returns and in the face of low and negative interest rates.[43] Two aspects of the Canadian model that are frequently touted as strengths are its governance and investment management model.[44] Both are reflected in the Home Capital story.

VI. From Government to Independent Governance

In a recent review of the development of the Canadian model, a key aspect of this model is described as being "independent governance."[45] This term refers primarily to independence from the public sector employers who contribute to the plans and a resulting "singularity of purpose" focusing on risk and returns to the exclusion of other considerations.[46] The Canadian model takes pains to avoid the perception of government interference with its operation. This feature of the model is partially intended to enhance investor confidence and for counter-parties in its investing activities. As a result, government policy and its cousins, political and regulatory risk, are closely monitored by the funds and are responded to quickly.[47] Their position as large pools of investable assets that are directly or indirectly controlled by governments and their status as independently governed institutional investors free of government control or direction are constantly in tension with each other.

A relevant recent example is the infrastructure agenda of current Canadian governments.[48] Direct public investment in infrastructure has, for a variety of reasons not considered here, ceded to a policy promoting the co-investment of pension funds and other pools of capital in privatized forms of infrastructure development.[49] For pension funds, this infrastructure policy may or may not involve opportunities to invest. Where the funds' interests diverge from those of the government, there is a concern that the funds may be requested or pressured into making loans that do not support their core mission. Most recently, for example, the Alberta government passed Bill 22, which removed the option for the province's "independently" governed jointly sponsored pension plans to discontinue using the state-sponsored and state-administered asset manager, AIMCO. The Alberta public sector pension funds are required to use that asset manager, regardless of performance or – as some trade union organization allege – the potential for political interference in AIMCO investment policy and options.

VII. Changing Investment Patterns, Changing Roles

The Canadian model developed from a tradition of active investment, which has garnered expectations about pension plan involvement in Canadian capital markets. Pension funds have traditionally and popularly been considered conservative and risk-averse investors.[50] Yet by the 1980s, funds began investing in publicly listed equities to such an extent that by the 1990s, corporate governance experts began to speculate about their role in encouraging market integrity by issuers.[51] The prudential regulation of pension fund investment rules has adapted to these activities.[52] This share ownership led to a "soft power" of influence on corporate boards.[53] This mode of influencing investments was organized and formalized in the early 2000s through the Canadian Coalition for Good Governance, which has a mandate to approach individual companies to urge changes.[54] Following the dot-com crash, the large pension funds began diversifying their portfolios to avoid prolonged low-interest rates.[55] They started making investments into emerging markets, private equity, hedge funds, infrastructure, and real estate.[56] This change effectively expanded into what became known as "alternative asset classes" beyond the standard model portfolio of 60% equities and 40% fixed income.[57] Today, smaller Canadian pension funds might allocate roughly 10% to alternative investments, including hedge funds. This figure is still higher than their allocations prior to the 2007–09 financial crisis.[58] The larger the fund, the greater and more important the share devoted to alternative assets tends to be.[59] The most frequent choice is Canadian real estate, but increased allocations in private equity and infrastructure have also become increasingly common.[60]

As a result of these changes, pension funds have been urged to expand their investment activities and take on new roles in capital market governance and fiscal policy by assuming a greater role in infrastructure investments domestically (they are already invested abroad) and through emphasis on "real economy" investment.[61] In making such investment, it has been suggested that pension fund boards take on new public interest dimensions, building on fiduciary concepts and related critiques of over-concentration and intermediation in financial markets.[62]

The theoretical justification for this role for pension funds in Canada is that of a "fiduciary society."[63] Fiduciary society theory emphasizes that, in an increasingly complex world that requires specialized functions and greater interdependence among social and economic actors, the incidence of fiduciary relationships will rise. Capital markets are a key example, as a result of the introduction of new market actors and through more complex activities and longer chains of intermediation. These conditions, it is argued, warrant the application of fiduciary duties on more and diverse relationships, even relationships such as arm's-length commercial relations that were previously thought to preclude most fiduciary obligations. This concept has been adapted and employed by the Kay Report, which reviewed long-term decision-making in British capital markets, and appears in a series of articles by Ed Waitzer and Doug Sarro that describe large Canadian institutional investors as "public fiduciaries."[64]

These new roles can give rise to tensions and contradictions.[65] As noted above, the government infrastructure agenda may give rise to opportunities but also to the perception of government influence on an arm's-length investor. There is some work on the awkward transitions for pension funds when pressed into privatizations and infrastructure development.[66] In different contexts, some have even described pension plans and funds as modern forms of "public utilities."[67] Despite these proposals and critiques, there remains relatively limited discussion of the role of Canadian pension funds in emergent market crises or as managers and mitigators of systemic risk.[68]

By contrast, in the recent global financial crisis, banks, finance firms, and insurance companies were pressed into service by the U.S. Treasury and Federal Reserve.[69] Similar coordination occurred between central banks and large systemically important financial institutions in European states and other countries.[70] In the crisis, the everyday mechanisms for monetary policy and prudential financial regulation were called upon to synchronize extraordinary measures, including emergency lines of credit and lending, swaps, and acquisitions in extreme cases.[71] The crisis, especially in Europe, was intrinsically a banking crisis, so the close intertwining of central banks, state treasuries, and the commercial and investment banking system was vital to ultimately stabilizing financial markets.

Missing in this global financial architecture, and later discussions of it, were pension funds – except to the extent that they have been victims of losses, low-for-long interest rate policy, and "financial vandalism."[72] While the role of these institutions in mitigating systemic risk has been understood for some time, their potential function in managing financial crises that have already broken out (or are threatening to break out) and limiting contagion is under-examined by financial authorities and other commentators.[73]

Their size, longer-term investment horizons, the diversity of their investment strategies, and the stability of their members' contributions may make these funds better able to invest counter-cyclically, thus acting as a stabilizing force in the Canadian financial system.[74] From a financial system perspective, the largest pension funds are of interest for their presence in these markets, the composition of their asset holdings, and for their interconnections with other financial institutions.[75]

Financial regulators and those concerned with systemic risk think of pension funds as having long-term investment horizons and an inattention to short-term instabilities.[76] Unlike capital accumulation plans, most major Canadian pension funds are defined benefit plans and can absorb liquidity risk and avoid the herd mentality that can drive financial crises.[77]

Their size also means that pension funds are significant employers of investment services, producer services, and in the financial sector as a whole. One estimate projects that the largest funds employ 5,500 people directly (11,000 including subsidiaries) and internally manage 80% of the assets of the funds.[78] These figures do not reflect the wider array of producer services they engage, which includes investment advisors, actuarial services, and legal advisors, among others. We can expect such large market actors, who have evolved to adopt and even internalize a wide array of global investment activities, to have an ongoing and steady exchange of ideas and personnel with other market actors and with their regulatory counterparts.

One well-known example of their importance in a crisis was during the collapse of the asset-backed commercial paper (ABCP) market in 2007. During those events, a Quebec public fund, the Caisse de dépôt du placement, held almost half the total market in ABCP, and led an eighteen-month restructuring. One lesson of that crisis was how exposed pension funds were to certain risks in Canadian capital markets, and the sophistication of their risk management.[79]

Drawing back in perspective, a longer-term and more fundamental tension – perhaps even contradiction – is at work on pension funds and central bank policy responses to crises. The Home Capital events occurred between two major global economic events: the global financial crisis of 2008–09 and the economic impacts of the response to the COVID-19 pandemic. In both, central bank interest rate policy and quantitative easing played important roles in stabilizing asset values in the short term, and in the aftermath of the 2008 crisis these rates remained at historically low levels for what is now the long term.[80] As noted above, pension funds with their size and ability have sought new strategies to cope with the "low for long" environment, but it remains a significant challenge in funding and investing pension assets.[81] Low interest rates drive up the valuation of projected pension liabilities, triggering funding requirements, which can be exacerbated when asset values themselves are falling. Put bluntly, central bank policy of ultra-low interest rates places enormous stresses on pension funds and insurance funds and, ultimately, can provide incentives to change the structure of the liabilities (e.g., to no longer provide an annuity during retirement but rather convert the payment stream to one contingent on funding – essentially shifting market risks to individuals and defeating the advantages of pooling market and longevity risks).[82]

On the one hand, we have large pools of patient capital with the potential to act in counter-cyclical modes and the ability to assist in capital market stabilization, potentially assisting in replacing public funding for fiscal expansion and working closely with market regulators. On the other hand, central bank interest policy, in seeking to have similar stabilizing effects on asset prices and even promote fiscal expansion through direct lending or quantitative easing, maintains a policy that threatens the viability of the model of the most successful Canadian pension funds.

At the time of writing in the fall of 2020, pension funds have avoided a sharp and immediate crisis in asset values, perhaps in part as the result of extraordinary central bank and government intervention into capital markets in response to the COVID-19 pandemic.[83] However, the much-observed disengagement between stock market asset values and indicators of the health of the "real economy" such as unemployment rates or consumer debt levels[84] and debates over the "shape of the recovery" suggest that there may yet be significant challenges ahead.[85]

VIII. HOOPP, Home Capital, Market Integrity, and Systemic Risk

In this light, we could say HOOPP played an almost expected role in the Home Capital events. What is remarkable about Home Capital's story for pension funds is that it appears to foreshadow a new role for pension funds – one that perhaps they are already playing. A good investment opportunity presented itself to the fund, which later allowed HOOPP to manage more systemic market integrity issues without compromising its core mission or independence.

Even if that risk became manifest in losses, HOOPP would still have protected its core mission. Recovery might have become awkward as it sought to enforce, or more likely sell, its collateral to recover its investment. Profiting from such circumstances contributes to one of the political risks mentioned above, and one that Canadian pension funds are very sensitive to, given the reduction in employer-funded pensions in the private sector. But those risks were correctly judged to be remote.

HOOPP's role also highlights some of the anxieties about this form of soft power or informal regulation in capital markets and the focus on the integrity and independence of the key actors. Just as Home Capital's founder was "retired" for his role, the board appointees to HOOPP and Home Capital took appropriate and even extraordinary steps to ensure the perception of independence. There is reason for that caution, given past allegations that senior executives of pension funds profited from such conflicts. This sensitivity provides an example of another anxiety about government-sponsored entities that are intended to act independently as private actors.[86]

There is a high probability that the officials in the Ontario Ministry of Finance and federal Department of Finance were in contact with Home Capital, HOOPP, and perhaps others when the crisis was mounting. Their story is yet to be told. What did they counsel? What were government officials' chief concerns? Has this experience changed their thinking about addressing future turbulence in the mortgage and residential home lending market? The involvement of pension funds in promoting infrastructure development and restructuring the ABCP market adds evidence to the proposition that large Canadian pension funds can be partners with the state in the pursuit of economic ends. Historically this has meant strategic investment and regional development objectives. As public finance becomes inextricably conjoined with private finance in the pursuit of economic development, is it impossible to imagine that pension funds could coordinate with public authorities during a financial crisis?

Pension funds are rapidly growing and innovating as dominant financial powers. The large Canadian pension funds are rivals, but they regularly communicate among themselves and with senior financial managers in government. What sort of contradictions would arise from a greater role for pension funds in financial system management? Do pension funds and supervisory authorities have a choice in the matter? Do contributors and plan members have any say?

Securities Regulators and Investor Education

*Gail E. Henderson**

Introduction

Financial literacy is "having the knowledge, skills and confidence to make responsible financial decisions."[1] At first glance, the story of Home Capital is not a story about the importance of financial literacy. Improving Canadians' financial literacy is unlikely to prevent public companies from making misrepresentations to investors, as Home Capital did when it misled investors about the cause of a decline in mortgage originations in 2015.[2] Following the revelations about Home Capital's misrepresentations, there were no media reports of unsophisticated investors losing their life savings because they had "put all their eggs in one basket."[3] But in an era of historically low interest rates on traditional bank savings deposits, more Canadians are putting their money in banking and investment products without fully understanding the risks, including the high-interest savings accounts and guaranteed income certificates offered by Home Capital and its subsidiaries.[4]

* Associate Professor, Queen's University Faculty of Law. The author wishes to express thanks to Alexandra Richmond (Queen's University, JD candidate 2021) for her excellent research assistance. Any errors or omissions are the author's own.

Home Capital has another connection to financial literacy, specifically the rise in government-mandated financial literacy efforts in the last ten years. Home Capital is a lender of non-prime – formerly known as subprime – mortgages.[5] One popular narrative explains the global financial crisis of 2008 as caused, at least in part, by individuals not understanding the terms of the subprime mortgages to which they had agreed, leading to an unexpectedly high number of defaults.[6] In response, governments around the world stepped up financial literacy and investor education efforts.[7] In Canada, the federal government struck a task force to create a national financial literacy strategy.[8] The final report of the Task Force on Financial Literacy called on regulators, including provincial securities commissions, "to be proactive in disseminating consumer education materials and messages."[9] Provincial securities commissions have heeded the call. The Ontario Securities Commission (OSC) merged the Office of the Investor and Investor Education Fund to create the Investor Office, which "sets the strategic direction and leads the OSC's efforts in investor engagement, education and outreach."[10] The other provincial securities commissions all engage in some amount of investor education.[11]

Although investor education efforts have increased in the last decade, regulatory mandates to educate investors predate the global financial crisis of 2008.[12] Their rise coincided with the shift in responsibility for retirement and post-secondary funding from employers and governments to individuals – a shift that has greatly increased the proportion of Canadians investing directly in capital markets.[13] The continuing low interest rate environment has also collapsed the distinction between savings and investments: for savings to generate sufficient returns to cover the cost of education and provide an adequate income in retirement, they must be invested in the capital markets, rather than left in a simple savings account. This requires choosing from an array of increasingly complex investment products. In its 2017–18 annual report, the OSC noted the need for investors to make "complex financial decisions, sometimes later in life with higher stakes than may have been the case for previous generations."[14]

Investor education goes beyond providing investors with relevant information through mandatory disclosure, generally considered the primary mechanism by which securities laws regulate the capital markets and protect investors.[15] The International Organization of Securities Commissions describes investor education as a subset of financial literacy.[16] Investor education focuses on helping individuals develop the specific knowledge and skills needed to invest in the capital markets.[17] James Fanto defines investor education as education about savings (i.e., the value of putting some money aside for future use), education about investing (i.e., the different types of investment products and the role and regulation of investment professionals), and education about investment fraud.[18]

Investor education might be a worthwhile endeavor that individuals should be encouraged to pursue, but this does not necessarily make it a sound regulatory strategy for protecting investors. This chapter takes a closer look at what securities regulators are doing to educate investors and whether they should be doing things differently.

Part I of this chapter describes the measures provincial securities regulators have taken to educate investors, including the content, delivery methods, target audiences, and sources of funding for their investor education. Part II examines whether securities regulators should be educating investors. First, does it fall within their regulatory mandate? Second, does it serve to shift the burden of regulatory responsibility onto investors? Third, is it effective? The chapter concludes with a look at two future developments in Canadian securities regulation that might affect future investor education initiatives.

A few words on scope and terminology. The chapter focuses on investor education by the Canadian provincial securities commissions.[19] Self-regulatory organizations also engage in investor education, but their work is not discussed in detail here.[20] Although this chapter discusses whether securities regulators should be educating investors, it does not discuss the question of who else has responsibility for this aim, or if another body is more appropriately placed to achieve it.[21] This chapter also does not assess investor education from the perspective of adult education, or theories of adult learning. The "investor" in "investor education" means retail investors in this chapter, not institutional investors.

I. What Are Provincial Securities Commissions Doing to Educate Investors?

Provincial securities commissions deliver investor education primarily through their investor education websites.[22] The content of these websites is similar and includes information about saving, investing, and fraud. There are web pages educating investors on different types of investments, on investment fees, and on the need for investors to do their own due diligence.[23] Several regulators provide a glossary of investment terms.[24] There are web pages to help investors identify and make a plan to meet their financial goals.[25] These pages generally advise consulting a registered financial adviser.[26] In addition to this type of general information, the securities commissions also engage in specific and timely investor education campaigns, such as those accompanying the introduction of new regulations. For example, to coincide with Ontario's equity crowdfunding rules, the Investor Office "developed CrowdfundOntario. ca, an interactive guide to help Ontario investors understand how equity crowdfunding works and learn about the risks."[27]

Securities commissions also deliver investor education in person, although this mode of delivery has been discontinued in the wake of the COVID-19 pandemic and its restrictions on in-person indoor gatherings. Even before COVID-19, some regulators had shifted their focus to online delivery.[28] The OSC's "OSC in the Community" program takes the regulator's mandate "From Bay Street to Main

Street,"[29] visiting towns across the province, often in partnership with other government and non-profit organizations.[30] The program is "aimed primarily at seniors, new Canadians and vulnerable investors."[31] The British Columbia Securities Commission (BCSC) delivers investor education workshops, also aimed at "seniors and pre-retirees."[32] The Nova Scotia Securities Commission's "Student Connections" program involves visits to schools and post-secondary institutions.[33] The Alberta Securities Commission offers its "Investing 101" classes in Calgary and Edmonton, for which it charges a fee.[34]

Provincial securities commissions also engage in investor protection under the auspices of the Canadian Securities Administrators (CSA). In 2016, the CSA conducted an awareness campaign to educate investors on the new disclosure rules relating to investment fees, using short videos, among other tools.[35] Several provincial investor education branches were involved in the CSA's work combatting binary options fraud, discussed further below. The OSC and the Autorité des marchés financiers also participate in investor education at the international level through International Organization of Securities Commissions' Committee on Retail Investors (also known as Committee 8).[36]

One of the main goals of investor education by provincial securities regulators is fraud prevention, a goal shared by the National Strategy for Financial Literacy.[37] According to the CSA 2020 Investor survey, 4% of respondents approached with a fraudulent investment reported that they had invested in a fraud, a rate that has been "steady" since 2006 when this survey was first conducted.[38] One major national effort by provincial securities commissions has been to encourage investors to check the national registration database to ensure that the investment dealers and advisors they are dealing with are registered.[39] Several securities commissions list "red flags" to help investors "spot scams."[40] Numerous provincial commissions also participate in Fraud Prevention Month.[41]

The focus on informing investors about frauds and scams has intensified in the wake of the COVID-19 pandemic.[42] COVID-related frauds come primarily in the form of companies "claiming to have products or services that would prevent, detect or cure COVID-19."[43] The CSA also warned the public about scams advertising opportunities to work from home as a securities trader without having to register.[44]

Seniors are a key target demographic of these fraud prevention and other investor education efforts.[45] The CSA and provincial securities commissions also have published materials to help seniors and caregivers identify, prevent, or intervene in the financial abuse of seniors.[46] Provincial securities commissions also offer help to seniors and their families with retirement planning.[47]

Newcomers to Canada are another focus of financial literacy and investor education at both the federal and provincial levels.[48] Newcomers are among the target market for Home Capital's non-prime mortgages, since many do not qualify for a mortgage from a mainstream bank.[49] Newcomers may not understand the Canadian financial system, making this demographic a target market for questionable financial products.[50] The OSC's Introduction to Investing website, which covers much of the information available on its main investor education website, is available in nineteen languages.[51] BCSC's InvestRight website is offered in three languages.[52]

In addition to investor education that securities commissions deliver directly, they also have developed financial literacy curriculum resources for use in schools. In 2004, the BCSC produced a resource for high school teachers called "The City," which became more widely available through a partnership with the Financial Consumer Agency of Canada.[53] The Manitoba Securities Commission has created lesson plans for instructors that can be used to incorporate financial literacy into other subjects,[54] including a lesson plan on "frauds and scams." The Manitoba Securities Commission also developed a guide for parents, which the Alberta Securities Commission investor education website also links to as a resource for parents to teach children about money.[55] The Autorité des marchés financiers has a web page for teachers.[56] This focus has also received recent political attention, including the 2019 Ontario budget, which called on the OSC to work with the Ministry of Education to develop a new financial literacy curriculum.[57]

Where provincial securities commissions are self-funded through fees and other revenues,[58] investor education is financially supported by the regulated entities. In some provinces, investor education by provincial securities commissions is funded by administrative penalties and settlements.[59] In Ontario, the legislative authority for funding investor education from these sources was added in 2012.[60] For example, in Home Capital's case, the individual defendants paid $2 million in administrative penalties, $1 million of which was allocated for the OSC to use either for the benefit of third parties or for investor education.[61]

Commissions' budgets for investor education are relatively small. For the year ending 31 March 2018, the OSC recovered $1.475 million in investor education costs from settlements and orders, representing approximately 1% of the OSC's expenses for the year.[62] In 2018, the BCSC spent $1.3 million on "education," most of which was on investor education, which represented 3% of its budget.[63] In fiscal 2019, the Alberta Securities Commission spent $813,000 on investor education, or just under 2% of expenses.[64] The expenses for the Alberta Securities Commission Communications and Investor Education division were a third of those for the Enforcement division.[65]

At least for the foreseeable future, investor education is likely to continue to be a prominent part of the work of provincial securities commissions. [66] In its 2019 budget, the government of Ontario called on the OSC to implement its Seniors Strategy, which includes a significant investor education component.[67] The Alberta Securities Commission's current strategic plan includes investor education in one of its three strategic pillars.[68] The Nova Scotia Securities Commission lists educating investors as one of its "core responsibilities."[69] Improving investors' financial literacy, "particularly as regards management of personal finances and retirement planning" is a priority of the Autorité des marchés financiers as well.[70] The CSA and some provincial commissions have plans for their investor education to reach a greater number of investors, through the use of social media and online resources, by more targeted messaging, or by adapting content for mobile devices.[71]

II. Should Provincial Securities Commissions Be Educating Investors?

The amounts being spent on investor education are not large relative to the size of the securities commissions' total budgets, and it does not appear from the reporting of any of the commissions or the CSA that investor education is replacing other regulatory actions. That said, the resources that the securities commissions are directing to investor education are not insignificant, and so it should be asked whether this work properly falls under their regulatory mandate. I also examine the extent to which investor education seeks to "empower" investors to further their own financial goals through better decision-making or whether it seeks to shift some regulatory responsibility onto the shoulders of investors. Finally, divisions of securities commissions involved in investor education, such as the OSC's Investor Office, promote investor protection in other ways, which may be more effective. This raises questions about whether investor education is the most effective way to achieve its stated goals, including preventing fraud.

A. The Mandate of Securities Regulators

The purpose of securities regulation and the mandate of securities regulators is to protect investors "from unfair, improper or fraudulent practices," "to foster fair and efficient capital markets"[72] and confidence in those markets, and, at least in Ontario since 2017, "to contribute to the stability of the financial system and the reduction of systemic risk."[73] Investor education is expressly included in the statutory purposes only for the Autorité des marchés financiers. Section 4(1) of the *Act Respecting the Regulation of the Financial Sector* makes it part of the "mission" of the Autorité des marchés financiers to "provide assistance to consumers of financial products and services, *in particular by setting up consumer-oriented educational programs on financial products and services*, processing complaints filed by consumers and giving consumers access to dispute-resolution services" (emphasis added).[74] In the aftermath of the global financial crisis, governments attempted to link financial literacy and investor education to market stability.[75] The more common justification for investor education offered by securities commissions, however, is investor protection and promoting confidence in capital markets.[76] The section of the OSC's annual report dealing with market stability does not mention investor education.[77]

Campaigns about checking that advisers are registered and avoiding fraudulent investment schemes connect directly to securities commissions' investor protection mandate. The latter also can be viewed as an extension of enforcement.[78] This is consistent with the historical focus of investor education by securities regulators,[79] but some investor education seems to go beyond protecting investors to "improving" the "outcomes" of their investment decisions to meet "their financial goals."[80] Some investor education also seeks to influence those goals by, for example, encouraging investors to save more. The OSC's *Investor News* June 2019 newsletter warns readers not to let vacation planning undermine their savings goals and links to its Get Smarter about Money web page on saving money.[81] The Alberta Securities Commission's CheckF1rst retirement savings calculator shows users the "additional growth" in your retirement savings from giving up "daily coffee purchases" and "weekly restaurant visits."[82] In response to the COVID-19 pandemic and its negative impact on investors' incomes, securities commissions also shared advice on how to budget and cut back on spending.[83]

It is difficult to argue that the securities regulators' investor protection mandate extends to encouraging Canadians save more of their disposable incomes for future use. It could be argued that this type of general interest information helps to lead investors to other web pages on checking the national registration database and recognizing the red flags of fraud. It is also arguable that this information supports Canada's National Strategy on Financial Literacy, one of the goals of which is to increase savings.[84] James Fanto argues that regulators should engage in such investor education to reinforce the key messages of financial literacy education in schools and workplaces, or arrange its delivery by private firms.[85]

Some might view encouraging investors to think about their financial goals as a means to further investor protection by helping them navigate the financial marketplace. The types of questions posed to investors on these web pages are similar to the questions an adviser might ask in fulfilling regulatory requirements to "know your clients" and sell them only investment products that are "suitable" to their investment goals and financial position.[86] This raises the question of whether investor education, perhaps unavoidably, seeks to shift some of the burden of regulating market intermediaries from the regulator and the industry to the investor.

B. Using Investor Education to Shift the Regulatory Burden from Registrants and Securities Commissions to Investors

Investor education by provincial securities commissions could focus on correcting the potential (and actual) market failure of information asymmetry between investors and intermediaries, helping to protect investors and create confidence in the capital markets.[87] It could do so by helping to ensure that investors make fully informed decisions about what to do with their money, should they decide to invest it in capital markets. The Manitoba Securities Commission describes its public education efforts as "help[ing] members of the public understand investing and market issues and to be able to make appropriate investment decisions."[88] Much of what commissions are doing, including educating investors about calculating the amount and impact of investment fees, fits within this description.[89] Investor education with this focus corresponds with what Toni Williams defines as the "empowerment" narrative.[90] Some commissions' educational materials speak explicitly of "empowering investors."[91]

But, as described above, investor education by securities commissions seems to be doing more than "empowering investors." Williams also describes a "responsibilization" strategy of investor education, which seeks to shape investor preferences, steering them toward self-reliance (e.g., encouraging Canadians to save more), and to enlist them in helping to regulate capital markets by identifying, and then avoiding, fraudulent or non-compliant dealers and advisers.[92] Investor education encouraging investors to save more for retirement and to check the registration of their dealer or adviser before they invest seems to further this agenda.[93] So too does investor education aimed at ensuring that investors buy only investment products that are "suitable" for them. For example, the "goal" of the Alberta Securities Commission's "CheckF1rst" investor education initiative "is to ... empower Albertans to make safe, *suitable* and informed investment decisions."[94] The requirement to sell investors only investment products that are "suitable" to them is a condition of registration of dealers and advisers, enforced by provincial securities regulators, including through compliance reviews. Some investor education materials explain this as a dealer/adviser responsibility.[95]

There is obvious overlap between investor education that "empowers" and that "responsibilizes." Being able "to recognize questionable products and practices"[96] allows investors to make decisions that are more likely to further the investors' self-selected goals and help to keep illegal and incompetent players out of the market.[97] The concern is that making investors responsible for policing themselves and the market will allow regulators to reduce their policing functions.[98] In this way, investor education serves the interests of the sellers of investment products rather than the buyers.[99] There is nothing in securities commissions' reporting on investor education to indicate that they view gains made in this area as allowing them to reduce monitoring and enforcement. Nor is investor education discussed in relation to the commissions' recent efforts to reduce "regulatory burden" on issuers and other market participants. [100] Other messages to investors, however, suggest that their failure to "self-regulate" in this way will limit their recourse to the state for assistance if things go wrong. For example, investor education materials of the BCSC suggest that working with an unregistered advisor means that "you forego the protection of [securities] laws."[101]

At least for seniors, securities regulators acknowledge that lower financial literacy and diminished capacity should be mitigated by the role of regulated professionals.[102] That said, the OSC Seniors Strategy also includes providing seniors with guidance on questions to ask their financial advisers to "help older Ontarians feel more prepared when they talk to a firm representative and more confident understanding and acting on the information and choices they are given."[103] This apparent contradiction might be explained as not treating seniors as a homogenous group.[104] It also might demonstrate that investor education necessarily pushes an agenda of individual responsibility.[105] Such an approach might be defensible if it worked. The next section examines the current impact and potential effectiveness of provincial securities commissions' investor education efforts.

C. Impact and Effectiveness

When trying to measure the impact of provincial securities commissions' investor education, some numbers look better than others. In the OSC's 2015–16 reporting year, its "Get Smarter about

Money" website had 4.5 million visits.[106] The Alberta Securities Commission reached almost 3,500 Alberta seniors "through targeted campaigns and initiatives" in its 2019 fiscal year.[107] Over 1,600 individuals attended OSC in the Community programs, with an additional 2,000 participating in "teletownhall" events – albeit out of 80,000 invitees.[108]

The CSA and the provincial securities commissions face an uphill battle in getting investors' attention. According to the CSA's 2020 investor survey, only 39% of Canadians are "aware of" their provincial securities regulator, up 3% from the 2017 survey, but down from 42% in 2016.[109] Awareness is higher (50%) among seniors and in Quebec (47%). The BCSC has acknowledged that "low public awareness of the BCSC is a significant challenge when it comes to delivering investor education to the B.C. public."[110] In 2017, among investors who were aware of their provincial securities regulator, only 15% had visited its website.[111] This statistic is not reported in 2020. Only 33% of respondents who have an adviser "checked [their] background in any way" (up 4% from 2017), and only 3% "checked with their provincial regulator," down from 4% in 2017.[112] Only 10% of respondents said they would report a suspected fraud to the securities commission.[113]

As noted above, one of the main goals of investor education by provincial securities regulators is fraud prevention. The BCSC used to measure the effectiveness of its in-person seminars through follow-up surveys. In 2017/18, 67% of survey respondents recalled four out of five warning signs of fraud, and an additional 33% recalled all five.[114] The BCSC has since shifted from in-person to online seminars and discontinued this performance measure in favor of simply tracking number of views.[115] Between March 2015 and November 2020, the BCSC's *Investment Fraud Explained: Recognize, Reject, and Report Investment Fraud* video was viewed just under 26,000 times.[116] Annual views were 1,383 in the BCSC's 2016/17 reporting year.[117] In 2017/18, annual views more than doubled to 2,834, and increased 46% the next year to 4,137.[118] Of course, number of views is not evidence of improved ability to "recognize" and "reject" investment fraud. Some demographics may prefer in-person seminars.[119]

Increases in the number of annual views is some evidence, at least, that the BCSC is reaching "a wider audience," which was the goal of focusing on online content rather than in-person seminars.[120] It is doubtful, however, that any amount of promotion done by provincial securities regulators can compete with advertising by for-profit companies, legitimate or otherwise, seeking investors' dollars.[121] Certainly, they would have to spend much more time and resources than they do now. To provide just one comparison, in its 2017–18 fiscal year, the Ontario Lottery and Gaming Corporation spent over $280 million on marketing and promotion.[122]

The justification for investor education as a main fraud-prevention strategy is that by the time fraud is detected, the perpetrators – and the money – are usually long gone.[123] But concerns about the ineffectiveness of after-the-fact enforcement does not mean that investor education is the only tool left to securities regulators. The campaign against binary options fraud is a good example. The United States Securities and Exchange Commission describes binary options as "a yes/no proposition" – hence the name – which "typically relates to whether the price of a particular asset will rise above or fall below a specified amount."[124] The OSC similarly describes them as "like an 'all or nothing' wager on how an underlying asset will perform in a limited amount of time."[125] The underlying asset could be a currency or stock, and the limited amount of time could be mere minutes.[126] For example, "The price of gold will be below $1082 at 3:42 pm on a particular day."[127] Once a binary option is purchased, investors either win the bet – or, more frequently, they do not. In some cases, the wager is rigged: the binary options trading platforms will do things such as extend the amount of time until the investor is on the losing side of the wager.[128] These high-risk investments are dangerous enough, but "in many instances,... no actual trading occurs and the transaction takes place for the sole purpose of stealing money" or the investor's identity.[129] In other words, they are not an investment product at all – they are merely a "vehicle to commit fraud."[130]

The CSA, including its Investor Education Committee, supported by the provincial securities commissions, took steps to protect investors from binary options fraud, in addition to investor education. In 2016 and 2017, these included persuading Apple, Facebook, Google, MasterCard, Twitter, and VISA to restrict binary options sellers from using their products for advertisement and payment.[131] In 2017, seven provincial securities commissions, including Alberta, Ontario, and Quebec, signed on to Multilateral Instrument 91-102, which made it illegal to "advertise, offer, sell or otherwise trade a binary option" to or with any individual investor, regardless of their level of wealth or sophistication, when the binary option matures less than thirty days from the date of purchase.[132] After an initial surge of complaints following implementation of the ban, the number of complaints fell, which the CSA attributed to "an actual decrease in this form of fraud."[133]

This example suggests that focusing on adjusting the behavior of a smaller number of private actors, who can help to keep such products from reaching investors in the first place, may be more effective at preventing fraud than trying to educate widely dispersed investors on potentially fraudulent products. The 2020 CSA Investor Index survey notes a decrease in investors reporting that they have been approached with a fraud, but the percentage of those approached who ultimately invested in a fraud has not declined.[134] This might suggest that regulators should focus prevention efforts on advertisers, rather than investors, in responding to new investment frauds seeking to capitalize on current market trends, such as cryptocurrencies.[135] This type of response also does not depend on "responsibilizing" investors to protect themselves. On the other hand, two commenters on the rule banning short-term binary options argued that *only* more investor education would help prevent binary options fraud.[136]

Even if securities regulators had the resources to reach a mass audience, investor education might deter investors only from the most easily recognizable frauds, and, as the CSA's website on binary options warns, "Scams aren't always obvious."[137] Part of the difficulty investors face is the complexity of the financial marketplace – complexity caused by the industry and, perhaps in some cases, exacerbated by mandatory disclosure rules.[138] This complexity likely makes the job of fraudsters easier: if investors do not understand the products sold to them at a mainstream bank, why would it be a "red flag" if they do not understand the product being sold to them by a con artist? It is not only the products that are difficult to understand. The BCSC's guide to be an empowered investor notes that market participants work under an "array of titles, qualifications, certifications, and licensing or registration," which "limit or expand what they can do."[139] An empowered investor needs to know "the services your advisor is legitimately permitted to offer, and what limitations they work under."[140] One solution to this problem is investor education; the other is to take steps to simplify the use of these titles.[141]

Furthermore, tips such as "Never buy an investment product without disclosure on the product" must be followed up with "But look out for fake disclosure."[142] The Autorité des marchés financiers instructs investors to make sure the documents have been filed on the System for Electronic Document Analysis and Retrieval (SEDAR). But this system was not built with retail investors in mind, and investors might fail to find disclosure documents for perfectly legitimate investment products. The broader concern is that sophisticated scams will be difficult for even educated investors to detect.

The OSC has stated that it will adopt "consumer-centric principles in a variety of work areas."[143] A consumer-centric approach could mean a greater focus on educating registrants on the needs of vulnerable investors, which is part of the OSC Seniors Strategy, and increasing compliance reviews of registrants, as the Nova Scotia Securities Commission plans to do.[144] It also could mean less emphasis

on educating investors, and more on rules intended to keep inherently unsafe products, such as binary options, out of the retail
investor market entirely.[145] Even in a climate of reducing the regulatory burden on the investment industry, substantive regulation
of inherently risky or harmful investment products is likely a more
cost-effective means of protecting investors than increasing investor education.[146] It also may foster investor confidence in the capital
markets. Former U.S. presidential candidate Elizabeth Warren has
famously compared financial products to toasters: consumer product safety standards allow "consumers [to] enter the market to buy
physical products confident that they won't be tricked into buying
exploding toasters and other unreasonably dangerous products."[147]

Conclusion: Looking Ahead

Despite the concerns described above, investor education by provincial securities commissions seems here to stay, at least for the
immediate future.[148] Two ongoing developments in the Canadian
securities landscape may affect its scope and content. First, seven
of the provincial and territorial securities commissions, including
British Columbia, Ontario, and Nova Scotia, have signed on to the
proposed new "national" regulator, the Cooperative Capital Markets Regulatory Authority (CCMRA).[149] Supporting the transition
to the CCMRA was one of the OSC's priorities for the 2020–1 fiscal
year.[150] Combining the resources dedicated to investor education
by thirteen regulators into one office likely would result in national
investor education campaigns of greater impact. However, investor education is not mentioned in the memorandum of agreement
governing the CCMRA, nor is it included in either of the proposed
pieces of legislation, and there is no planned equivalent of the OSC's
Investor Office.[151] It is unclear whether the CCMRA will include investor education in its mandate, or whether the federal government
will push this over to the financial literacy education mandate of the

Financial Consumer Agency of Canada.[152] When, or if, the transition to the CCMRA is completed, this could reduce the overall level of investor education activity by securities regulators in Canada.

Another development that could affect the amount and/or content of investor education is securities regulators' recent embrace of the field of behavioral finance.[153] The OSC is the most active provincial regulator on this front.[154] Research in this field reveals that human investors are subject to cognitive limitations and biases that likely affect their ability to make decisions in their own best interests.[155] Old and new insights in this field could move regulators away from the "empowering" model of investor education, although recent reports on "behavioural insights" focus on continuing to work within this model, but with improved messaging and disclosure to investors.[156]

Putting aside the concerns about securities regulators and investor education expressed above, Canadian investors looking for unbiased and helpful information about saving, investing, and fraud can turn to their provincial securities regulator. As long as individual investors continue to bear primary responsibility for financing their retirement and their children's post-secondary education, the ability to access such information is important. More than ten years out from the global financial crisis, triggered, in part, by the subprime mortgage market served by institutions like Home Capital, financial literacy remains a policy priority of many governments. Nevertheless, concerns about mandate, the shift of the regulatory burden onto investors, and the effectiveness of investor education mean that securities regulators should continue to critically assess their investor education efforts and consider whether funds currently being spent on investor education could be reallocated in other ways that would better protect investors.

Home Capital and Cross-Border Lessons in Mortgage Regulation

*Stephanie Ben-Ishai**

Introduction

Home ownership remains a major financial and personal mile-stone for many Canadians. In a recent survey of millennials, 86% of non-homeowners surveyed reported having a goal of home-ownership.[1] For many Canadians, this ambition also represents the biggest financial commitment that they will make in their life-time. Mortgages are the single largest item of debt held by most Canadians, representing 114% of household income on average.[2] In Canada's largest cities, Toronto and Vancouver, the mortgage-to-income ratios are much higher than the national average, at 145.2% and 176.9% respectively.[3] In 2018, the total outstanding mortgage balance in Canada was roughly $1.5 trillion held through six mil-lion loans. Approximately 80% of this market was held by Canada's big five banks, with the remaining share split among non-bank fi-nancial institutions, including credit unions (CUs) and private lend-ers.[4] While Toronto-based Home Capital, and its subsidiary Home Trust, comprise a small part of this total, they are the largest single

---

* Professor and Distinguished Research Professor at Osgoode Hall Law School

alternative mortgage lender, holding approximately $20 billion of mortgages.[5]

Home Trust is a federally regulated trust company that primarily offers uninsured residential mortgages.[6] Home Capital Group's residential mortgage business consists of two portfolios: accelerator mortgages, the majority of which are insured, and conventional mortgages, which are not insured. Home Capital targets customers without established credit histories[7] and charges higher rates on its mortgages than the established banks.[8] Despite its diminutive market share, there are good reasons why the Home Capital debacle merits further attention. Aside from the corporate governance shortcomings and securities law violations mentioned in the preceding chapters of this volume, Home Capital serves as a cautionary example of the system-wide destabilizing effects that risky lending practices, inadequate external controls, and ineffective regulatory interventions can produce.

As demonstrated by the current case study, the health of even the smallest players in the mortgage sector can have profound impacts on mortgage markets, stakeholders, and the economy more generally. This is a particularly salient consideration in times of system-wide economic fragility, such as the current global recession triggered by the COVID-19 pandemic. Many lenders are facing unprecedented numbers of customer relief requests, pressures from government-mandated deferral programs, and seek new ways to address borrower challenges. Mortgage lenders and regulators alike can capitalize on many of the lessons learned from Home Capital to address current economic conditions and use the current crisis as an opportunity for reform through designing recovery efforts that will ensure more stable and sustainable mortgage markets in the long term. With this in mind, this chapter considers the regulatory framework for the mortgage market in Canada and the United States, both before and after the 2008 financial crisis. It then moves on to evaluate the effects of the new regimes on the stability of the mortgage market and assess their overall efficacy. The focus will then shift to non-bank financial institutions by laying out the current regulatory framework, before closing with a note about Home Capital and what it might mean for the current economic crisis.

I. Regulation of Financial Institutions

Canada's lending system is often lauded as more stable than its American counterpart, partially because it has avoided the degree of irresponsible lending that led to the 2008 U.S. subprime housing market collapse. These assertions were called into question by the actions of Home Capital in recent years. Not only did these events shake some investors' confidence in Canadian non-bank lending institutions, but they also inspired greater scrutiny of the interventions (or failures to intervene) by regulatory bodies tasked with overseeing the mortgage sector in Canada. The regulatory oversight of financial services in Canada is largely split among a few federally constituted institutions. Each is responsible for different elements of the market, but all have joint protocols in place to ensure a comprehensive response in the event of a crisis.[9] The following section will set out the regulatory actors in Canada, describe their functions in greater detail, and briefly compare them to equivalent American institutions.

A. The Canadian Context

Office of the Superintendent of Financial Institutions (OSFI)
The OSFI is an independent government agency that reports to the minister of finance and is responsible for publishing industry guidelines and ensuring that federally regulated financial institutions and pension plans are sound and in compliance with the law governing their conduct.[10] These federally regulated lenders, often referred to as "traditional mortgage lenders," consist of financial institutions incorporated, continued, or regulated under the *Bank Act, Trust and*

Loan Companies Act, Insurance Companies Act, and *Cooperative Credit Associations Act.*[11] Examples of institutions currently regulated by OSFI include banks, trust companies, property and casualty insurance companies, and foreign bank representative offices.[12] Lenders falling under OSFI's purview account for nearly 80% of all residential mortgages issued in Canada.[13] As the sole regulator of banks and the primary regulator of several other financial institutions such as loan companies, OSFI is also responsible for "monitoring system-wide or sectoral issues that may have a negative impact on the financial conditions of financial institutions" and examining financial institutions for solvency, liquidity, safety, and soundness.[14] The regulator's overarching objective is to instill public confidence in the Canadian financial system. OSFI also represents Canada in wider international discussions on banking stability at fora including the Financial Stability Board and the Basel Committee on Banking Supervision.[15]

Deposit Insurance Regime

Deposit insurance provides protection for deposits in a financial institution if the institution fails.[16] In Canada, this responsibility is jointly shared between the federal and provincial governments. Banks and trust and loan companies are regulated by the Canada Deposit Insurance Corporation (CDIC), and credit unions are covered under provincial regulatory schemes.[17] After the global financial crisis, the CDIC was given expanded powers to forcibly restructure a non-viable member institution, or create a "bridge institution" to preserve the value of its remaining assets.[18] The CDIC ensures deposits up to $100,000 in six categories: registered retirement funds, registered retirement income funds, tax-free savings accounts, checking accounts, deposits held in trust, and deposits held for paying taxes on mortgaged properties.[19]

In Ontario, deposit insurance is managed by the new Financial Services Regulatory Authority (FSRA), which launched in June 2019.[20] The FSRA is an independent agency that replaced the

Financial Services Commission of Ontario (FSCO) as the regulator for mortgage brokers, insurance, credit unions, loan and trust corporations, and pensions. At the time of the crisis, the FSCO conducted a review of Home Capital's suspension of several brokers in its network for allegedly inflating applicants' incomes and falsifying employment details to secure mortgages.

Financial Consumer Agency of Canada (FCAC)

The FCAC's focus is on ensuring that customers of federally regulated financial institutions and payment card network operators have recourse in the event of a dispute.[21] FCAC has a mandate for education through the promotion of financial literacy and consumer awareness about their rights when dealing with financial institutions.[22] In the mortgage context, the FCAC has made information available to the public on a variety of topics such as mortgage deferrals during the pandemic, reverse mortgages, and informing them more generally about financial institutions' consumer protection obligations. FCAC also works directly with financial institutions and uses a variety of enforcement mechanisms such as the imposition of fines to ensure that they are compliant with voluntary codes of conduct and other public commitments.[23] The FCAC, through the minister of finance, presents an annual report to Parliament on institutions' compliance with consumer protection measures.[24]

Canada Mortgage and Housing Corporation (CMHC)

The CMHC is a Crown corporation that was established to promote housing "affordability ... competition and efficiency in the provision of housing finance, ... contribute to the well-being of the housing sector in the national economy," and carry out research on housing financing.[25] Mortgage default insurance is available to borrowers purchasing a home worth less than $1 million, with at least a 5% down payment.[26] The *National Housing Act* Mortgage-Backed Securities and Canada Mortgage Bonds are fully guaranteed by the CMHC to improve public access to these instruments.[27] The CMHC has stringent regulations for lenders governing mortgage insurance eligibility and relies on these same lenders to comply with the rules. CMHC can deny lender claims to recoup losses if the lender is found to have committed fraud or provided inaccurate or misleading information when submitting the mortgage insurance application. Affordable and public housing initiatives are also coordinated through the CMHC, often in conjunction with the relevant provincial legislatures.[28]

Canadian Regulatory Framework for Credit Unions (CUs) – Split Jurisdiction

CUs, or caisses populaires in Quebec, are non-profit financial institutions that perform many of the same operations as traditional banks, including offering mortgages and checking accounts.[29] Rather than being accountable to shareholders, CUs are member owned.[30] This shift in focus often results in better interest rates and lower fees than at major banks.[31] However, these institutions tend to be locally based, and that restriction can be a challenge for highly mobile customers.[32]

The regulation of Canadian CUs fits into two categories. Those that are federally registered, or operate in more than one province, are governed by the both the *Bank Act*[33] and the *Cooperative Credit Associations Act*[34] and are overseen by OSFI. CUs and caisses populaires that are organized to operate in only one province are governed by the provincial statutes and regulator in that jurisdiction.[35] In 2018, there were 252 provincial credit unions and two federal credit unions serving roughly 5.7 million Canadians.[36] Credit unions are the largest source of residential mortgages behind the major banks, holding 13% of the market.[37]

The growth in credit unions has led to two major institutes, Central 1 Credit Union and Caisse Desjardins, being deemed "domestically systemically important" by their regulator.[38] This term refers to the risk that problems in one institution can have negative material effects on the real economy.[39] With increasing pressure on credit unions to merge their operations, it is likely that more of these nationally important credit unions will emerge.[40] Ineffectual regulation of credit unions can have consequences beyond the single province in which they operate. However, the number of institutions regulating credit unions can result in uneven regulatory oversight. British Columbia's regulator, FICOM, was condemned in 2014 by the BC auditor general, who found that the regulator lacked important competencies, which negatively affected timely reviews.[41] A year later, FICOM provided a submission to the minister of finance indicating that there were major gaps in its governing statute compared to international standards that hindered its performance.[42] In 2019, the provincial government introduced legislation to establish the British Columbia Financial Services Authority (BCFSA), an independent Crown agency accountable to the minister of finance. Later that year, BCFSA replaced FICOM in regulating financial institutions, the Credit Union Deposit Insurance Corporation, pension plans, and mortgage brokers in the province.

B. The American Context

There are more entities regulating the American financial system than in Canada. Some, such as the Federal Deposit Insurance Company, the Consumer Financial Protection Bureau, and the Office of the Comptroller of the Currency, have mandates similar to those of their Canadian counterparts. Others reflect the different regulatory regime. The Federal National Mortgage Association (or Fannie Mae) and the Federal Home Loan Mortgage Corporation (or Freddie Mac) promote affordability in the American mortgage market.[43] Both institutions provide liquidity to thousands of banks and mortgage companies that finance housing, before buying the mortgages from lenders to either be held or repackaged into mortgage-backed securities, thus making a secondary market that makes the resale of mortgages feasible.[44] Key differences between these institutions are their target markets and products. While both assist banks in making more loans available and keeping interest rates low through purchasing mortgages, Fannie Mae focuses on large retail banks and Freddie Mac frees up bank funds by targeting smaller financial institutions. By 2009, Fannie Mae, Freddie Mac, and the Federal Home Loan Bank provided 90% of the financing for new mortgages in America.[45]

The Government National Mortgage Association (GNMA or Ginnie Mae) provides guarantees to mortgage lenders to allow them to obtain a better price on the secondary mortgage market, freeing up additional capital for new loans.[46] The Federal Housing Administration has a role similar to that of some elements of the CMHC's mandate by providing mortgage insurance on mortgages made from pre-approved lenders in the United States.[47] The differing regulatory regimes for mortgages in the United States and Canada may help explain some of the divergent reforms that will be examined in the next section.

II. Changes since the Global Financial Crisis

The regulatory response in both countries saw the introduction of measures to ensure that the size and terms of the mortgage were appropriate for the consumer. In the United States, the response was to place additional requirements on the lenders, while the focus in Canada was on the borrower. Though there are substantive differences in the Canadian and American systems and they tend to view the problem from different perspectives, both regimes encourage home ownership and are ultimately aimed at ensuring that past excesses will not be repeated.

A. Canada: Focus on Hot Spots and Borrower Solvency

Since the global financial crisis, a number of changes have been made to reduce the risk in the Canadian mortgage market. Many were made with an eye to overheated property markets in To-ronto and Vancouver, which have become widely viewed as a bubble.[48] Some of the new restrictions include: increasing the premiums on mortgage default insurance, nearly halving the maximum amortization period for insured mortgages, and lim-iting the maximum gross debt service and maximum total debt service ratios.[49] Homes worth at least $500,000 received further restrictions, including the requirement that an additional 10% be placed on the down payment for the value of the house between $500,000 and $999,999, mandating a minimum 20% down pay-ment on homes bought for over $1 million, and restricting gov-ernment-backed mortgage insurance for homes with a purchase price of less than $1 million.[50] These measures will apply to many new mortgages in both Toronto and Vancouver, where the aver-age price of a house at the beginning of 2019 was $761,800 and $1,019,600 respectively.[51]

Further measures were introduced as an attempt to cool those heated markets, including making it more expensive for foreign investors and people who don't intend to live in the property to purchase them. This includes a 15% foreign buyer's tax, a 1% tax on vacant homes that remain unrented, and a minimum down payment of 20%.[52] OSFI has also implemented guidelines for resi-dential mortgage insurance underwriting policies and procedures, commonly known as B-20, for banks, federally regulated mortgage lenders, and insurers.[53] This framework will be discussed in more detail below.

The New Canadian Regime: Stress-Tested Mortgages

Canadian financial regulators have enacted several changes to as-sist in the stability of the mortgage market, particularly in the event of a financial downturn or a rise in interest rates. The first major change took place in 2012, when OSFI announced the B-20 Guide-lines, which outlined the key principles mortgage lenders were ex-pected to adhere to.[54] A major change to B-20 took place in 2016, when the federal government announced stress testing for insured mortgages.[55] Mortgage insurance is mandatory when a home is purchased with a down payment of less than 20% of the purchase price.[56] This change mandates that to be eligible for a mortgage with that smaller deposit, borrowers will need to qualify for the greater of their contract mortgage rate, or the Bank of Canada's five-year posted rate.[57] Borrowers are also restricted from having a gross debt service (GDS) ratio of 39% or higher, or a total debt service (TDS) ratio of 44% or more.[58] The GDS ratio is calculated by adding the carrying costs of the home, including the mortgage payment, property taxes, condo fees, and heating costs, relative to borrowers' income.[59] The TDS ratio takes a wider view of borrowers' commitments, looking at the carrying costs of the home and all other debt payments relative to borrowers' income.[60]

In October 2017, the stress-testing regime was expanded to uninsured loans through the B-20 Guidelines on residential mortgage underwriting practices and procedures.[61] Among the new requirements was updating the minimum qualifying rate for uninsured mortgages to the greater of the five-year Bank of Canada benchmark rate or the contracted mortgage rate plus 2%.[62] Before the implementation of B-20, the stress test was restricted to insured borrowers with a down payment of less than 20%.[63] In practical terms, this means that for borrowers to purchase an average-priced home, currently valued at approximately $500,000, they would need to have a minimum household income of 18%, or $16,000 higher than they needed before the implementation of B-20.[64] This change affects a significant portion of the Canadian mortgage market, since 45% of domestic bank mortgage portfolios and roughly 70% of new loans are non-insured.[65]

Since the stress-testing regime was implemented, there have been criticisms about the intensity of the tests and claims that the stress tests are harmful to consumers.[66] Following the introduction of the B-20 guidelines, the Bank of Canada raised interest rates by 0.75%, sparking questions about whether the current 2%

figure in the guidelines is still appropriate.[67] The stress-testing regime also applies unevenly across the country as the result of standard requirements. What may be an asset in overheated markets, such as Toronto, has hindered the mortgage market for young people and in depressed markets like Calgary's.[68] Especially controversial is the requirement that borrowers re-financing their mortgage must stay with their existing lender if they fail the stress test – even if they have no history of default or late payments.[69] A new lender may offer a more competitive rate or more favorable terms than the existing one, or simply give borrowers more options in how they choose to organize their financial affairs.[70] An estimated 100,000 renewers annually are at risk of not passing the stress test.[71]

Despite criticisms of the stress-testing regime, the federal government is still largely supportive of the policy, saying in the 2019 federal budget that they are "having their intended impacts."[72] To soften the effects for first-time home buyers, the budget contained additional assistance. The first requires CMHC to begin offering shared equity mortgages to first-time home buyers with household incomes under $120,000 to increase the size of the down payment.[73] If the home being purchased is a new build, 10% of the house's purchase price will be offered, or 5% if the house has been previously owned.[74] This measure is designed to make it easier for first-time home buyers to qualify for an insured mortgage within the stress-testing regime.[75] The second measure increased the amount that may be removed from a registered retirement account to go toward a down payment without incurring tax consequences.[76] Canadians are able to privately save for retirement through registered accounts and are permitted to deduct the value of contributions from their income taxes. Normally withdrawals are taxed at the recipient's marginal tax rate, although it is not treated as income if the sum is used toward a down payment and is repaid within fifteen years.[77] The 2019 budget increases this sum to $35,000 from $25,000.[78]

Stress Testing and the CUs

With the majority of credit unions falling under provincial regulation, the industry is generally exempt from OSFI's B-20 guidelines. Quebec has elected to require its caisses populaires to adhere to the B-20 guidelines, although it remains the only regulator to do so.[79] This is partially due to the perceived stability of provincial credit unions.[80] A recent study found that the ninety-day delinquency rate at credit unions is less than half the comparable figure for the major banks.[81] Individual credit unions are also electing to adhere to the guidelines voluntarily, with the CMHC estimating that approximately 58% were compliant as of October 2018.[82] While there is substantial anecdotal evidence of a migration to credit unions in the wake of the implementation of the B-20 guidelines, there is limited evidence about the scope of the shift. Though federal regulators are monitoring CU participation in the mortgage market, they acknowledge that "the cost of levelling that playing field may not be worth the effort."[83]

B. The United States: New Institutions and Lender Requirements

The United States also took steps following the financial crisis to reform its role in the mortgage market. The *Housing and Economic Recovery Act* created the Federal Housing Finance Authority (FHFA), which is organized along the same lines as the FDIC.[84] Since the crisis, both Fannie Mae and Freddie Mac have shrunk their investment portfolios by half and continue to work with the FHFA to minimize their credit risk.[85]

The Consumer Financial Protection Bureau (CFPB), an independent bureau within the Federal Reserve System, was created as part of the *Dodd-Frank Wall Street Reform and Consumer Protection Act* (*Dodd-Frank*) to protect Americans from unfair or abusive financial practices.[86] The bureau has power over any person or institution that offers or provides financial services, including mortgages, to prevent "unfair, deceptive, or abusive acts or practices."[87] This phrase "unfair practices" has been defined by the *Federal Trade Commission Act* and associated decisions as practices where there is a reasonable basis to conclude that the "practice causes or is likely to cause substantial injury to customers which is not outweighed by countervailing benefits to consumers or to competition."[88] This definition has been accepted by the CFPB.[89] An "abusive practice" was defined by *Dodd-Frank* as a practice that "materially interferes with the ability of a consumer to understand a term or condition" or "takes unreasonable advantage of" consumers' lack of understanding about the risks or costs of a product, inability to protect their interests by using a consumer financial product, or a reasonable reliance on someone covered under *Dodd-Frank* to act in their interests.[90] The CFPB can enforce its standards by beginning a civil action against an offender.[91] Much like the FCAC in Canada, the CFPB, in addition to monitoring the marketplace, seeks to empower consumers to make informed decisions by providing information about mortgages and other consumer financial products and services.

On the lending side, additional regulations were put in place to require more thorough documentation and verification. *Dodd-Frank* requires that before a loan is approved, lenders must disclose all costs involved in the loan, ensure that the borrower can repay the mortgage, and validate the borrower's employment and debt levels.[92] Highly risky products, such as negative amortization mortgages or an interest-only period, have been banned altogether.[93] *Dodd-Frank* also created the concept of a "qualified mortgage," which will be explored in more detail in the next section of this paper.[94]

Some of the regulations brought forward in *Dodd-Frank* were subsequently watered down by the Trump administration. S.2155 eliminated reporting requirements for many mortgage lenders, which may have consequences on identifying predatory lending.[95] Obtaining a mortgage from a smaller bank or credit union could become easier, as they are no longer subject to the more stringent underwriting requirements and will be able to issue qualified mortgages.[96]

The New American Regime: Qualified Mortgages

Qualified mortgages (QMs) were added to the American mortgage regime through *Dodd-Frank*.[97] QMs are grounded in the idea that there was a systemic mismatch in the mortgage market where risky complex mortgages were being sold to people who were not suitable for that product.[98] In the view of many legislators, lenders targeted poor, less-educated consumers with these products, knowing that securitization would minimize their down-side risk.[99]

In response, QMs require the lender to make a good-faith effort to verify that the borrower has the ability to repay the loan before it is extended.[100] In return for adhering to certain requirements, lenders are given protections from future claims from the borrower that the loan was unsuitable.[101] Without protections in place, the lender could be vulnerable to judicial proceedings and fines, which are typically collected in the context of a class action suit.[102] The "safe harbor" provisions, while beneficial, alter a previously arm's-length relationship between the borrower and lender to one that imposes a general duty on lenders.[103] *Dodd-Frank* was the first American federal law to impose such an obligation on mortgage lenders.[104]

Restrictions for QMs include a limit on the debt-to-income (DTI) ratio and a prohibition on risky loan features, excess upfront points, or fees.[105] The factors that must be considered are: current or expected income and assets, current employment status, monthly mortgage payment for the loan, monthly payment on loans secured by that property, monthly payments related to the property including applicable taxes and homeowners association fees, other debts including child support obligations, monthly debt-to-income ratio, and credit history.[106]

The appropriate level of the DTI ratio for qualified mortgages has recently become a subject of debate. The CFPB has set the general requirement for a QM that the borrower should have a DTI of no more than 43%.[107] However, under the rules for QMs, any loan can be a QM as long as it is eligible for purchase by Fannie Mae or Freddie Mac.[108] This exemption from CFPB guidelines was effective until January 2021.[109] This is commonly referred to as the "GSE [government sponsored entity] patch."[110] On 29 July 2017, the exemption was used when Fannie Mae raised the acceptable DTI ceiling to 50%, citing "other factors" in borrower risk profiles that reduce the potential for default with the higher DTI.[111] Approximately one-third of Fannie Mae's current loans exceed the CFPB-recommended 43% DTI ratio.[112] Discussions on the resolution of the GSE patch have raised questions about the appropriate stringency for the DTI ratio, whether it should be amended to include other factors, or if the cap should be eliminated altogether.[113]

III. Home Capital and the Threat of a Blind-Side Hit

The saga at Home Capital illustrates how, despite the new regulatory requirements around the mortgage industry, turmoil can still emerge from unexpected places. These events also highlight how the bad behavior of market actors can exacerbate the enforcement issues caused by fragmented and ineffective regulatory frameworks and transform the unsafe practices of a single lender into systemic risks. Responding to this systemic risk, depositors and investors could lose faith in other financial institutions and send the country into the sort of crisis that threatens the entire housing market or the economy writ large.

Home Capital's problems originated from allegations of fraud dating to July 2015. After an internal investigation revealed fraudulent activity from forty-five of its brokers, Home Capital parted ways with those brokers.[114] The terminations and subsequent implementation of quality controls had a direct effect on Home

Capital's mortgage originations.[115] The terminated brokers generated roughly 10% of Home Capital's total new mortgages in 2014, and new internal controls and more stringent underwriting checks increased the amount of time to process a mortgage, causing a slowdown in business. This reduction in activity was explained in Home Capital's annual disclosure as "external vagaries such as macroeconomics, seasonality, and competitive markets."[116] It took five months for Home Capital to fully disclose the reasons behind the decline. By 2017, the Ontario Securities Commission (OSC) alleged that Home Capital made a misleading disclosure by failing to disclose the fraud to their shareholders in their annual disclosure.[117] Despite the strength of Home Capital's capital base and underlying fundamentals, the OSC's release prompted a $600 million drop in deposits and the commencement of a class action lawsuit against it, as well as a drop in share price for other non-bank lenders.[118] In fact, subsequent to the "collapse" of Home Capital's share price on 26 April 2017, shares in Equitable Bank, Home Capital's closest competitor, fell more than 25% in large part as the result of fear of contagion from the Home Capital crisis. The drop in deposits reduced Home Capital's ability to lend, ultimately requiring the intervention of a Warren Buffet–led consortium to provide a $400 million equity loan and a $2 billion line of credit.[119]

It is worth noting that Home Capital's troubles began before the major B-20 guidelines had been announced or had come into force.[120] However, if anecdotal evidence is correct that an increasing number of borrowers are flocking to provincially regulated institutions to avoid the stress-testing regime, the regulatory action around Home Capital leaves something to be desired.[121] The reaction to a charge of regulatory non-compliance appeared to catch regulators off-guard and sparked calls for a reconsideration of how such information is disclosed in the future.[122] Home Capital's woes have also raised questions about the transparency and regulatory compliance of financial institutions.[123] Although the CMHC and other actors can deny lender claims to recoup losses if that lender committed fraud or provided inaccurate information, it is impossible to effectively police wide swaths of the mortgage market in real time.[124] If, or when, a correction in housing begins elsewhere, it may be worse than anticipated if lenders are succumbing to the moral hazard of granting loans with relaxed standards to gain more business, as the risk of potential default lies with the CMHC.[125] The cost of the failure of an institution like Home Capital, however, is not borne by its shareholders alone. Any slowdown in lending caused by the failure of non-bank lending institutions will ultimately weigh on home prices through rising mortgage rates and could make it harder for some individuals, often those already financially marginalized, to secure a home loan.

Conclusion

As the economic reverberations of the COVID-19 crisis proliferate across the globe, the pandemic's impact on the financial services sector and individuals' wealth and debt levels becomes more apparent. Mortgage debt, as the single largest source of debt for most homeowners, has a significant impact on their ability to stay solvent through wage decreases or unemployment. Similarly, lenders' profitability and liquidity are also acutely affected by changes in repayment schedules and default rates for residential mortgages. As such, maintaining the continued health of the global residential mortgage market is critical to ensuring that individuals, firms, and countries can recover from the COVID-19 crisis. As demonstrated by the events surrounding Home Capital and the 2008 financial crisis before it, this recovery can be either hastened or delayed by the regulatory responses of relevant actors. Home Capital was regarded as "small enough to fail," but regulators must consider "what happens if a few becomes several or many, and [they] don't see it coming."[126] If smaller institutions are more exposed to a crashing mortgage market, we may find out just how prepared Canada's institutions are to weather that storm.

CHAPTER FIVE

Tax Reform: A Missing Piece in Canada's National Housing Policy

Jinyan Li*

Introduction

Housing occupies a special place in Canadian society. Over two-thirds of Canadian families own a home, which is one of the highest homeownership rates among OECD countries.[1] As well as being a home, housing is a financial asset: it is the biggest family asset for most households, and housing-related expenditures (mortgages, property taxes, and maintenance) are the main cause of household debts.[2] The housing sector accounts for about 7.5% of the Canadian economy, and new housing is an important indicator of the state of the economy.[3] Any "crisis" associated with housing can have a profound impact on Canadians. Governments often put fiscal and regulatory policies in place to affect the supply and/or demand of housing for social and economic reasons.

This chapter considers the role of tax policy in Canada's housing policy. Drawing on the literature and publicly available data, it claims that current tax policy is biased in favor of homeownership,

* Professor at Osgoode Hall Law School. The author thanks Cameron Smith, Jin Bao, and Lucas Colantoni for their research assistance, and Stephanie Ben-Ishai, Patrick Egit, and anonymous reviewers for their comments on earlier drafts.

which has propelled demand for housing as a speculative investment asset. This, in turn, potentially contributes to rising housing
prices and less access to affordable housing. Despite the profound
impact it has on this area, tax policy has not been well integrated
into Canada's national housing policy. This chapter argues that it
should be. Tax instruments can be redesigned to help address, although not necessarily prevent, housing vulnerabilities in terms of
financial risks and affordable housing.

Research on the importance of tax policy in housing was inspired
by the "scare" of a housing bubble being punctured by Home Capital's
crisis in 2017[4] and possible connections between tax policy, speculative investments, and the secondary mortgages market. This research
is important for two reasons. First, it contributes to the housing policy
debates by drawing attention to the role of tax policy. It shows that,
even though the existing tax instruments were intended to promote
economic activities in the housing sector, they are now likely contributing to the housing crisis. These tax instruments can be redesigned
to reduce speculative investments in housing while encouraging investment in affordable housing.[5] Second, this research contributes to
Canadian literature on housing by examining the significance of tax
policy on the demand and supply of housing. Literature in this area
is limited (e.g., Dowler,[6] Fallis,[7] Steele,[8] Bird,[9] and Hulchanski[10]) and
rather dated. This chapter seeks to remedy this gap.

This chapter's subject matter is also timely. The COVID-19 pandemic amplifies the health risk associated with housing because housing has become "the front line defense against the coronavirus,"[11] and
poor housing conditions are correlated to higher infection rates. For
example, the number of COVID-19 cases is nearly four times higher
among people living in areas of Toronto with high levels of overcrowd-
ing.[12] These communities also tend to house a higher concentration
of impoverished and racialized individuals than their less-crowded
counterparts. The post-pandemic era will likely see broader political
support for a more coherent public policy framework to reduce such
inequity at the top (e.g., reducing speculative investment in oversized

housing or second or third homes) as well as the bottom (more access to affordable housing). As in other major public policy areas, tax policy can be a major element of the national housing policy framework. This chapter illustrates how that can be the case.

Following this introduction, parts I to III provide the context for developing the central argument. Part I discusses the importance of housing in Canada. It also examines the housing situation from a market perspective: demand for housing driven by the fundamental need of a home and by speculative investments that regard housing as an investment asset or commodity, and supply of housing out of profit motivations and for social policy reasons. Part II presents the existing federal, provincial, and municipal taxes on housing and notes that the most significant tax measures are those in the *Income Tax Act*,[13] such as the Principal Residence Exemption, first-time home buyers tax credit, tax-free treatment of imputed rent, and the availability of self-help tax shelters through investment in rental housing. Part III considers the impact of the tax bias for homeownership on speculative investment in housing and the supply of affordable housing. Part IV makes the case for using tax policy to advance housing policy objectives. It identifies main options and teases out potential challenges. The chapter closes with concluding remarks.

I. Housing and Housing Crisis

A. Home Ownership

Housing has a unique place in Canadian society because of its multifaceted relationship with home owners. A housing unit can be a family residence, an instrument of savings, or an object of speculation. For most Canadians, housing is a hybrid of consumption and savings. According to Statistics Canada, the decision to own or rent one's home is "one of the most important decisions for a household" as it "affects household finance, the ease with which people can relocate, the choice of location and type of dwelling, and other important factors related to how people live."[14]

About two-thirds of Canadian households own their home. For example, in 2016, more than 67.8% (9.5 million of the 14.1 million) Canadian households owned their home, while about 26% of households rent at market rate, 6% participate in social housing, and 25,000 Canadians are chronically homeless.[15] Some Canadian households own more than one residential property. In 2018, 1.2 million multiple-property owners in British Columbia, Nova Scotia, and Ontario owned around 2.1 million properties and these non-owner-occupied properties were used to generate income, capital gains, or for personal use.[16] The majority of multiple-property owners were concentrated in Toronto and Vancouver, and most own two single-detached houses.[17]

Since housing wealth is the most important form of wealth for ordinary Canadians, disparities in homeownership widen the wealth inequality gap in Canada. Home ownership is concentrated in higher-income groups and with older Canadians. For example, in 2017, the lowest-quintile households held 7% of total housing assets, compared to a 46% share among top-quintile households.[18] Among households in the top-income quintile, net worth rose by 56% from 2010 to 2017.[19] During recent decades, the growing gap between high-income and low-income Canadian households has increasingly manifested itself in the housing system, with households that cannot afford to buy their homes remaining in the rental market.[20]

Inter-generational inequality between baby boomers and younger Canadians is also evident. Canadian families with a major income earner aged sixty-five and older reported the largest median value in home equity in 2016 at $300,000, where those aged thirty-five to forty-four had median home equity of $168,000.[21] In 2016, the home-ownership rate was 74.6% for households aged sixty-five and over, but only 43.1% for households under thirty-five.[22] Millennials are purchasing homes at a slower rate than baby boomers did when they were young adults, and those purchases are more likely to be condos, rather than detached homes.[23]

Homeownership in Canada has social and economic implications. In general, housing is considered to have significant linkages with children's education, health, sense of security, community life, and environment, and has been considered the "root of human flourishing" and critical to "personhood."[24] Access to affordable housing is considered a basic human right.[25] When housing becomes a speculative investment asset or trading commodity, it may create financial risks.

B. Affordability Crisis

The Current Crisis

Affordability is "the sum of a range of factors including the ability to access affordable housing, trade-offs made on quality and location and the range of other costs associated with housing consumption such as taxes and utilities."[26] There are different methods used to calculate housing affordability in Canada.[27] A minimum income threshold is the conventional method that uses "the shelter-cost-to-income ratio, which most commonly sets the affordability threshold at 30% of before-tax household income."[28]

Research commissioned by the CMHC found that affordability pressures are acute for both single adults and lone-parent households across several of the largest metropolitan areas.[29] According to a recent RBC Economic Brief, the share of income a household would need to cover homeownership costs is 84.7% in Vancouver, 66.1% in Toronto, 44.5% in Montreal, and 40.6% in Ottawa in the last quarter of 2018.[30] The down payment for an "average" home in most major Canadian cities exceeds the average annual household income, and was more than 150% of this figure in Vancouver.[31] The time required to save for the down payment on a representative home at a savings rate of 10% is 342 months in Vancouver, 33 months in Montreal, and 92 months in Toronto.[32] Exorbitant down payments particularly affect the ability of younger Canadians to purchase a home.

The challenges in affordable rental housing are well recognized. For example, over 50% of Ontario households headed by someone aged twenty-five to thirty-four rent their home, and nearly half of Ontario renters pay more than the affordability threshold of 20% of before-tax income.[33] Across Canada, 1.7 million people are in core housing need; living in homes that are either inadequate or unaffordable.[34] For many Canadians, shelter costs grow faster than incomes. Low-income and private rental households are particularly vulnerable to "housing stress."[35] On average, a full-time worker needs to make $22.40/hour to be able to rent an average two-bedroom apartment using no more than 30% of her income.[36] In some cities, the hourly wage needed is much higher: $35.43 in Vancouver and $33.70 in Toronto.[37] The minimum wage in 2019 was $13.85 in Vancouver and $14.00 in Toronto.

It can be said that there is an affordability crisis in many parts of Canada and that this has serious social consequences.[38] A recent study found that, on average, immigrants face more severe housing challenges than non-immigrants, homeowners tend to fare better than renters, and non-couples tend to face greater housing difficulties than couples.[39] The most vulnerable Canadians include "women and children fleeing family violence, Indigenous peoples, seniors, people with disabilities, those dealing with mental health and addiction issues, veterans and young adults."[40]

Government Intervention

All levels of government have intervened in an attempt to improve the affordability of housing. Conquering the lack of affordable housing is key to solving rising poverty levels in Canada. A government housing policy is therefore a necessary ingredient in a comprehensive social policy as well as economic, health, and environmental policies.[41] The first modern example of a housing program is from 1918, when the federal government made $25 million available to build new homes for "young returning soldiers of modest income who needed help to purchase a small home."[42] At the end of the Second World War, the *National Housing Act* was introduced and the Central Mortgage and

Housing Corporation (later renamed the Canada Mortgage and Housing Corporation, or CMHC) was created to provide returning war veterans with homes and to lead Canada's housing programs.[43] Today, the CMHC exists for a single reason: "to make housing affordable for everyone in Canada."[44] The most recent example is the National Housing Strategy, which was launched in 2017 to increase investment in social housing and help vulnerable Canadians.[45] The strategy contains a ten-year, $55 billion investment initiative to help ensure that "Canadians have housing that meets their needs and [that] they can afford."[46]

C. Financial Risks

Potential Crisis

Risks related to housing can have significant impact on the Canadian economy because of the size of the housing sector. In fact, the housing and real estate sector is a major pillar of the Canadian economy.[47] In 2019, residential real estate represented 7.5% of the Canadian economy, compared with 4.9% in the United States, and 4.1% in the United Kingdom.[48] About one-fifth of the Canadian economy is related to real estate, including construction, rental and leasing, finance, and insurance sectors.[49]

The Canadian housing market comprises three segments: ownership, private market rental, and the social and non-profit sector where rents are administratively set below market rates.[50] Outside the social housing sector, the price of housing is a function of supply and demand, which, in turn, is influenced by many factors, including government policies, regulatory measures, the general state of the economy, employment rates, and population growth. A buoyant housing market contributes to sustained economic activity.[51]

Meanwhile, household debt and overvaluation in the housing market are among Canada's largest domestic economic risks.[52] Canadians have a propensity to view housing as a "can't lose" investment[53] and to maximize debt to finance home ownership. Mortgage debt accounts for two-thirds of all outstanding household debts in

Canada.[54] In 2018, 51.9% of household income was needed to cover ownership costs.[55] High housing prices make homeowners believe they are wealthier than they are and increase consumer spending. This mindset poses some risks, particularly because a growing share of the mortgage market is made up of less-regulated financial institutions beyond the big banks, such as Home Capital. Some recent data show that "nearly a quarter of new borrowers hold debt exceeding 450% of their income – a level far beyond the 170% debt-to-income ratio at the national level that is normally quoted – making them significantly more vulnerable to the current rising interest rate environment."[56]

The COVID-19 pandemic does not appear to have pronounced effects on housing markets thus far, as housing sales bounced back in the summer after an initial drop in the spring of 2020. On the other hand, it temporarily "cooled" the rental markets in some large cities such as Toronto, Montreal, and Vancouver.[57] The economic shock of the pandemic and the uncertainty of post-pandemic economic recovery can cause financial strain on homeowners, thus posing a risk for the residential housing market.

A downturn in housing may trigger a de-leveraging episode among Canadian households, which could adversely affect the financial system and the broader economy.[58] The Bank of Canada recently noted that the "vulnerabilities associated with high household debt and imbalances in housing market have declined modestly but remain significant."[59] Younger homeowners would suffer disproportionately if prices subsequently fall, since they are more likely to have outstanding debt secured against their homes.[60] As suggested by the Home Capital case, the residential mortgage market is tied to the overall financial system of Canada, and its risk may affect the Canadian economy in significant ways.[61]

Regulatory Policies

Policy interventions in the ownership and rental markets tend to be behavior-inducing measures to encourage demand or supply of housing, or establishing and enforcing the rules of the game through regulation. "Most of the history of the role of Canadian government housing policy and programs is a history of efforts targeted at the house-ownership sector."[62] Behavior-inducing measures include tax subsidies to first-time home buyers and homeowners.[63] An example of a regulatory regime is the "stress test" for obtaining mortgages and mortgage insurance where the down payment is less than 20% of the total purchase price, a framework that is given a detailed examination in Stephanie Ben-Ishai's chapter.[64] As discussed below, income tax instruments are geared mostly toward home owners.

II. Taxation of Housing

Three types of taxation affect housing in Canada: income taxes, GST, and property taxes.[65] While income taxes and GST are imposed by the federal and provincial governments, property taxes are imposed by provinces or municipalities. Housing-related income tax and GST measures are predominantly tax expenditures,[66] as they provide preferential treatment for owner-occupied housing. In contrast, property taxes are designed to target housing directly and are an important source of revenue for local governments. Property taxes take the form of land transfer tax, property tax, vacancy taxes, and the foreign buyers' tax.[67] All of these taxes can be viewed as part of Canada's housing tax system, even though they were not introduced with much, if any, coordination. The impact of these tax instruments on the demand or supply of housing is explored in part III.

A. Income Tax

The *Income Tax Act* provides several tax subsidies to owner-occupied housing, including the Principal Residence Exemption and first-time home buyers' plan.[68] The *Income Tax Act* does not tax imputed rent, namely the economic value derived by owners from living in their home[69] while taxing imputed income from some other forms of investments (such as long-term debts or shares of controlled foreign affiliates).[70] Finally, the *Income Tax Act* contains opportunities for owner-investors to create "tax shelters" where investment in housing creates "losses on paper" to offset income from other sources, thus making the after-tax return on such investments higher. The *Income Tax Act* is markedly biased in favor of homeownership.

The Principal Residence Exemption

The Principal Residence Exemption is a popular tax subsidy. It, in effect, exempts gains realized from the sale of a principal residence by resident individuals from taxation.[71] It makes buying a home much more attractive than buying investment assets, such as bonds or stocks, since gains from the sale of these assets are taxable. A principal residence is a home that was ordinarily inhabited during the year by taxpayers, their spouse or common-law partner, their former spouse or common-law partner, or their child under eighteen years of age.[72] The property can be located outside Canada. There is no limitation on the amount of capital gains eligible for the exemption.

The Principal Residence Exemption was introduced during the 1972 tax reform, which added a tax on capital gains.[73] The main justifications for this exemption were the social and economic implications of residential housing. "Homeownership is part of the Canadian way of life,"[74] and the exemption "recognizes that principal homes are generally purchased to provide basic shelter and not as an investment, and increases flexibility in the housing market by facilitating the movement of families from one principal residence to another in response to their changing circumstances."[75] The Department of Finance gave a commentary in the explanatory booklet that accompanied the legislation:

> Many who commented on the [white paper] provisions felt that substantial tax liabilities would still occur in areas where pressure on the housing market pushed prices up strongly and that homeowners would continue to face uncertainty about their tax position. It was also argued that the

economic use of our housing stock might be inhibited if families could not "move up" to larger houses as they grew and established themselves.

The Government has decided that these arguments can best be met by a complete exemption. This will save homeowners from valuation problems and meet the very strong views of Canadian homeowners and many other Canadians who aspire to home ownership.[76]

The Principal Residence Exemption is the second most expensive federal tax expenditure,[77] costing the government roughly $5 to $7 billion in revenue each year from 2013 to 2018.[78] This figure dwarfs federal direct spending on social housing. For example, CMHC plans to spend an average of $2.8 billion per year on assisted housing programs over the ten-year term ending in 2027, and Employment and Social Development Canada plans to spend $225 million per year on homelessness programs.[79]

The tax exemption benefits homeowners, especially the top 20% of income earners who receive 55% of the benefit from this exemption. Only 10% of the tax benefit goes to the bottom half of income earners.[80] The distributional effect is thus regressive: the more capital gains realized from the sale of homes an individual has, the more government subsidy he or she receives. Renters do not benefit from this tax subsidy; owners of smaller homes benefit less. The tax exemption thus subsidizes the higher end of the housing market. It favors investment in housing over other types of investments. This tax exemption, coupled with low interest rates, makes "investing in our homes an irresistible means of savings."[81] As will be explained in part IV, the tax exemption has the effect of encouraging accumulation of housing wealth on a tax-free basis, which may cause speculative investment or house flipping.

First-Time Home Buyers Tax Credit
The First-Time Home Buyers Tax Credit and the tax-free withdrawal from a Registered Retired Savings Plan (RRSP) under the Home Buyers Plan[82] assist those purchasing a residential property for the

first time. The First-Time Home Buyers' Tax Credit was introduced in 2009 following the 2008 global financial crisis. It provides an annual tax relief of $750[83] and is tied to an estimated foregone tax revenue of roughly $100 million per year.[84] The Home Buyers Plan is available to individuals who have money accumulated in an RRSP. While withdrawals from RRSPs before retirement age are taxable,[85] withdrawals of up to $35,000 are tax-free if the money is used for a down payment on the purchaser's first home.[86] This initiative was found to encourage Canadians under the age of forty-five to use the RRSP to save for home ownership.[87]

Non-Taxation of Imputed Rent

Imputed rent is not regarded as taxable income. Non-taxation of imputed rent is not even counted as a tax expenditure in the annual tax expenditures report in Canada.[88] The *Income Tax Act* is biased in favor of investment in a home, as opposed to other forms of investments, even if such investments are sheltered in an RRSP or a Tax-Free Savings Account (TFSA). There are two main reasons for this: (1) the money spent on residential rent is not tax deductible, while income from investment (such as interest or dividend) is taxable; and (2) capital gains from the sale of the investment assets is taxable. The following example shows the favorable treatment of owner-occupied homes:[89]

> A taxpayer (the homeowner in table 5.1) with a marginal tax rate of 50% owns a house, free and clear, which could be rented for $12,000 per year, and he lives in the house. Assume that he moves to another city and becomes a renter (the renter in the table). He leases his house in the old city for $12,000 per year and rents an equivalent house in the new city for $12,000 per year. See how this move leaves him worse off to the tune of $6,000 per year.

In this example, the homeowner paid no rent and received no rental income for tax purposes, but the renter paid rent of $12,000 and

Table 5.1. Tax Bias for Homeowners

	Homeowner ($)	Renter ($)
Salary	100,000	100,000
Rental income (old city)	0	12,000
Taxable income	100,000	112,000
Tax (at 50%)	(56,000)	(50,000)
Cost of rent (old city)	0	(12,000)
Discretionary income	50,000	44,000

received rental income of $12,000. For tax purposes, the $12,000 paid by the renter is not deductible from taxable income, while the $12,000 received by renter is subject to tax at 50%. Therefore, the renter had a tax liability of $6,000 and is thus worse off by $6,000 each year.

The non-taxation of imputed rent has a distributional effect similar to that of the Principal Residence Exemption: higher-income and older taxpayers who can afford to buy valuable homes benefit the most. An earlier study found that the non-taxation of imputed rent "tends to favour taxpayers with the greatest amounts of equity in a house, and who have owned the dwelling for the longest period of time."[90]

Rental Housing as a Tax Shelter

While there are currently no specific subsidies for rental housing investors, the *Income Tax Act* permits self-created tax shelters. Previously, a tax incentive for multiple unit residential buildings (MURBs) allowed taxpayers to deduct capital cost allowance (CCA)-generated losses on a rental property from income derived from other sources.[91] The MURB program was criticized for being too costly, inefficient, and prone to abuse; it was repealed in 1981.[92] Now, taxpayers can help themselves in using rental housing as tax shelters.[93] The CCA regime is based on the idea that assets will depreciate in value and that a portion of that loss should be reflected on the individual's or corporation's tax returns as an expense.[94] This regime makes sense for assets with a finite useful life, such as a piece of manufacturing equipment, but is less reasonable when the asset holds its value or appreciates, as is almost always the case with housing. However, under the current regime, the landlord can deduct CCA as an expense, even when the asset has not lost its value.[95] These losses can then be used to offset income earned by the landlord's other operations, reducing the overall tax burden.[96] The *Income Tax Act* requires only that a loss arise from either business or property, leaving it to the courts to determine if a rental loss is from an eligible source. The courts have adopted a very low threshold.

For example, in *Stewart v Canada*,[97] the Supreme Court of Canada held that a highly leveraged investment in a rental housing, which was designed to generate paper losses, constituted a source of income, thus rendering the losses tax deductible. In the *Stewart* case, the taxpayer bought four condos that he then rented to unrelated parties. There was no evidence that the taxpayer intended to make use of any of the properties for his personal benefit. Rather, it appeared that Mr. Stewart intended to later sell the condos after they had appreciated in value. In the year after he purchased the condos, Mr. Stewart claimed losses on his taxes for the interest he had to pay on the mortgages to acquire those condos. The loss was denied as an expense by the minister of national revenue. Both the Tax Court and the Federal Court of Appeal found that there was no reasonable expectation of profit from property because the scheme held out no expectation of profit from the rental income. The scheme was promoted by the vendor/developer as a tax shelter to "use rental losses to offset other income and realize a gain at the end of the day from the expected appreciation in the value of the property."[98] The Supreme Court of Canada reversed the lower courts' decisions and ruled that there was a source of property income because the investment was in pursuit of profit. It further held that "the motivation of capital gains accords with the ordinary business person's understanding of 'pursuit of profit,' and may be taken into account (as one of several factors) in determining whether the taxpayer's activity was commercial in nature."[99] *Stewart* is just one example of the favorable treatment tax planning receives by the courts.[100]

B. Goods and Services Tax

The GST is a multi-stage value-added tax.[101] It is collected by businesses that supply goods and services, but the tax burden falls on consumers. Businesses that purchase goods and services to be used in the course of their commercial activities can claim input tax credits and receive a tax refund. The current federal GST tax rate is 5%. Housing is eligible for special treatment.

Canadians who sell their principal residence or who purchase a used home are not required to pay GST. However, new housing, including newly constructed or substantially renovated housing, is subject to GST.[102] To encourage home ownership, individuals who buy new housing may be eligible for a tax rebate to recover some of the GST paid on the purchase.[103] When the pre-tax price exceeds a threshold (currently $450,000), the rebate is not available, suggesting that the tax rebate was intended to assist lower-income homeowners. The estimated annual amount of revenue cost to the government is over $500 million from 2013 to 2019.[104]

Canadians who rent a house, apartment, or condo for a period of at least one month are exempt from the GST.[105] This exemption "is intended to preserve the affordability of housing."[106] The estimated annual cost to the government rose from $1.8 billion in 2013 to $2.2 billion in 2019.[107] Short-term accommodation is also exempt from GST where the daily charge is less than $20.[108] The new housing rebate also applies to new residential rental property.[109] As such, owner-occupants and owner-landlords receive identical GST treatment.

C. Property-Related Taxes

Property-related taxes include land transfer taxes and recurring taxes on the assessed value of homes and other municipal-level vacancy taxes. The main policy objectives of these taxes are to raise revenue, combat restate estate speculation, increase the supply of rental housing, and reduce the wealth gap.[110]

Land Transfer Taxes

Land transfer tax is imposed by all provinces except Alberta and Saskatchewan, which levy a nominal transfer fee.[111] In most provinces, the tax is calculated as a percentage of property value, using the closing price as a close estimate. These tax rates are also progressive. For example, the marginal rate in Ontario and Toronto is 0.5% of the first $55,000 of the purchase price, 1.0% of $55,000.01 to $250,000, 1.5% of $250,000.01 to $400,000; 2% of $400,000.01 to $2 million; and 2.5% of more than $2 million.[112] The rates in British Columbia are slightly higher: 1.0% of the first $200,000; 2.0% of $200,001 to $2 million; and 3.0% of over $2 million. First-time home buyers can be partially exempted from this tax. For example, the rebate of the Toronto land transfer tax effectively exempted the first $400,000 of the purchase price from the tax.[113]

Non-resident buyers are liable to pay an additional land transfer tax in British Columbia and Ontario. This tax was introduced as a response to the skyrocketing housing prices in Vancouver and Toronto, which were believed to be caused, in part, by housing speculations by foreign buyers.[114] In both British Columbia and Ontario, this tax was among a number of measures adopted to improve the affordability and stability of housing market in specified areas.[115] The tax rate is currently 15% in Ontario and 20% in British Columbia.[116]

Recurring Taxes on Property

A property tax is a tax on the assessed value of real property[117] at provincial and/or municipal levels.[118] A portion of the tax is earmarked for educational funding or the municipal budget, and that is why the tax is often referred to as a "school tax." The rates of property tax can be either flat or progressive, depending on the jurisdiction. For example, in Toronto, the total property tax rate was 0.63% in 2018, with 0.46% being allocated to the city, 0.17% to education, and 0.002% to the city building fund.[119] British Columbia recently introduced progressive property tax rates on high-value homes: starting in 2019, the value of homes between $3 and $4 million are subject to an additional school tax of 0.2%, and any value assessed at $4 million or more is subject to a 0.4% school tax.[120]

An anti-speculation tax targeting out-of-province home owners was introduced by the British Columbia government in its 2018 budget.[121] It is an annual property tax applicable in specified areas, such as Metro Vancouver and the Fraser Valley. The tax rate for 2019 is $20 per $1,000 of assessed value. This tax is creditable against British Columbia's income tax up to $2,000, so that only homeowners who do not pay income tax in BC pay this tax. The tax is aimed at individuals residing in foreign countries, other provinces, and "satellite families – households with high worldwide income that pay little income tax in BC."[122] Long-term rental housing as well as principal residences are exempt from the tax.

Vancouver also levies an additional Empty Homes Tax.[123] This tax does not apply to principal residences or homes rented for at least six months of the year. Each year, homeowners in Vancouver must submit a property status declaration to determine if their property is subject to this tax. Properties deemed empty are taxed at the rate of 1% of the property's assessed taxable value. Revenues collected from this tax are earmarked for investment in affordable housing.[124]

III. Tax Policy and Housing Crisis

A. Tax Bias for Homeownership

The income tax and GST treatment of housing is biased in favor of homeownership. For example, the *Income Tax Act* does not "see" any capital gains from the sale of a principal residence, regardless of the value and length of ownership or the imputed income from owning the property. As such, owner-occupied housing is a "nothing" for tax purposes. Such policy is particularly striking in light of the fact that housing is the biggest asset for most Canadian households and the 1972 tax reform principle that all revenues should be treated and taxed equally.[125] This bias for homeownership goes beyond tax exemptions. Through the Home Buyers Plan and First-Time Home Buyers' Tax Credit, the *Income Tax Act* grants "free capital" to home buyers. For example, when taxpayers withdraw funds from their RRSP through the First-Time Home Buyers Plan, they are using money on which no tax has been payable, representing a significant government subsidy. As such, governments contribute monetarily to owner-occupied housing.

The *Income Tax Act* contains no explicit tax subsidies to suppliers of housing. Allowing self-help tax shelters could be viewed as an implicit tax subsidy to the supply of rental housing, but it was arguably not intended as such. The government introduced draft legislation in 2003 to shut down such tax shelters, but the proposal was withdrawn after concerns about its potential adverse impact on the market and businesses.[126]

B. Tax-Induced Financial Risks

The tax bias induces demand for housing, including "harmful demand," which may lead to rising prices and financial risks.[127] Demand for housing is "harmful" if the housing is an over-sized property, the second or third "home" of a household, a speculative investment, or a tax shelter. Conceptually, harmful demand is associated with investors who buy housing to multiply the tax exemptions, to accumulate wealth in a tax-preferred form, or to flip housing as commodities. This is in contrast to "natural demand," which arises when a home is bought to accommodate non-investment reasons, such as a larger home to accommodate a growing family or relocation. Even though people are motivated by different factors to buy a housing property, tax incentives may entice some people to become first-time home buyers and others to buy more valuable homes.[128]

There is no conclusive evidence on the exact effect of tax incentives on increasing homeownership rate in Canada, nor is there an explicit link in the data between tax schemes and encouraging harmful demand for housing.[129] Inferences can be drawn from research on the United States and Australia, which have largely similar housing markets and homeownership-biased tax policies.[130] For example, research on American housing tax policies suggests that they have encouraged "over-investment" in the form of buying bigger houses, or buying homes before the buyers were financially prepared, and that the value of the tax subsidies changes the taxpayer's marginal tax rate, leading to a rise in housing prices and increased loan-to-value ratios.[131] Similarly, Australian research shows that their housing tax incentives result in "inflated housing prices"[132] and that rising housing prices are "driven in large part by the commodification of established housing and growing demand for housing assets by 'mum and dad' investors."[133]

Also, the Principal Residence Exemption was found to be one of the causes of housing price inflation during the 1970s:[134]

> Since other assets are subject to capital gains tax, the attractiveness of housing as an investment increases, particularly during periods of inflation (since when inflation rises, higher nominal gains on assets held by investors are subject to capital gains tax). Therefore, demand rises and house prices increase as investors seek to avoid the rising margin of capital gains tax on other investments. Existing homeowners experience substantial capital gains and potential homebuyers find the opportunity of purchasing moving out of reach. No detailed evaluation of the effects of these tax subsidies on housing markets is presently available.[135]

The technical design of the Principal Residence Exemption allows the exemption to be used for multiplying the number of tax exemptions by a household or maximizing the amount of a tax exemption. For example, the exemption is limited to each household consisting of a taxpayer, the taxpayer's spouse or common-law partner, and children under the age of eighteen. As such, a property can be "owned" by the taxpayer's parent or adult child and qualify for the exemption. There is no maximum limitation on the amount of gain to be exempted, which, in effect, promotes demand for more valuable housing and more "trading" or flipping of houses. As such, higher-income earners, who pay higher rates of marginal tax, have the most to gain by investing capital in housing.

Demand pulled up by the tax incentive causes higher prices when supply is constant. Local "counter-speculation" tax measures are not significant enough to offset the effect of the bias in the *Income Tax Act*. Housing debts, market shocks, and price fluctuations driven by investors can pose major risks to the Canadian economy.

C. Affordability

The issue of affordability is directly related to housing prices. As such, tax policies that drive up harmful demand reduce affordability for first-time buyers and renters. The affordability of homeownership is tied to affordability of private rentals. If renters can afford to buy homes, they create more rental spaces on the market, which may reduce the price of rent. Higher costs related to purchasing a property by the landlord is translated into higher rental charges. Prior to the outbreak of the COVID-19 pandemic in early 2020, increases to condo prices in major cities drove up demand for rental units: rent increased by an average of 6.4% in Vancouver, 4.4% in Toronto, and 7.6% in Victoria in the past three years.[136] The impact of the pandemic on the rental market is unknown at the time of writing in November 2020.

The *Income Tax Act* offers no explicit subsidies to renters or businesses that supply low-cost housing.[137] Municipal vacancy taxes may encourage the supply of rental spaces, but the effect is unknown and presumably negligible.

Overall, there is sufficient evidence to show that the tax bias for homeownership is likely a contributing factor in Canada's housing crisis. Consequently, it would make sense to consider tax policies as part of broader housing policies in order to address the fiscal risks and affordability problems. These characteristics of the tax system also have the potential to negatively impact the economy as a whole, since housing-sector vulnerabilities pose a significant risk to financial markets.

IV. Tax Reform as Part of Housing Policy

A. Why?

Canada's National Housing Strategy focuses on increasing the supply of housing to address the problem of affordability for the most vulnerable.[138] This is undoubtedly an important mission; however, it is not enough to achieve the vision of affordable housing for all Canadians. This is especially true for younger working Canadians,[139] since current policies do not address the economic risks associated with speculative investments and inequity issues. Because the three segments of the housing market (ownership, rental, and social housing) are interconnected, a national housing strategy would ideally address the system as a whole through a combination of tax and non-tax measures. Housing tax policies are outdated, ineffective, and in desperate need of reform.

Tax Reform and the New Housing Reality
The *Income Tax Act* currently regards housing mainly as a personal consumption property for owners. Profits on the sale of a home are treated as a recovery of the personal expenses of the owner, and thus should not be taxable like profits from sale of investment assets.[140] Not taxing owners means that tax policy treats housing as a unique product and sets the housing market apart from other markets. Such treatments of housing may have made sense when the problems of income and wealth inequality were not as pronounced, and at a time when owning a home was achievable without government intervention.[141] However, this is no longer the reality in Canada. As

discussed in part II, housing is a complex and multifaceted issue that requires urgent reform.

The current housing crisis presents an opportunity for Canada to modernize the housing tax system. There appears to be increasing awareness of the housing crisis and political support for improving affordability. "Polling data show that housing affordability is now a top issue for the electorate, especially for younger Canadians."[142] Major political parties seem to recognize the problem of housing and signal commitment to addressing it.[143] The COVID-19 pandemic only heightens the importance of housing, given the intimate links between adequate housing, population health, and individual well-being.

The Pathway to Affordable Housing for All Canadians

Tax reform is a pathway to achieving the goal of affordable housing for all Canadians, including the middle class. In the current system, middle-income earners miss out because social housing spending benefits Canadians in low-income groups, and indirect government spending through tax subsidies disproportionately benefit those with high incomes. Few housing tax benefits are extended to middle-income households.[144] To improve equity in housing and help the middle class, tax reform is necessary.

Reducing the tax bias for homeownership at the top may help reduce housing prices so that housing is more affordable to Canadians in the middle class. It would also improve tax equity in housing because the bias results in a "upside-down subsidy" to those who are already better off. Only 10% of the benefits from the $5–7 billion per year Principal Residence Exemption[145] went to the bottom half of tax filers, while 35% of the benefits went to the top 10% of income earners.[146] Inter-generational inequality is aggravated by housing tax policies to the extent that the tax subsidies benefit older homeowners and raise housing prices beyond the reach of younger Canadians. In fact, "for an individual aged 25–34, the ratio of median fulltime, full-year income relative to average home costs increased from 4:1 in 1976 to 10:1 as of 2017."[147] Even if younger Canadians can benefit from the tax subsidies for first-time homebuyers, the front-end tax subsidy pales in comparison to back-end tax subsidies available through the Principal Residence Exemption. Savings from a more strategically targeted Principal Residence Exemption can be re-deployed to improve equity, such as increasing the subsidy to low-income first-time home buyers.

Tax Reform and Additional Funding for Social Housing

Direct and indirect spending through tax expenditures on housing are not integrated at the moment. In 1990, the Liberal Task Force on Housing led by Paul Martin and Joe Fontana recognized the importance of tax policies in housing policy, and recommended a review of all forms of taxation on housing in order to create a "fair and integrated reform of the entire tax system."[148] That recommendation has not been heeded. Current housing taxes were introduced on a piecemeal basis and can be redesigned to promote national housing objectives.

A redesigned housing tax system can also generate extra revenues that can be earmarked for improving affordable housing. Funding for investment in social housing may be insecure or unsustainable. There is no assigned revenue source for the $55 billion investment in the National Housing Strategy. A change in government or policy could put this funding at risk. It would make sense to "recycle" or redirect the fiscal resources from the generous tax expenditures on high-income homeowners and/or speculative housing investments to funding affordable housing.

B. How?

Redesigning the Principal Residence Exemption

The Principal Residence Exemption should be retained but redesigned. Its abolishment is not politically feasible or necessary. However, additional safeguards are necessary to ensure that it remains true to its original aim of helping Canadian families. Possible new safeguards include tightening up disqualifying conditions for the exemption and putting a lifetime limit on the amount of gains eligible for exemption.

The qualifying conditions for the exemption can be better targeted at "ordinary homes" to prevent taxpayers from multiplying the exemption. For example, governments could institute a condition that the qualifying property must be actually used by the taxpayer as a home, and any housing property owned by a taxpayer's parent or adult child and bought with the taxpayer's money should be treated as owned by the taxpayer. The latter test is akin to an attribution rule that, in effect, assigns the ownership of the property registered in the name of a parent or adult child to be the taxpayer's for purposes of the Principal Residence Exemption. As a result, gains from such attributed property would not qualify for the exemption unless it is designated as the principal residence of the taxpayer.

In recognition of the fact that a home is both a personal consumption and a key investment asset, the Principal Residence Exemption should be limited to the portion of gains attributable to the "home" aspect. Conceptually, the portion of gains attributable to the "investment" aspect will be taxable, just like capital gains from the sale of other investment assets. The practical difficulty in bifurcating the capital gains (as accruing to the home and to investment) is that it is administratively impossible to do this on a property-by-property basis. A presumptive rule must be used: any gain below the chosen limit is presumed to be personal gains from the home, and any amount above the limit is presumed to be investment gains.

The design of the limitation can be informed by research on the value of an "average" home in Canada. Since housing prices vary greatly from region to region, it may be possible to have the limit "indexed" to reflect regional differences.[149] If it is impossible to reach a consensus on such a "nuanced" limitation, a national arbitrary amount can be used. This is the case with the current lifetime capital gains exemption for owners of small businesses.[150] The Carter Commission recommended a lifetime exemption for each family unit or individual up to a $25,000 (a present value is close to $200,000).[151] The United States also imposes a limit: the first $250,000 of gain from the sale of a home is exempt from tax of a single individual, or $500,000 for a married couple filing jointly.[152]

Imposing a cap on the Principal Residence Exemption would improve tax equity and reduce harmful demand. It would place Canadians who invest in housing on a footing equal to those who invest in other assets, and thus reduce investment distortions and improve efficiency of the capital market. More importantly, it would improve tax equity, especially inter-generational equity, because homeowners are predominantly from older demographics.[153] Limiting the amount of the tax exemption is also sound tax policy, as the excessive gains are mostly "windfalls" arising from the location and societal environment. Furthermore, limiting the tax exemption will also bring this expensive tax subsidy in line with other major tax subsidies to individuals, none of which are presently open-ended. For example, the child care expense deduction is limited to a fixed amount per child, and the tax-free contribution to an RRSP is limited to $14,500 per year.[154] It is difficult to predict the effect of the proposed lifetime limitation on reducing harmful demand. It is hoped that the limitation reflects a balance between preserving Canadian attitudes toward housing, without stimulating speculative investment in Canadian housing or using housing as a wealth accumulation vehicle.

New Tax Incentives for Supplying Affordable Housing

Increasing supply is a possible solution to the "serious middle-income housing affordability crisis."[155] The private market alone has not worked efficiently, and public policy interventions are necessary. Tax policy should be in the mix of policy instruments to incentivize the supply of more affordable housing, especially residential rental units.[156] A new tax incentive can be introduced for this purpose.

Several options can be considered. One is to revive and redesign the MURB program.[157] This program provided a tax subsidy to promote the building of rental housing in urban areas, and allowed investors to deduct losses by offsetting the capital cost allowance associated with the construction of new residential buildings against other income. The effect was to create a tax shelter for investors, which would lower the cost of capital or increase the rate of return. Lessons could be learned from this earlier program on how to minimize abuse of the tax shelter.[158]

Another option is an American-style low-income housing tax credit.[159] This tax credit is the primary federal program for encouraging the investment of private equity in the development of affordable rental housing for low-income households.[160] Qualifying rental properties include apartment buildings, single-family dwellings, townhouses, and duplexes. More specifically, this credit supports the construction and rehabilitation of affordable rental units by allowing an investor to take a federal tax credit equal to a percentage of the development cost. To obtain funding, developers generally sell tax credits awarded from state housing agencies to private investors who claim the tax credit when the rental property is made available to tenants.[161]

To encourage owners to rent, the capital cost allowance deduction can be redesigned as a tax incentive through increasing the rate of depreciation or accelerating the deduction if the property has a tenant. When a rental property is sold, a rollover can be allowed to defer the taxation on capital gains and the recaptured capital cost allowance, on the condition that the former and new property provide affordable housing.

The main justification for the above measures is to correct the homeownership bias of the current tax policy and to solve the affordable housing problem through a private market mechanism. Tax incentives to provide housing support to low- or middle-income individuals would encourage more stable communities and neighborhoods and are defensible on the basis that they encourage behavior with positive externalities. There are numerous tax expenditures of this type in the *Income Tax Act*, such as the small business deduction[162] or the scientific research and experimental development tax credit.[163]

Considering Taxation of Imputed Rent

Non-taxation of imputed rent is a major tax advantage for investing in a principal residence. This benefits homeowners only. The economic value of living in one's own house is a significant source of implicit income. A Statistics Canada research study found that, on average, "this implicit source of earnings raised the incomes of retirement-age households (aged 70 and over) by 16% from 1969 to 2006," and that the implicit returns to housing have risen over time.[164] It is reasonable to assume that the recent surge in housing prices raised these implicit returns even more.

Taxing imputed rent is supported by economic theory – income should measure a person's consumption plus savings, the principle of ability to pay, and tax neutrality between housing and non-housing investment assets.[165] The economic advantage of not having to pay rent for accommodation out of after-tax earnings constitutes income in the broad sense. It aggravates the tax bias for owner-occupied homes. This can be explained by a simple example. Two individuals, X and Y, have a net worth of $100,000. X invests $100,000 in buying a house as a principal residence. Y invests $100,000 in stocks, earning $10,000 dividend annually and pays $12,000 rent to the landlord. Each year, taxable income for X would be zero, but $10,000 for Y. If both X and Y sell their assets for a gain of $20,000, this gain is exempt for X, but taxable for Y. In this example, Y must pay rent with after-tax income while X enjoys housing tax-free. Taxing X's imputed rent, and removing the Principal Residence Exemption, would remove the bias for X and treat X and Y the same.

Imputed income is taxable in other areas. For example, when a corporation supplies rent-free housing to its controlling shareholder, the shareholder is deemed to receive a benefit from the corporation and is required to include the value of the benefit in her income.[166] In a sense, the shareholder becomes an owner-occupier of the house, albeit through her corporation, and must pay tax on the value of the housing or the imputed rent. Another example is the annual imputation of interest on long-term investment contracts for tax purposes.[167] A third example is imputing dividends to the Canadian resident controlling shareholder of a foreign corporation in respect the corporation's foreign accrual property income.[168] Several OECD countries, including Iceland, Luxembourg, the Netherlands, Slovenia, and Switzerland, tax imputed rent. [169]

The main reasons why imputed rent taxation has not been pursued in Canada are administrative and political in nature. The administrative difficulties involved in valuing annual imputed rent can be formidable. These difficulties are presumably not insurmountable, as other countries have done so. Imputed rent is taken into account in measuring national income and gross national product (GDP).[170] Political pressures and entrenched interests that led to the current homeownership-biased tax policy are expected to block any reform to remove such bias.

If a general taxation on imputed rent is not feasible, Canada should at least consider recognizing imputed rent as "income" for the purposes of qualifying for means-tested social assistance programs, such as the Canada Child Benefit and Old Age Security. House-rich and income-poor households should, ideally, not be able to qualify for social assistance payments that are designed as poverty-relief measures.

Conclusion

Housing is important to all Canadians, owners and renters alike. The tax treatment of housing affects homeowners and renters differently. Federal tax policies are structurally biased in favor of owners, especially those with high incomes. This chapter has offered evidence on the implications of this bias for demand for housing and speculative investment. Even though local property taxes may help "correct" the effect of such bias through transfer taxes or property taxes, the bias remains significant.

This chapter argues that housing policy and housing tax reforms should not be viewed in isolation, because tax bias is at play in the housing market. Addressing this bias would help advance Canada's housing objectives and move us toward affordable housing for all. Further, by addressing the tax bias, the housing tax regime would be updated to better suit the complex reality of today's housing market and the integral role that it plays in Canadian society and the economy. Tax reforms should ideally take place in conjunction with, or at least in the context of, the national housing policy. More specifically, the Principal Residence Exemption should be redesigned to encourage "natural" demand for homes and remove those elements that induce speculative investments and increase housing risks. That can be done through limiting the amount of the tax-exempt gains and tightening the eligibility of homes for the exemption. Specific tax incentives should be seriously considered to increase the supply of affordable housing. Any savings from the tax reform can be earmarked for investment in social housing to contribute to the policy's overarching goals.

It is important to note, however, that while this chapter argues for an enhanced role for tax considerations in Canada's housing policy and offers some ideas for tax reform, it also urges more research be done on the costing of tax reform options and the impact these reforms might have on housing prices and affordability. For example, insights should be gathered regarding the impact of tax reform on harmful demand for housing, the linkage between harmful demand and the secondary mortgage market, and the financial risks associated with both.

Dangerous Opportunities: Lessons Learned for the Pandemic Recovery Efforts

Stephanie Ben-Ishai*

As the reader has learned from the preceding chapters, the Home Capital crisis played out in manifold and unexpected ways. This complexity was partially attributable to the fragmented regulatory framework within which Home Capital operated, but was also compounded by the actions of the firm's senior executives, stakeholders, and regulators. These actors and institutions not only affected the way the crisis played out in real time, but also established future standards of conduct for other businesses occupying the same markets as Home Capital.

As Poonam Puri demonstrates in her chapter, decisions were made by Home Capital's board of directors that directly contributed the firm's downfall during the period in question. She argues that corporate governance mechanisms in securities laws were insufficient in this case and that governance judgments could have been improved internally had Home Capital's board of directors been more independent and diverse. Puri also explains how factors such as board diversity and independence complement a board's long-term perspective on decision-making and work together to improve

---

* Professor and Distinguished Research Professor at Osgoode Hall Law School

corporate governance in ways that avert crises rather than functioning as a crucible for them.

Regarding Home Capital's senior executives and its conspicuous governance shortcomings as the sole source of the calamity paints an incomplete picture and obfuscates some of the key lessons that can be gleaned from this episode. Simon Archer's chapter helpfully lays out how the actions of lenders such as HOOPP can have a stabilizing effect during crises and improve chances of a firm's recovery. He argues that the Home Capital crisis, particularly through the role HOOPP assumed during the firm's distress, is an example of the role stakeholders can assume in promoting integrity in Canadian capital markets. Though Home Capital will be accurately classified as a cautionary tale by many, Archer offers a positive lesson on how pension funds can use investment opportunities to address systemic market integrity issues.

Any account of the Home Capital saga would be remiss without including considerations of the impact crises of this kind have on small retail investors. Gail Henderson's chapter provides this invaluable perspective. Through her discussion of current government-mandated financial literacy and investor education initiatives, she explains how these initiatives lead to uneven protections, since they tend to shift the regulatory burden onto investors who have varying degrees of sophistication and resources. She also illustrates how many individuals placing their money in banking and investment products, including high-interest savings accounts and guaranteed income certificates offered by financial institutions such as Home Capital, still have an incomplete understanding of the risks tied to these investments, despite decades of investor education initiatives.

In addition to exposing the inadequacy of investor education in upholding the investor protection regime, the Home Capital crisis exposed many cracks in the regulatory foundation of the mortgage sector in Canada. Stephanie Ben-Ishai gives a persuasive account of the ways in which inadequate external controls and ineffective regulatory interventions exacerbated the Home Capital crisis and amplified its effects. Added to her analysis is a comparison of U.S. and Canadian regulatory frameworks, both pre- and post-2008 financial crisis, and an evaluation of the efficacy of these regimes in stabilizing the mortgage market. Ben-Ishai makes a compelling case for viewing the Home Capital saga as a justification for regulatory reform to reduce fragmentation and to better address the bad behaviors of market actors.

Taxation policy is another area intimately linked to the housing sector that requires reform to better structure incentives for market actors. Jinyan Li shows how current tax policy's bias toward homeownership propels demand for housing as a speculative investment asset and contributes to affordable housing shortages and other issues that destabilize mortgage markets. Li explains that a redesign of tax instruments is central in addressing housing risk, in both financial risks and the supply of affordable housing. Integrating tax policy into conversations about crisis prevention and market stability is an essential step in post-crisis reform.

All of the chapters in this volume, and the areas of expertise that they draw upon, point toward the centrality of a multi-disciplinary and multi-stakeholder dialog in anticipating challenges, building resilience, and forming effective solutions to financial crises. Home Capital made it clear that the status quo is no longer tenable. As the COVID-19 pandemic sends the economy into a tailspin, we are likely to become acutely aware of this need for reform. An important aspect of any effective approach is looking back at the lessons learned from past failures and previous disruptions. Governments and stakeholders should capitalize on the inevitability that things become clear through hindsight. Post-crisis, it is essential that we employ past lessons in our design of solutions if we wish to help reduce the severity of future financial crises and place our regulatory and policy responses on better footing this time around. Every crisis offers an opportunity to both capture lessons learned and to identify areas requiring improvement for use in future crises.

The abject failure of the relevant laws and regulatory bodies in fulfilling their preventative role is the most obvious lesson here. Improved surveillance and monitoring of the financial sector help to alert regulators to an impending crisis and can empower them to work to prevent it from happening in the first place. While investor education may help prevent demand-side risks, it does very little in practice to prevent firms from engaging in risky or illegal behaviors. Regulators' ability to catch crises before they form is closely linked to public confidence in, and the stability of, financial systems. The effective regulation of financial institutions requires that oversight mechanisms promote standards of sound business and financial practice and that firms see these as mandatory legal requirements. It also necessitates that recovery efforts have built-in deterrents to prevent history from repeating itself, including that the consequences of non-compliance are sufficiently severe.

The Home Capital crisis also brought beneficial instructions on crisis preparedness and management. It may be trite to say that financial crises and firm misconduct occur regularly with similar causes; however, the Home Capital experience suggests that very little attention has been given to how best to manage them. The failure of regulators to curtail the crisis quickly once it began and to prevent negative impacts for depositors and investors was glaring in this case. The OSC's delayed reaction and enforcement actions in relation to Home Capital's failure to properly disclose information on their financial statements represents a misspent opportunity that prolonged the crisis and may have magnified its negative effects on certain stakeholders. Again, as was the case with crisis prevention, ongoing surveillance is key. Regulators must be fully apprised of developments as they occur in order to tailor effective responses. Laws should also give regulators sufficient discretion and resources to appropriately manage crises as they unfold.

Even the strongest regulatory framework cannot prevent crisis or wrongdoing in all circumstances. At the heart of this volume, however, is a recognition that a broad understanding of the current state of regulatory controls and the possible consequences of these laws is crucial so that society can make informed decisions about how best to manage market risks and protect itself from the next crisis. As the financial fallout from the pandemic increases and damages people's lives and the economy, teasing out more of the lessons learned from the Home Capital crisis becomes an increasingly urgent and worthwhile exercise.

Notes

Introduction

1 See Home Capital, "About Home Capital Group" (last visited 13 September 2019), online: <https://www.homecapital.com/about-home-capital /our-story/default.aspx>.

2 See Matt Schuffham, "Canada Watchdog Sets New Mortgage Rules, Acknowledges Risks" (17 October 2017), online: *Reuters* <https://www .reuters.com/article/canada-mortgages/update-3-canada-watchdog-sets -new-mortgage-rules-acknowledges-risks-idUSL2N1MS0HE>; Mark S Bonham, "Royal Bank of Canada" (22 February 2019), online: *The Canadian Encyclopedia* <https://www.thecanadianencyclopedia.ca/en /article/royal-bank-of-canada>.

3 See Armina Ligaya, "What Exactly Is Home Capital and Why Is It so Important to the Mortgage Industry?" (27 April 2017), online: *Financial Post* <https://business.financialpost.com/news/fp-street/what-exactly -is-home-capital-and-why-is-it-so-important-to-the-mortgage-industry>.

4 See Kareen Brown & Kevin Veenstra, "Home Capital Group – The High Cost of Dishonesty" (2018) 17:2 Accounting Perspectives 307 at 315–16.

5 *Ibid* at 316.

6 *Ibid* at 317.

7 See generally *Disclosure Standards*, OSC NI 51-201 (2002) 25 OSCB 4492.

8 *Ibid* at Part IV.

9 Brown & Veenstra, *supra* note 4 at 318.

10 *Ibid* at 317.

11 *Ibid*.

12 *Ibid*.

13 *Ibid* at 321.

14 Ligaya, *supra* note 3.

15 *Ibid*; Brown & Veenstra, *supra* note 4 at 319.

16 Brown & Veenstra, *supra* note 4 at 319.

17 See Jeremy Kronick, "Home Capital: How Did We Get Here?" (15 May 2017), online (blog): *C.D. Howe Institute* <https://www.cdhowe.org /intelligence-memos/jeremy-kronick-home-capital-how-did-we-get-here>.

18 Brown & Veenstra, *supra* note 4 at 319.

19 Ligaya, *supra* note 3.

20 Brown & Veenstra, *supra* note 4 at 322.

21 See *Re Home Capital Group Inc, Gerald Soloway, Robert Morton and Martin Reid Statement of Allegations,* (2017) at paras 25–29, online (pdf): *OSC* <https://www.osc.gov.on.ca/documents/en/Proceedings-SOA/soa _20170419_home-capital.pdf>.

22 See Michelle Zaidikan, "Home Capital Emergency Loan Was a 'Win-Win': HOOPP CEO", *Business News Network Bloomberg* (30 October 2017), online: <https://www.bnnbloomberg.ca/home-capital-emergency-loan-was-a -win-win-hoopp-ceo-1.900233>.

23 See Armina Ligaya, "Equitable Group CEO Says $2 Billion Credit Line a 'Sign of Confidence,' Stems Contagion from Home Capital", *The Financial Post* (1 May 2017), online: <https://business.financialpost.com/news/fp -street/equitable-group-rushes-to-contain-contagion-risk-from-home -capital-maelstrom>.

24 See Barbara Shecter, "'Better Not to Sit in Two Places': HOOPP Board Overlaps Raise Concerns", *The Financial Post* (28 April 2017), online: <https://business.financialpost.com/news/fp-street/better-not-to-sit-in -two-places-hoopp-board-overlaps-raise-concerns>.

25 See Lauren E Willis, "Against Financial-Literacy Education" (2008) 94 Iowa L Rev 197 at 282 (citing President George W Bush).

26 See Carly Sawatzki, "Lessons in Financial Literacy Task Design: Authentic, Imaginable, Useful" (2017) 29 Mathematics Education Research J 25 at 25.

27 See Department of Finance Canada, News Release, 2009-067, "Minister of Finance Launches Task Force on Financial Literacy" (26 June 2009), online: *Department of Finance Canada* <https://www.canada.ca/en/news /archive/2009/06/minister-finance-launches-task-force-financial-literacy .html>; Task Force on Financial Literacy, "Final Report of the Task Force on Financial Literacy, Canadians and Their Money: Building a Brighter Financial Future" (2010) at 21, online (pdf): *FCAC* <https://www.canada .ca/content/dam/fcac-acfc/documents/programs/financial-literacy /canadians-and-their-money.pdf>.

28 See Canadian Securities Administrators (CSA) Investor Education Committee (IEC), "Annual Activity Report 2018 (Apr 2017–Mar 2018)" at 7, online

(pdf): *CSA* <https://www.securities-administrators.ca/uploadedFiles /General/pdfs/CSA_InvestorEd_AnnualReport_2018_EN_VF.pdf>.

29 See Canada Mortgage and Housing Corporation & Deloitte, "Impact of Credit Unions and Mortgage Finance Companies on the Canadian Mortgage Market" (August 2018) at 10, online (pdf): <http://publications .gc.ca/collections/collection_2018/schl-cmhc/nh18-33/NH18-33-4-2018 -eng.pdf>.

30 See Dan Andrews & Aida Caldera Sánchez, "Drivers of Homeownership Rates in Selected OECD Countries" (2011) at 8–11, online (pdf): *Organisation for Economic Co-operation and Development* <https://www .oecd.org/officialdocuments/publicdisplaydocumentpdf/?cote=ECO /WKP(2011)18&docLanguage=En>.

1. Governance Challenges in Times of Crisis

1 See generally *National Instrument 52-110 – Audit Committees*, OSC NI 52-110, (2004) 27 OSCB 3252 [NI 52-110].

2 Home Capital's predecessor company, Sonor Petroleum Corporation, a *Canada Business Corporations Act* corporation, changed its name to Home Capital Group Inc. on 31 December 1986. See Home Capital Group Inc, "Annual Information Form for the Year Ended December 31, 2017" (28 March 2018) at 4, online (pdf): *SEDAR* <https://s2.q4cdn.com/668293721/files/doc _financials/annual_meetings/2018/AnnualInfoForm2017.pdf> [Annual Information].

3 Gerald Soloway ceased to be CEO in 2016 and a director in 2017. See Home Capital Group Inc, News Release, "Home Capital Group Announces CEO Succession" (29 February 2016), online: *SEDAR* <https://s2.q4cdn.com /668293721/files/doc_news/archive/SuccessionNR_HCG_final.pdf>; Home Capital Group Inc, "Annual Information Form for the year ended December 31, 2016" (31 March 2017) at 11, online (pdf): *SEDAR* <https:// s2.q4cdn.com/668293721/files/doc_financials/annual_meetings/2017 /AnnualInfoForm2016.pdf>.

4 Until 1988, Home Capital was governed by the *Canada Business Corporations Act*. Annual Information, *supra* note 2 at 4; Home Capital Group Inc, "About Home Capital," online: <https://www.homecapital.com/about -home-capital/our-story/default.aspx>.

5 See *Home Capital Group Inc (Re)*, 2017 ONSEC 32 at paras 17, 54 [OSC Settlement].

6 *Ibid*.

7 OSC Settlement, *supra* note 5 at paras 18–21 (given that Home Capital's primary business dealt with residential mortgages, the number of new mortgages issued was a critical measure of the company's performance).

8 See Home Capital Group Inc, News Release, "Home Capital Provides Update on Q2 Origination Volumes" (10 July 2015), online (pdf): *SEDAR* <https://s2.q4cdn.com/668293721/files/doc_news/archive/press -release-Q2-disclosure-final.pdf>.

9 *Ibid*.

10 See Markets Insider, "Home Capital Group Stock", online: <https:// markets.businessinsider.com/stocks/home_capital_group-stock>.

11 See Home Capital Group Inc., "Annual Report 2014" (2014) at 68, online (pdf): *SEDAR* <https://s2.q4cdn.com/668293721/files/doc_financials /annual_meetings/2015/HomeCap-2014AR_full_sedar.pdf>.

12 See *Re Home Capital Group Inc, Gerald Soloway, Robert Morton and Martin Reid Statement of Allegations*, (2017) at para 25, online (pdf): *OSC* <https://www.osc.gov.on.ca/documents/en/Proceedings-SOA/soa _20170419_home-capital.pdf> [Statement of Allegations].

13 *Ibid* at para 27.

14 *Ibid* at para 28.

15 *Ibid* at para 29.

16 *Ibid*.

17 *Ibid* at para 30.

18 *Ibid* at para 36.

19 *Ibid* at para 37.

20 *Ibid* at para 38.

21 *Ibid*; Siskinds LLP, "Class Actions: Home Capital Group Inc" (last visited 26 September 2019), online: <https://www.siskinds.com/class-action /home-capital-group-inc/> [Siskinds Class Action].

22 OSC Settlement, *supra* note 5 at paras 21, 33.

23 *Ibid* at paras 36–37.

24 *Ibid* at paras at 23–24.

25 Siskinds Class Action, *supra* note 21.

26 See Ontario, *Five Year Review Committee Final Report: Reviewing the Securities Act (Ontario)*, Chair: Purdy Crawford (Toronto: Queen's Printer, 2003) at 22 [Crawford Report]; SO 1945, c 22.

27 See Ontario, Committee on Securities Legislation, *Report of the Attorney General's Committee on Securities Legislation in Ontario*, Chair: JR Kimber (Toronto: Queen's Printer, 1965) [Kimber Report].

28 Crawford Report, *supra* note 26 at 22; SO 1966, c 142.

29 Kimber Report, *supra* note 27 at 28.

30 See Toronto Stock Exchange, Committee on Corporate Disclosure, *The Toronto Stock Exchange Committee on Corporate Disclosure, Final Report: Responsible Corporate Disclosure: A Search for Balance*, Chair: Thomas IA Allen (Toronto: Toronto Stock Exchange, 1997).

31 See Poonam Puri, "Securities Class Actions in Canada: Ten Years Later" in Sean Griffith, Jessica Erickson, David H Webber, & Verity Winship, eds,

Research Handbook on Representative Shareholder Litigation (Gloucestershire: Edward Elgar Publishing Limited, 2018) 482 [Puri, Class Actions]; *Securities Act*, RSO 1990, c S-5, s 1.1 [Ontario *Securities Act*]; Mary Condon, Anita Anand & Janis Sarra, *Securities Law in Canada: Cases and Commentary* (Toronto: Emond Montgomery, 2005).

32 Ontario *Securities Act, supra* note 31, s 2.1.

33 See generally *National Instrument 51-102 – Continuous Disclosure Obligations*, OSC NI 51-102, (2004) 27 OSCB 3439 [NI 51-102].

34 Ontario *Securities Act, supra* note 31, ss 75(1), 75(2); *ibid* at Part 7.

35 *Ibid*, ss 75(1), 75(2); NI 51-102, *supra* note 33 at Part 7.

36 See Borden Ladner Gervais LLP, *Securities Law and Practice*, 3rd ed (Toronto: Carswell, 2003) at 18–19; *McLaughlin v S.B. McLaughlin Associates Ltd.* (1981), 14 BLR 46 (OSC) at 59; *AiT Advanced Information Technologies Corporation et al*, (2008) at para 199, online (pdf): *OSC* <https://www.osc .gov.on.ca/documents/en/Proceedings-RAD/rad_20081009_ait.pdf>.

37 See Christopher C Nicholls, *Securities Law*, 2nd ed (Toronto: Irwin Law, 2018) at 325.

38 Ontario *Securities Act, supra* note 31, s 1(1). See also NI 51-102, *supra* note 33, s 1.1.

39 Ontario *Securities Act, supra* note 31, s 1(1); NI 51-102, *supra* note 33, s 1.1.

40 See e.g. *National Instrument 51-101 – Standards of Disclosure for Oil and Gas Activities*, OSC NI 51-101, (2003) 26 OSCB 5560; *National Instrument 43-101 – Standards of Disclosure for Mineral Projects*, OSC NI 43-101, (2005) 28 OSCB 8165 [NI 43-101]; *CSA Staff Notice 51-357 – Staff Review of Reporting Issuers in the Cannabis Industry*, OSC CSA Notice, (10 October 2018), online (pdf): *OSC* <https://www.osc.gov.on.ca/documents/en /Securities-Category5/csa_20181010_51-357_staff-review-reporting -issuers-cannabis-industry.pdf> [Cannabis Industry Notice].

41 NI 43-101, *supra* note 40, s 2.1.

42 Cannabis Industry Notice, *supra* note 40.

43 See *CSA Staff Notice 51-354 – Report on Climate Change-Related Disclosure Project*, OSC CSA Notice, (5 April 2018), online (pdf): *OSC* <https://www .osc.gov.on.ca/en/SecuritiesLaw_csa_20180405_51-354_disclosure-project .htm#N_1_1_1_45_>.

44 2013 ONSC 1310 [*Coventree*].

45 *Ibid.*

46 *Ibid* at paras 98–99.

47 See *Kerr v Danier Leather Inc*, 2007 SCC 44 at para 55.

48 *Coventree, supra* note 44 at para 55; *Rex Diamond Mining Corp v Ontario (Securities Commission)*, 2010 ONSC 3926 at para 6.

49 OSC Settlement, *supra* note 5 at para 3. See also *Coventree, supra* note 44 43.

50 OSC Settlement, *supra* note 5 at para 14.

51 Kimber Report, *supra* note 27 at 28.

52 Settlement Agreement, *supra* note 5 at paras 7, 26.
53 *Ibid* at para 7.
54 Crawford Report, *supra* note 26 at 126.
55 See e.g. *OSC Staff Notice 51-722 – Report on a Review of Mining Issuers' Management's Discussion and Analysis and Guidance*, OSC Notice, (2014) 37 OSCB 1361, online: <https://www.osc.gov.on.ca/en/SecuritiesLaw_sn _20140206_51-722_rpt-mining-issuers-mdag.htm>.
56 See *CSA Staff Notice 51-312 – Harmonized Continuous Disclosure Review Program*, OSC CSA Notice, (2004) 27 OSCB 6475, online: <https://www.osc .gov.on.ca/en/SecuritiesLaw_csa_20040716_51-312_harm-con-dis.htm>.
57 See e.g. *CSA Staff Notice 51-355 – Continuous Disclosure Review Program Activities for the Fiscal Years Ended March 31, 2018 and March 31, 2017*, OSC CSA Notice, (2018) 41 OSCB 5852, online (pdf): *OSC* <https://www.osc .gov.on.ca/documents/en/Securities-Category5/csa_20180719_51-355 _continuous-disclosure-review-program.pdf>.
58 *Ibid.*
59 See generally Luzi Hail & Christian Leuz, "International Differences in the Cost of Equity Capital: Do Legal Institutions and Securities Regulation Matter?" (2006) 44:3 J Accounting Research 485; Poonam Puri, "A Model for Common Enforcement in Canada: The Canadian Capital Markets Enforcement Agency and the Canadian Securities Hearing Tribunal" Commissioned Reports and Studies Paper (2008), online: *Osgoode Digital Commons* <https://digitalcommons.osgoode.yorku.ca /reports/111> [Puri, Common Enforcement]; Utpal Bhattacharya, "Enforcement and Its Impact on Cost of Equity and Liquidity of the Market" in *Taskforce to Modernize Securities Legislation in Canada, Canada Steps Up Final Report* Volume VI (Toronto: Task Force to Modernize Securities Legislation in Canada, 2006) 131.
60 See Department of Finance Canada, *It's Time: Report of the Committee to Review the Structure of Securities Regulation in Canada*, Chair: Michael EJ Phelps (Ottawa: Department of Finance Canada, 2003) at vii; Peter deCarteret Cory & Marilyn L Pilkington, "Critical Issues in Enforcement" in *Task Force to Modernize Securities Legislation in Canada, Canada Steps Up Final Report* Volume VI at 196–197 (Toronto: Task Force to Modernize Securities Legislation in Canada, 2006); Puri, Common Enforcement, *supra* note 59; Poonam Puri, "Securities Litigation and Enforcement: The Canadian Perspective" (2012) 37:3 Brooklyn J Intl L 967 [Puri, Securities Litigation].
61 Puri, Securities Litigation, *supra* note 60.
62 See generally Canadian Securities Administrators, "2008 Enforcement Report" (2008), online (pdf): <https://www.securities-administrators.ca /uploadedFiles/General/pdfs/CSA_Enforcement_Report_English_2008 .pdf>; Canadian Securities Administrators, "2009 Enforcement Report"

(2009), online (pdf): <https://www.securities-administrators.ca
/uploadedFiles/General/pdfs/CSAReportENG09[FA].pdf>; Canadian
Securities Administrators, "2010 Enforcement Report" (2010), online (pdf):
<https://www.securities-administrators.ca/uploadedFiles/General/pdfs
/CSA2010EnforcementReportEng.pdf>.

63 However, in 2018, this figure increased exponentially to nearly 44%,
    almost nine times the figure from earlier years. However, 2018 may be an
    outlier as a result of the OSC's sanctions against Sino-Forest Corporation
    that year.

64 See generally Ontario Securities Commission, *2017–2018 Report Card,*
    (Toronto: Ontario Securities Commission, 2018), online (pdf): <https://
    www.osc.gov.on.ca/documents/en/Publications/rpt-on-sop_fiscal-2017
    -2018.pdf>.

65 See generally Ontario Securities Commission, *2018 Annual Report*, (Toronto:
    Ontario Securities Commission), online (pdf): <https://www.osc.gov.on.ca
    /documents/en/Publications/Publications_rpt_2018_osc-annual-rpt
    _en.pdf>.

66 See Ontario Securities Commission, "OSC Compliance Reviews" (last
    visited 27 September 2019), online: <https://www.osc.gov.on.ca/en
    /Dealers_compliance-review_index.htm>.

67 See *OSC Staff Notice – 15-704 Request for Comments on Proposed Enforcement
    Initiatives*, OSC Notice, (2011) 34 OSCB 10720 at 10720, online (pdf):
    <https://www.osc.gov.on.ca/documents/en/Securities-Category1/sn
    _20111021_15-704_rfc-enforcement-initiatives.pdf> [Notice 15-704].

68 See generally *OSC Staff Notice – 15-702 Revised Credit for Cooperation
    Program*, OSC Notice, (2014) 37 OSCB 2583, online (pdf): <https://www
    .osc.gov.on.ca/documents/en/Securities-Category1/sn_20140311_15-702
    _revised-credit-coop-program.pdf>.

69 *Ibid.*

70 *Ibid.*

71 *Ibid.*

72 Notice 15-704, *supra* note 67.

73 OSC Settlement, *supra* note 5 at para 13.

74 See Anita Anand, Andrew Green & Matthew Alexander, "Are No-Contest
    Settlements in the Public Interest?", *The Globe and Mail* (19 July 2017),
    online: <https://www.theglobeandmail.com/report-on-business/rob
    -commentary/are-no-contest-settlements-in-the-public-interest
    /article35735938/>.

75 See Bill 173, *Jobs for Today and Tomorrow Act (Budget Measures), 2016*, 1st
    Sess, 41st Leg, Ontario, 2016 (assented to 19 April 2016), online: <https://
    www.ola.org/en/legislative-business/bills/parliament-41/session-1
    /bill-173>.

76 See *OSC Notice and Request for Comment Proposed OSC Policy 15-601 –
    Whistleblower Program*, OSC Notice, (28 October 2015), online (pdf): *OSC*
    <https://www.osc.gov.on.ca/documents/en/Securities-Category1
    /rule_20151028_15-601_rfc-whistleblower-program.pdf>; *OSC Policy 15
    -601 – Whistleblower Program*, (14 July 2016), online (pdf): <https://www
    .osc.gov.on.ca/documents/en/Securities-Category1/20160714_15-601
    _policy-whistleblower-program.pdf>.
77 See Ontario Securities Commission, News Release, "OSC Whistleblower
    Program Contributing to a Stronger Culture of Compliance" (29 June
    2018), online: <https://www.osc.gov.on.ca/en/NewsEvents_nr_20180629
    _osc-whistleblower-program-contributing-to-a-stronger-culture-of
    -compliance.htm>.
78 Puri, Class Actions, *supra* note 31; Puri, Securities Litigation, *supra* note 60.
79 Puri, Class Actions, *supra* note 31.
80 Statement of Allegations, *supra* note 12 at para 8.
81 See Rafael LaPorta, Florencio Lopez-de-Silanes & Andrei Shleifer,
    "What Works in Securities Laws?" (2006) 61:1 J Finance 1; Poonam Puri,
    "Enforcement Effectiveness in the Canadian Capital Markets" Com-
    missioned Reports and Studies, (2005), online: *Osgoode Digital Commons*
    <https://digitalcommons.osgoode.yorku.ca/reports/3> [Puri, Enforce-
    ment Effectiveness].
82 Puri, Class Actions, *supra* note 31.
83 Puri, Securities Litigation, *supra* note 60; Puri, Enforcement Effectiveness,
    supra note 81.
84 OSC Settlement, *supra* note 5 at paras 23–24.
85 Siskinds Class Action, *supra* note 21.
86 See Poonam Puri, "Converging Numbers: Harmonization of Accounting
    Standards with the Context of the Role of the Auditor in Corporate Gov-
    ernance" in *Responding to Globalization: Papers Presented at the 8th Queen's
    Annual Business Law Symposium 2001* (Kingston: Queen's University,
    2002) at 1; Poonam Puri, "The Hallmarks of Good Corporate Law: A Per-
    formance Evaluation of the Canadian Business Corporations Act" Report
    Commissioned by the Government of Canada, Industry Canada (2004)
    at 12, online (pdf): *Osgoode Digital Commons* <https://digitalcommons.
    osgoode.yorku.ca/cgi/viewcontent.cgi?article=1114&context=reports>.
87 See *Canada Business Corporations Act*, RSC 1985, c C-44, s 122 [CBCA].
88 *Ibid*, ss 106(3), 162(1), 239(1) – (2), 241(1) – (2).
89 *Ibid*.
90 2008 SCC 69 [BCE].
91 *Ibid* at paras 37, 40. For more on the stakeholder interest view, see
    generally Stephanie Ben-Ishai, "A Team Production Theory of Canadian
    Corporate Law" (2006) 44:2 Alta L Rev 299; PM Vasudev, "The

Stakeholder Principle, Corporate Governance, and Theory: Evidence from the Field and the Path Onward" (2012) 41:2 Hofstra L Rev 399; Stephanie Ben-Ishai, "The Promise of the Oppression Remedy: A Review of Markus Koehnen's Oppression and Related Remedies" (2005) 42:3 Can Bus LJ 450.

92 *BCE, supra* note 90 at para 38. For more on *BCE*, see generally Edward J Waitzer, "Peoples, BCE, and the Good Corporate 'Citizen'" (2009) 47:3 Osgoode Hall LJ 439; Jeremy Fraiberg, "Fiduciary Outs and Maximizing Shareholder Value following BCE" (2009) 48:2 Can Bus LJ 213; Camille Paquette, "Promoting the Long-Term Management of Public Corporations through a Reform of Canadian Corporate Law" (2019) 24 Appeal 19.

93 *CBCA, supra* note 87, s 122(1.1).

94 See Business Roundtable, "Business Roundtable Redefines the Purpose of a Corporation to Promote 'An Economy That Serves All Americans'" (19 August 2019), online: <https://www.businessroundtable.org/business-roundtable-redefines-the-purpose-of-a-corporation-to-promote-an-economy-that-serves-all-americans>. The Business Roundtable is an association of 181 CEOs of America's leading companies.

95 *Ibid*.

96 *Ibid*. The statement's signatories have also committed to: (i) delivering value to customers, including meeting or exceeding customer expectations; (ii) investing in employees, through fair compensation and important benefits, supporting training and education initiatives, and fostering diversity, inclusion, dignity, and respect; (iii) dealing fairly and ethically with suppliers; and (iv) supporting the communities in which the companies operate, by respecting people in the communities and protecting the environment by embracing sustainable business practices.

97 See Reuters, "Trump's Pitch to End Quarterly Reports Would Follow EU, Australia", (20 August 2018), online: <https://www.reuters.com/article/us-usa-sec-trump-factbox/trumps-pitch-to-end-quarterly-reports-would-follow-eu-australia-idUSKCN1L51ZN>.

98 *Ibid*.

99 See Thompson Reuters, "Trump Asks SEC to Consider Getting Rid of Quarterly Reports", *CBC* (17 August 2018), online: <https://www.cbc.ca/news/business/trump-sec-earnings-1.4788913>.

100 See US, Securities and Exchange Commission, *Request for Comment on Earnings Releases and Quarterly Reports* (Release No 33-10588) (Washington, DC: Securities and Exchange Commission, 2018) at 1, online (pdf): <https://www.sec.gov/rules/other/2018/33-10588.pdf>.

101 *Ibid* at 12.

102 See *Financial Times*, "Trump Proposal to Axe US Quarterly Reporting Gets Tepid Reception", (22 March 2019), online: <https://www.ft.com/content/10144538-4cc2-11e9-bbc9-6917dce3dc62>. For all comment letter

submissions, see US, Securities and Exchange Commission, *Comments on Earnings Releases and Quarterly Reports* (Release Nos 33-10588, 34-84842) (Washington, DC: Securities and Exchange Commission, 2020) online: <https://www.sec.gov/comments/s7-26-18/s72618.htm>.

103 *Ibid.*
104 See US, Securities and Exchange Commission, "SEC Adopts Rule Amendments to Modernize Disclosures of Business, Legal Proceedings, and Risk Factors under Regulation S-K" (26 August 2020), online: <https://www.sec.gov/news/press-release/2020-192>.
105 *Ibid.*
106 See US, Securities and Exchange Commission, "Modernizing the Framework for Business, Legal Proceedings and Risk Factor Disclosures" (26 August 2020), online: https://www.sec.gov/news/public-statement/clayton-regulation-s-k-2020-08-26>.
107 *Ibid.*
108 Robert C Pozen, Suresh Nallareddy, & Shiva Rajgopal, "Impact of Reporting Frequency on UK Public Companies" (March 2017), online: CFA Institute <https://www.cfainstitute.org/en/research/foundation/2017/impact-of-reporting-frequency-on-uk-public-companies>.
109 *Ibid.*
110 *Ibid.*
111 *Ibid.*
112 See Chris Isidore & Cristina Alesci, "President Trump Asks SEC to Study Abolishing Quarterly Earnings Reports" (17 August 2018), online: *CNN Business* <https://money.cnn.com/2018/08/17/news/companies/trump-drop-quarterly-reports/index.html#:~:text=President%20Trump%20asks%20SEC%20to%20study%20abolishing%20quarterly%20earnings%20reports,-By%20Chris%20Isidore&text=President%20Donald%20Trump%20says%20he,companies%20to%20report%20quarterly%20earnings.&text=In%20a%20statement%20to%20reporters,a%20six%2Dmonth%20reporting%20schedule>; *CSA Consultation Paper 51-404 – Considerations for Reducing Regulatory Burden for Non-Investment Fund Reporting Issuers*, (2017), online (pdf): *OSC* <https://www.osc.gov.on.ca/documents/en/Securities-Category5/csa_20170406_51-404_considerations-for-reducing-regulatory-burden.pdf>.
113 See Ontario Securities Commission, "Reducing Regulatory Burden in Ontario's Capital Markets" (2019), online: <https://www.osc.gov.on.ca/documents/en/20191119_reducing-regulatory-burden-in-ontario-capital-markets.pdf> [Reducing Regulatory Burden].
114 See generally *OSC Staff Notice 11-784 – Burden Reduction*, OSC Notice, (14 January 2019), online: <https://www.osc.gov.on.ca/en/SecuritiesLaw_sn_20190114_11-784_burden-reduction.htm>.

115 *Ibid.*

116 Reducing Regulatory Burden, *supra* note 113.

117 Ontario Securities Commission, "Reducing Regulatory Burden: Decisions and Recommendations – Status Update" (May 2020), online: <https:// www.osc.gov.on.ca/documents/en/20200527_reducing-regulatory -burden-decisions-and-recommendations.pdf>.

118 *Capital Markets Modernization Taskforce* (2020), online (pdf): https://files .ontario.ca/books/mof-capital-markets-modernization-taskforce-report -en-2020-07-09.pdf.

119 *Ibid.*

120 *Ibid.*

121 See Ariel Fromer Babcock & Sarah Williamson, "Quarterly Earnings Guidance – A Corporate Relic?," Note, (2018) at 10, online (pdf): *Conference Board of Canada* <http://www.shareholderforum.com/access /Library/20180300_ConferenceBoard-DirectorNotes.pdf> (Unilever stopped this practice in 2009).

122 *Ibid*; Canadian Coalition for Good Government, *Building High Performance Boards* (Toronto, August 2013).

123 See Poonam Puri, "The Future of Stakeholder Interests in Corporate Governance" (2010) 48:3 Can Bus LJ 427 [Puri, Stakeholder Interests].

124 See generally Barry J Reiter, *Director Duties in Canada*, 6th ed (Toronto: LexisNexis Canada Inc, 2016).

125 Puri, Stakeholder Interests, *supra* note 123.

126 RSO 1990, c B16 [*OBCA*]. In the case of a corporation incorporated under the *Canada Business Corporations Act*, at least two of the directors of a distributing corporation must be independent, *CBCA, supra* note 87, s. 102(2).

127 *OBCA, ibid*, s 115(3).

128 *CBCA, supra* note 87, s 102(2).

129 See *National Policy 58-201 – Corporate Governance Guidelines*, OSC NP 58-201, (17 June 2005), ss 3.1–3.3.

130 See Institutional Shareholder Services, "Canada Proxy Voting Guidelines for TSX-Listed Companies" (12 December 2018) at 10, online (pdf): <https://www.issgovernance.com/file/policy/active/americas/Canada -TSX-Voting-Guidelines.pdf> [ISS Proxy Voting]; Glass Lewis, "2019 Proxy Paper Guidelines: An Overview of the Glass Lewis Approach to Proxy Advice, Canada" (2019) at 6, online: <https://www.glasslewis. com/wp-content/uploads/2018/10/2019_GUIDELINES_Canada.pdf> [Glass Lewis Proxy].

131 *OBCA, supra* note 126, s 158(1); *CBCA, supra* note 87, s 171(1); NI 52-110, *supra* note 1 (Both corporate and securities law require corporations to establish and maintain an audit committee composed of at least three members).

132 ISS Proxy Voting, *supra* note 130; Glass Lewis Proxy, *supra* note 130.

133 NI 52-110, *supra* note 1, s 1.4.

134 ISS Proxy Voting, *supra* note 130.

135 Glass Lewis Proxy, *supra* note 130.

136 See generally *CSA Staff Notice 58-306 – 2010 Corporate Governance Disclosure Compliance Review*, OSC CSA Notice, (2 December 2010), online (pdf): *OSC* <https://www.osc.gov.on.ca/documents/en/Securities -Category5/csa_20101203_58-306_2010-corp-gov-disclosure.pdf>.

137 See generally Home Capital Group Inc, "Management Information Circular, Notice of 2014 Annual Meeting of Shareholders" (14 May 2014), online (pdf): *SEDAR* <https://s2.q4cdn.com/668293721/files/doc _financials/annual_meetings/2014/MICircular2014.pdf>; Home Capital Group Inc, "Management Information Circular, Notice of 2015 Annual & Special Meeting of Shareholders" (13 May 2015), online (pdf): *SEDAR* <https://s2.q4cdn.com/668293721/files/doc_financials/annual_meetings /2015/MICircular2015.pdf>; Home Capital Group Inc, News Release, "Home Capital Group Inc. Announces Annual Meeting Results" (22 May 2014), online (pdf): *SEDAR* <https://s2.q4cdn.com/668293721/files /doc_news/2014/annual-meeting-05.22.2014.pdf> [Meeting Results 2014]; Home Capital Group Inc, News Release, "Home Capital Group Inc. Announces Annual Meeting Results" (22 May 2015), online (pdf): *SEDAR* <https://s2.q4cdn.com/668293721/files/doc_news/2015/ANNOUNCES -ANNUAL-MEETING-RESULTS.pdf> [Meeting Results 2015].

138 Meeting Results 2014, *ibid*; Meeting Results 2015, *ibid*.

139 OSC Settlement, *supra* note 5 at para 24.

140 See generally Irving Janis, *Victims of Groupthink: A Psychological Study of Foreign-Policy Decisions and Fiascos* (Oxford: Houghton Mifflin, 1972).

141 See Marleen A O'Connor, "The Enron Board: The Perils of Groupthink" (2003) 71 U Cin L Rev 1233.

142 *Ibid*.

143 ISS Proxy Voting, *supra* note 130.

144 Reiter, *supra* note 124.

145 OSC Settlement, *supra* note 5.

146 *Ibid*.

147 *Ibid* at paras 9, 64.

148 See generally Andrew Howard, "Groupthink and Corporate Governance Reform: Changing the Formal and Informal Decision-making Processes of Corporate Boards" (2011) 20 S Cal Interdisciplinary LJ 425.

149 See generally RS Burt, "Cooptive Corporate Actor Networks: A Reconsideration of Interlocking Directorates Involving American Manufacturing" (1980) 25 Administrative Science Q 557; MS Mizruchi, "What Do Interlocks Do? An Analysis, Critique, and Assessment

of Research on Interlocking Directorates" (1996) 22 Annual Rev Sociology 271.

150 See generally Gerald Davis, "The Significance of Board Interlocks for Corporate Governance" (1996) 4:3 Corporate Governance: Intl Rev 154; Johan SG Chu & Gerald F Davis, "Who Killed the Inner Circle? The Decline of the American Corporate Interlock Network" (2016) 122:3 American J Sociology 714.

151 Glass Lewis Proxy, *supra* note 130.

152 See Home Capital Group Inc, News Release, "Home Capital Announces Resignation of Jim Keohane from Board" (27 April 2017), online (pdf): *SEDAR* <https://s2.q4cdn.com/668293721/files/doc_news/archive /NRJimiKeohane-CL.pdf>.

153 Howard, *supra* note 148; O'Connor, *supra* note 141.

154 O'Connor, *supra* note 141.

155 Howard, *supra* note 148; O'Connor, *supra* note 141.

156 See generally David A Carter, Frank P D'Souza, Betty Jo Simkins, & W Gary Simpson, "The Diversity of Corporate Board Committees and Financial Performance" (2008) SSRN Electronic Journal 1; Cristian L Dezső & David Gaddis Ross, "'Girl Power': Female Participation in Top Management and Firm Performance" (2008), online (pdf): *CiteSeerX* <http://citeseerx.ist.psu.edu/viewdoc/download?doi=10.1.1.141 .5974&rep=rep1&type=pdf>; O'Connor, *supra* note 141; David A Carter, Betty J Simkins & W Gary Simpson, "Corporate Governance, Board Diversity, and Firm Value" (2003) 38 Financial Rev 33.

157 See generally Irene van Staveren, "The Lehman Sisters Hypothesis" (2014) 38 Cambridge J Economics 995.

158 See generally Vathunyoo Sila, Angelica Gonzalez & Jens Hagendorff, "Women on Board: Does Boardroom Gender Diversity Affect Firm Risk?" (2015) 36 J Corporate Finance 26.

159 Puri, Stakeholder Interests, *supra* note 123.

160 See generally RB Adams & D Ferreira, "Women in the Boardroom and Their Impact on Governance and Performance" (2009) 94:2 J Financial Economics 291; RB Adams, "Women on Boards: The Superheroes of Tomorrow?" (2016) European Corporate Governance Institute Finance Working Paper No. 466/2016; D Rhode & AK Packel, "Diversity on Corporate Boards: How Much Difference Does Difference Make?" (2014) 39 Del J Corp L 2; C Post & K Byron, "Women on Boards and Firm Financial Performance: A Meta-Analysis" (2015) 58:5 Academy Management J 1546.

161 See Barbara Schecter, "What's a Woman on the Board Worth to Stock Investors?", *Financial Post* (7 June 2017), online: <http://business.financialpost .com/news/fp-street/whats-a-woman-on-the-board-worth-to-investors -about-300-bps-according-to-cibc-study> (The S&P/TSX Composite Index

provides approximately 95% coverage of the Canadian equities market and includes 250 issuers. It is the primary gauge for Canadian-based, TSX listed companies. The TSX is the primary stock exchange in Canada.)

162 See generally Credit Suisse Research Institute, "The CS Gender 3000: The Reward for Change" (September 2016), online (pdf): *Credit Suisse* <https://evolveetfs.com/wp-content/uploads/2017/08/Credit-Suisse -Reward-for-Change_1495660293279_2.pdf>.

163 See generally *CSA Multilateral Staff Notice 58-310 – Report on Fourth Staff Review of Disclosure Regarding Women on Boards and in Executive Officer Positions*, OSC CSA Notice (27 September 2018), online (pdf): *OSC* <https://www.osc.gov.on.ca/documents/en/Securities-Category5/sn _20180927_58-310_staff-review-women-on-boards.pdf>.

164 *Ibid.*

165 See generally *National Instrument 58-101 – Disclosure of Corporate Governance Practices*, OSC NI 58-101, (2005) 28 OSCB 5377.

166 See Canada, Canadian Securities Administration, "Roundtable Discussion – Third Review of Women on Boards and in Executive Officer Positions" (Toronto: Ontario Securities Commission, 2017) at 8, online (pdf): *OSC* <https://www.osc.gov.on.ca/documents/en/Securities-Category5/sn _20171103_transcript-wob-roundtable.pdf> [CSA Roundtable Discussion].

167 See generally *An Act to Amend the Canada Business Corporations Act, the Canada Cooperatives Act, the Canada Not-for-profit Corporations Act and the Competition Act*, SC 2018, c 8 [C-8].

168 CSA Roundtable Discussion, *supra* note 166 at 10 (importantly, Canadian securities regulators may not have the authority to establish quotas).

169 C-8, *supra* note 167, s 24.

170 This was notwithstanding that it is relatively easier for a backbencher to bring a bill forward for debate in the Senate than the House of Commons.

171 Glass Lewis Proxy, *supra* note 130.

172 ISS Proxy Voting, *supra* note 130.

2. HOOPP and Home Capital: Pension Funds as Good Governors and Crisis Managers

1 Terms such as "market integrity" are not always well defined. In a narrower sense, it refers to the fair access and treatment of individuals to capital markets and protections against manipulations such as insider trading. Wider definitions include stability in market movements and addressing systemic risks, which may or may not involve questions of manipulation or fairness for individual market participants. In this chapter, the term will be used in the wider sense to include objectives of securities and prudential regulation of capital markets and in particular

to manage systemic risks. For discussion on the definition of market integrity and its scope, see generally Janet Austin, "What Exactly Is Market Integrity? An Analysis of One of the Core Objectives of Securities Regulation" (2017) 8:2 Wm & Mary Bus L Rev 215 at 231ff.

2 See, for example, David Parkinson, "Canadian Household Debt Soars to Yet Another Record", *The Globe and Mail*, (11 March 2016), online: <https://www.theglobeandmail.com/report-on-business/economy /canadians-debt-burden-still-growing-hits-record-in-fourth-quarter /article29172712/> [perma.cc/ WA5V-2H6V] reporting on Statistics Canada data. The article also mentions the Bank of Canada's monitoring of household debt, characterizing it as a persistent worry. Similar reporting occurs in prior years. See, for example, Gary Marr, "Canada Household Debt Ratio Hits New Record of 163.3%", *The Financial Post* (12 March 2015), online: <https://business.financialpost.com/personal -finance/debt/canada-household-debt-ratio-hits-new-record-of-163-3> [perma.cc/ NUD8-KBAR] noting that one measure of household debt ratios showed a greater household debt ratio in Canada than the United States, and reaching levels seen in the United States immediately prior to the general financial crisis in 2008–2009.

3 See, for example, Matt Scuffham and Allison Martell, "Bundles of Debt: How Lenders Sidestep Canada's Mortgage Rules", Reuters Special Report (11 January 2017), online: <https://www.reuters.com/article /us-canada-housing-insight/bundles-of-debt-how-lenders-sidestep -canadas-mortgage-rules-idUSKBN14V1DY> [perma.cc/ NJS5-BR2P] discussing the growth in subprime lending and new bundled loan formats. The article cites Ministry of Finance and Bank of Canada data showing the market share (approximately $125 billion in assets, including other consumer loans) of unregulated lenders at 12.5%, up from 6.6% ten years previously. Although contemporaneous with the Home Capital affair, see a useful summary of then-current views in Joe Castaldo, "What the Home Capital Crisis Reveals about the Housing Market", *Maclean's Magazine* (5 May 2017), online: <https://www.macleans.ca/economy/what-the -home-capital-crisis-reveals-about-the-housing-market/> [perma.cc / 5KU6-E3HJ].

4 Nearly ten years after the 2008 financial crisis there were dozens of popular accounts about the origins and events, particularly in the United States. For just three examples, see Atif Main and Amir Sufi, *House of Debt* (Chicago: University of Chicago Press, 2014); Andrew Ross Sorkin, *Too Big to Fail: The Inside Story of How Wall Street and Washington Fought to Save the Financial System* (Viking: New York, 2009); and for wider transatlantic scope, Tamim Boyoumi, *Unfinished Business* (Padstow, UK: International Monetary Fund, 2017).

5 See Castaldo, *supra* note 3; and generally for information and links on the Home Capital story see Kareen Brown & Kevin Veenstra, "Home Capital Group – The High Cost of Dishonesty" (2018) 17:2 Accounting Perspectives. On 31 December 2014, Home Capital reported total revenues of just over $1 billion, total assets of $20 billion, and mortgage loans of $18 billion, which Castaldo reports were about 1% of the total mortgage market in Canada. According to Brown and Veenstra, Home Capital's residential mortgage business consisted largely of two portfolios: accelerator mortgages, which were its main insured single-family product available to prime borrowers (the majority of whom are insured by the Canada Mortgage and Housing Corporation); and exchange conventional mortgages, which are not insured. Residential mortgages comprised approximately 90% of Home Capital's business. One of Home Capital's closest competitors is Equitable Bank Group (TSX: EQB), who also financed alternative lending through deposits. Equitable's share price dropped 50% between 7 April ($70) and 27 April ($36) in 2017. For detail, see TMX, "Price History for Equitable Group Inc. [TSE:EQB]" (27 August 2019), online: *TMX Group* <https://web.tmxmoney.com /pricehistory.php?qm_symbol=EQB> [perma.cc/ K4QH-FKLU].

6 See Barbara Shecter, "'Better Not to Sit in Two Places': HOOPP Board Overlaps Raise Concerns", *The Financial Post* (28 April 2017), online: <https://business.financialpost.com/news/fp-street/better-not-to-sit -in-two-places-hoopp-board-overlaps-raise-concerns> [perma.cc/9M3W -JYKQ].

7 See James Bradshaw, Jacqueline Nelson, Andrew Willis, & Christina Pellegrini, "Exclusive: Buffett on How He Struck the Home Capital Deal", *The Globe and Mail* (22 June 2017), online: <https://www.theglobeandmail .com/report-on-business/how-warren-buffett-struck-the-home-capital -deal-in-three-short-days/article35443101/> [perma.cc/2ZZ8-RJ8Y].

8 Staff, "Home Capital to Pay $1.65B Owed to HOOPP from Buffett Loan" (22 June 2017), online: *Benefits Canada* <https://www.benefitscanada .com/news/home-capital-to-end-hoopp-financing-after-new-deal-with -warren-buffett-99916> [perma.cc/ LEN9-25NY].

9 Home Capital Group Inc., News Release, "Home Capital Announces Agreements to Settle OSC and Class Action Matters" (14 June 2017), online: *CISION* <http://www.newswire.ca/news-releases/home-capital -announces-agreements-to-settle-osc-and-class-action-matters-628505203 .html> [perma.cc/4MKU-FLSJ].

10 *Ibid.*

11 See TMX, "Financial Statements for Home Capital Group Inc. [TSE:HCG]" (21 August 2019), online: *TMX Group* <https://web.tmxmoney.com /quote.php?locale=en&qm_symbol=HCG> [perma.cc/XT7W-CW4L].

The TSE:HCG share price is considered low compared to its balance sheet ratios and near competitors.

12 By the fall of 2018, the Canada Mortgage and Housing Corporation – the main insurer of residential mortgages – was forecasting slower growth in housing prices and slower mortgage activity overall. See CMHC, *Housing Market Outlook* (Fall 2018), online: <https://www.cmhc-schl.gc.ca/en /data-and-research/publications-and-reports/housing-market-outlook -highlights> [perma.cc/36TG-NR4F].

13 See e.g. Jason Kirby, "This Is How Canada's Housing Correction Begins", *Maclean's Magazine* (3 January 2019), online: <https://www.macleans.ca /economy/realestateeconomy/this-is-how-canadas-housing-correction -begins/> [perma.cc/6M8P-3986]. But see Chris Fournier, "Canada's Home Sales Rise for Third Month, Easing Concerns about Correction", *Financial Post* (14 June 2019), online: <https://business.financialpost. com/real-estate/housing-market-picks-up-steam-in-canada-after-slow -start-to-year> [perma.cc/W2DQ-AA6K].

14 For one among many examples, see Ben McLannahan, "Canada's Housing Market Flirts with Disaster", *The Financial Times* (8 February 2018), online: <https://www.ft.com/content/8cb9f0fa-0a61-11e8-839d -41ca06376bf2> [perma.cc/ 4RR3-ASA5].

15 See for example Stephen S Poloz, "Canada's Economy and Household Debt: How Big Is the Problem" (1 May 2018), online: *Bank of Canada* <www.bankofcanada.ca/2018/05/canada-economy-household-debt -how-big-the-problem/> [perma.cc/4BRZ-UCL8] [Poloz, Household Debt]; Stephen S Poloz, "Risk Sharing, Flexibility and the Future of Mortgages" (6 May 2019), online: *Bank of Canada* <www.bankofcanada. ca/2019/05/risk-sharing-flexibility-future-mortgages/> [perma.cc/K3YF -5FJ5]. See also Guillaume Bédard-Pagé, "Non-Bank Financial Intermedia- tion in Canada: An Update" (2019) Bank of Canada Staff Discussion Paper No 2019-2, online (pdf): *Bank of Canada* <www.bankofcanada.ca /wp-content/uploads/2019/03/sdp2019-2.pdf> [perma.cc/LH4V-4K5A].

16 See e.g. Armina Ligaya & Barbara Shecter, "'Like the Perfect Storm': An FP Investigation into the Events That Took Home Capital to the Brink", *The Financial Post* (22 September 2017), online: <http://business .financialpost.com/news/inside-the-rise-and-fall-of-home-capital> [perma.cc/B382-QZAG]; Editorial, "Home Capital Group: A Timeline", *The Globe and Mail* (last modified 15 June 2017), online: <https://www .theglobeandmail.com/report-on-business/home-capital-group-a -timeline/article34770189/> [perma.cc/4FAF-PJ4S]; Armina Ligaya & Barbara Shecter, "OSC Accuses Home Capital of Misleading Disclosure after Uncovering Fraud in Mortgage Broker Channel", *Financial Post* (last modified 20 April 2017), online: <http://business.financialpost.com

/news/fp-street/osc-accuses-home-capital-of-misleading-disclosure
-after-uncovering-fraud-in-mortgage-broker-channel> [perma.cc/5TNL
-D86P]; Kristine Owram, Doug Alexander & Katia Dmitrieva, "Home
Capital Defends Buffett as Investors Question Discount", *Bloomberg* (last
modified 28 June 2017), online: <https://www.bloomberg.com/news
/articles/2017-06-28/buffett-in-bag-home-capital-taps-canada-patriots
-for-funding> [perma.cc/5AKJ-SLAQ].

17 See Brown & Veenstra, *supra* note 5. The article outlines several possible
issues or lenses through which to see the events and contains a trove of
summary information about Home Capital and subprime lending drawn
on by this chapter.

18 See the article discussing the development of housing markets and
mortgage policy in Canada 1970 to present by Gideon Kalman-Lamb,
"The Financialization of Housing in Canada: Intensifying Contradictions
of Neoliberal Accumulation" (2017) 98:3 Studies in Political Economy
298 at 310 and 313. See also the mention of Home Trust in UK, Prudential
Regulation Authority, *Independent Review of the Prudential Supervision of
The Co-operative Bank Plc* (For the period 1 May 2008 to 22 November
2013) by Marc Zelmer (London: Her Majesty's Treasury & Bank of
England, 2019) at 34.

19 See Brown and Veenstra, *supra* note 5 at 6.

20 See Editorial, *supra* note 16.

21 *Ibid.*

22 *Ibid.* On 14 March 2017 that the OSC had issued enforcement notices to
current and former executives for non-disclosure of fraudulent activities
by certain mortgage brokers who had submitted mortgage applications
with falsified information.

23 See Ontario Securities Commission, News Release, "OSC Approves
Settlement Agreement with Home Capital Group Inc., Gerald Soloway,
Robert Morton and Martin Reid in Relation to Disclosure Violations"
(9 August 2017), online: *OSC* <https://www.osc.gov.on.ca/en/NewsEvents
_nr_20170809_settlement-home-capital.htm> [perma.cc/4CNW-VV27].

24 See Siskinds Law Firm, "Home Capital Group Inc." (last visited
25 August 2019), online: *Siskinds Law Firm* <https://www.siskinds.com
/class-action/home-capital-group-inc/> [perma.cc/2AZA-G5DT]. The
action was filed in February and settled 22 June 2017. The original claim
was for $200 million in alleged losses for the class being persons who
had losses between November 2014 and July 2015. The settlement was
for about 11% of that amount, which is consistent with shareholder class
proceeding settlements.

25 See Shecter, *supra* note 6.

26 *Ibid.*

27   Home Capital announced on 26 April 2017 that it had received a
      $2 billion line of credit lifeline from the HOOPP to compensate for
      withdrawals from its Home Trust High Interest Savings Accounts. See
      Editorial, *supra* note 16.

28   See Robert Benzie, "Home Capital Director Quits OPSEU Pension Board",
      The Toronto Star (18 May 2017), online: <https://www.thestar.com/news
      /queenspark/2017/05/18/home-capital-director-quits-opseu-pension
      -board.html> [perma.cc/49DD-HFD6].

29   See Armina Ligaya, "Equitable Group CEO Says $2 Billion Credit Line a
      'Sign of Confidence,' Stems Contagion from Home Capital" *Financial Post*
      (1 May 2017), online: <https://financialpost.com/news/fp-street
      /equitable-group-rushes-to-contain-contagion-risk-from-home-capital
      -maelstrom>. The terms included a 0.75% commitment fee and a 0.5%
      standby charge on any unused portion of the facility. The Home Capital
      terms were "significantly more onerous".

30   *Ibid.*

31   See <https://www.corporatemapping.ca/> [perma.cc/2QAD-M8MD].
      John Coates, "The Future of Corporate Governance Part I: The Problem of
      Twelve" Harvard Public Law Working Paper No. 19-07, online: <https://
      papers.ssrn.com/sol3/papers.cfm?abstract_id=3247337> [perma.cc
      /RY64-SQEP].

32   In the aftermath of the OSC accusations, Home Capital lost approximately
      9% of customer deposits in high interest savings, from $2 billion to
      approximately $100 million as of 25 June 2017: see Castaldo, *supra* note 3.
      See also Armina Ligaya, "Equitable Group CEO says $2 billion credit line
      a 'sign of confidence,' stems contagion from Home Capital" *supra* note 29.

33   "Home Capital Group Director Keohane Resigns after Fund Backs
      $2 Billion Loan", *Bloomberg News* (27 April 2017), online: <https://
      business.financialpost.com/news/fp-street/home-capital-group-director
      -keohane-resigns-after-fund-backs-2-billion-loan> [perma.cc/ W63H
      -E95D].

34   Michelle Zaidikan, "Home Capital Emergency Loan Was a 'Win-Win':
      HOOPP CEO", (30 October 2017), online: *Business News Network Bloomberg*
      <https://www.bnnbloomberg.ca/home-capital-emergency-loan-was-a
      -win-win-hoopp-ceo-1.900233> [perma.cc/ 2C2H-DFEY]; "Home Capital
      Not a Risky Investment for Us: HOOPP CEO", Interview with Jim Keohane
      (undated), online: *BNN Bloomberg,* <https://www.bnnbloomberg.ca/video
      /home-capital-not-a-risky-investment-for-us-hoopp-ceo~1111585> [perma
      .cc/ 5ZY8-6335].

35   BNN Bloomberg, *supra* note 34.

36   *Ibid.*

37   *Ibid.*

38 *Ibid.*; see also Editorial Board, "Home Capital Group Director Resigns after Fund Backs $2 Billion Loan", *Financial Post* (27 April 2017), online: <https://business.financialpost.com/news/fp-street/home-capital -group-director-keohane-resigns-after-fund-backs-2-billion-loan> [perma .cc/LCZ3-MQN6]

39 The Canadian model is widely discussed. For one example see Mary Childs & John Authers, "Canada Quietly Treads Radical Path on Pensions", *The Financial Times* (24 August 2016) online: <https://www .ft.com/content/99075c68-68f9-11e6-a0b1-d87a9fea034f> [perma.cc /2XNW-F5TX]; and for a recent report on the development and features of the model, see World Bank, "The Evolution of the Canadian Pension Model: Practical Lessons for Building World-Class Pension Organizations" (2017) World Bank Group Working Paper No 121375.

40 World Bank, *supra* note 39.

41 The largest public service pension funds and the mandatory publicly administered (but both public and private sector participation) pension arrangements are often referred to as the "group of ten" or the "group of eight". They are: Canada Pension Plan Investment Board; Caisse de dépôt et placement du Québec; Ontario Teachers' Pension Plan; British Columbia Investment Management Corporation; PSP Investments; Alberta Investment Management Corporation; Ontario Municipal Employees' Retirement System; HOOPP; Ontario Pension Board; and OPTrust: see World Bank, *ibid.* at 1–2, 7, and footnotes 6–8.

42 World Bank, *ibid.* at 3. Rivalry sometimes takes aim at the role of pension funds as competitors to private investors, and issues of "level playing fields" are raised, in particular the tax-assisted status of pension funds. See e.g. *4352238 Canada Inc v SNC-Lavalin Group Inc, et al*, 2019 ONSC 4423, in which SNC Lavalin challenges a pension fund as a "competitor". Low interest rates drive up the valuation of liabilities and require greater contributions from stakeholders.

43 See Gareth Gore, "Pension Giants Add Leverage as 30-Year-Old Canadian Model Flounders", *International Financing Review* (12 July 2019), online: <http://www.ifre.com/pension-giants-add-leverage-as-30-year-old -canadian-model-flounders/21394558.fullarticle> [perma.cc/E7HP -MZW6]. Traditionally, borrowing by pension funds to amplify returns was considered risky and was restricted to limited circumstances, such as avoiding an untimely liquidation of an investment.

44 World Bank, *supra* note 39 at 2–3.

45 *Ibid.*

46 See World Bank, *supra* note 39 at xii.

47 *Ibid* at 37.

48 See e.g. Bill Curry, "Will the $35-Billion Canada Infrastructure Bank Survive the Election?", *The Globe and Mail* (30 June 2019), online: <https://

www.theglobeandmail.com/politics/article-will-the-35-billion-canada
-infrastructure-bank-survive-the-election/> [perma.cc/C6UY-4BBM].

49 See generally Clive Lipshitz & Ingo Walter, *Bridging the Gaps: Public Pension Funds and Infrastructure Finance* (Independently Published, 2019).

50 See commentary on the evolution of Canadian pension funds in World Bank, supra note 39 at 7–8; and see Malcolm Rowan (Chair), *In Whose Interest?* Report from the Task Force on the Investment of Public Sector Pension Fund (Toronto: Queen's Printer Ontario, 1987) recommending private investment of public pension funds' assets.

51 For the main discussion in the Canadian context see Jeffrey MacIntosh, "Institutional Shareholders and Corporate Governance in Canada" (1996) 26:2 Can Bus LJ 145 at 162–3 and 167 on the barriers to pension fund activities promoting good governance, and 171ff on formal and informal influence of pension fund on investments.

52 For example, restrictions on foreign property ownership were slowly eliminated to eliminate forced bias to Canadian assets, which might account of only 2–3% of global market opportunities. Similarly, rules requiring passivity such as caps on voting securities have been relaxed or "worked around". See for example Mark Firman, "Government's Plan to Eliminate 30% Rule Should Concern Everyone" *Benefits Canada* (27 April 2016), online: <https://www.benefitscanada.com/investments/other -investments/governments-plan-to-eliminate-30-rule-should-concern -everyone-80404> [perma.cc/ HDJ6-XAWG].

53 See MacIntosh, supra note 51 at 171ff.

54 See Canadian Coalition for Good Governance website at www.ccgg.ca.

55 See Bank of Canada, *Large Canadian Public Pension Funds: A Financial System Perspective*, by Guillaume Bédard-Pagé, Annick Demers, Eric Tuer, & Miville Tremblay, Bank of Canada Financial System Review 2016 (Ottawa: Bank of Canada, June 2016), online (pdf): *Bank of Canada* <https://www.bankofcanada.ca/wp-content/uploads/2016/06/fsr -june2016-bedard-page.pdf> [perma.cc/RL2T-GR6D] at 34–37; see World Bank supra note 39 at 50–54.

56 *Ibid*.

57 Bank of Canada, *supra* note 55 at 34–37; see World Bank *supra* note 39 at 50–54. Another useful source for summary portfolio information on major Canadian pension funds is the website of the Pension Investment Association of Canada, which makes annual reports on portfolios available online at: https://www.piacweb.org/site/publications/asset-mix-report.

58 *Ibid*.

59 *Ibid*.

60 *Ibid*.

61 See Douglas Sarro & Edward Waitzer, "Fiduciary Society Unleashed: The Road Ahead for the Financial Sector" (2014) 69:4 Bus Lawyer 1081; Douglas

Sarro & Edward Waitzer, "Reconnecting the Financial Sector to the Real Economy: A Plan for Action" (2014) 7:2 Rotman Intl J of Pension Mgmt 28. See also Lipshitz & Walter, *supra* note 49; and for other examples of Canadian funds as leaders in infrastructure investing, see Matti Siemytacki, "Canadian Pension Fund Investors in Transport Infrastructure: A Case Study" (2015) 3:2 Case Studies on Transport Policy 166; Georg Inderst, "Pension Fund Investment in Infrastructure: Lessons from Canada and Australia" (2014) 7:1 Rotman International Journal of Pension Management 40.

62 *Ibid.*

63 See Sarro & Waitzer, *supra* note 61.

64 See UK, Department for Business, Innovation & Skills, *Kay Review of UK Equity Markets and Long-Term Decision Making*, (23 July 2012) online: *Department for Business, Innovation & Skills* <www.bis.gov.uk/kayreview> [perma.cc/ BK64-MPJG].

65 Kevin Skerrett, Johanna Weststar, Simon Archer, & Chris Roberts, *The Contradictions of Pension Fund Capitalism* (Ithaca, NY: Cornell University Press, 2018).

66 See Ellen Dannin, "Infrastructure Privatization Contracts and Their Effect on Governance" (2009) Penn State Legal Studies Research Paper No 19-2009. See also Ellen Dannin, "Crumbling Infrastructure, Crumbling Democracy: Infrastructure Privatization Contracts and Their Effects on State and Local Governance" (2011) 6:1 Nw JL & Soc Pol'y 47. For a historical overview of U.S.-based pension fund investments, including privatizations, see Michael McCarthy, *Dismantling Solidarity: Capitalist Politics and American Pensions since the New Deal* (Ithaca, NY: Cornell University Press, 2017).

67 That commentator is Gordon Clarke in "From Corporatism to Public Utilities: Workplace Pensions in the 21st Century" (2012) 50:1 Geographical Research 31. In discussing the evolution of pensions in Anglo-American economies, and with reference to continental Europe, Clarke characterizes the emergence of government-sponsored savings schemes intended to fill the gap left by declining workplace pensions as akin to public utilities. Although distinct from the public pension plans discussed in this chapter – which are workplace pension plans and not government sponsored utilities – they are close analogs.

68 For one discussion of pension funds from the financial system perspective, see Bank of Canada, *supra* note 55.

69 For popular accounts of these events, see works cited, *supra* note 5.

70 See Boyoumi, supra note 4.

71 See Sorkin, *supra* note 4.

72 For financial vandalism, see Anchalee Worrachate, "Pension World Reels from 'Financial Vandalism' of Falling Yields" (27 August 2019), online:

Bloomberg <https://www.bloomberg.com/news/articles/2019-08-27
/pension-world-reels-from-financial-vandalism-of-falling-yields>
[perma.cc/ UU4R-G43Z]. Discussions of local plans include locally, Keith
Ambachtsheer, Peter Dungan, Steve Murphy, James Pesando, & Dmitry
Sorochenko, "Risks of a Prolonged Low-Interest-Rate Environment
for the Pension Sector" (Report Submitted to the Global Risk Institute,
Rotman School of Management, University of Toronto, September 2013).
For an OECD survey, see J Yermo & C Severinson, "The Impact of the
Financial Crisis on Defined Benefit Plans and the Need for Counter-
Cyclical Funding Regulations" (2010), OECD Working Papers on
Finance, Insurance and Private Pensions, No. 3, OECD Publishing, DOI:
<10.1787/5km91p3jszxw-en>. There is a lot of commentary on the effect
of the general financial crisis on pension funds themselves; there is much
less discussion of how pension plans and funds operate during and
around financial market crises.

73 To the author's knowledge, the most recent Canadian discussion in
this vein is Bank of Canada, *supra* note 55. An earlier discussion was
Lawrence Schembri, "Double Coincidence of Needs: Pension Funds and
Financial Stability" (15 May 2014), online: *Bank of Canada* <https://www
.bankofcanada.ca/2014/05/double-coincidence-needs-pension-funds/>
[perma.cc/ A35P-9D2L] setting out several of the stabilizing features
pension funds have in capital markets and the alignment of interests in
market integrity and management of systemic risks. For international
discussions, see Andrew Haldane, "The Age of Asset Management?"
(Speech delivered at London business School, 4 April 2014), online:
<https://www.bis.org/review/r140507d.pdf> [perma.cc/8YWG-HRLN]
discussing evidence in the UK; and Taejin Han, Kyoung Gook Park &
Dariusz Stańko, "Are Pension Funds a Stabilising Factor in Financial
Markets? Evidence from Four Countries" (December 2018), IOPS
Working Papers on Effective Pensions Supervision, No. 31, online:
<http://www.iopsweb.org/WP-31-Are-pension-funds-a-stablising
-factor-in-financial-markets.pdf> [perma.cc/ 3QJA-53ED] examining the
operation of funds in Mexico, Chile, Poland and Italy.

74 See Bank of Canada, *supra* note 55 at 37–38.

75 *Ibid*.

76 See Schembri, *supra* note 73.

77 There is not a well-developed body of evidence of pension fund behavior
in market crises; Bank of Canada, *supra* note 55 at 37.

78 *Ibid* at 35.

79 See Paul Halperin, Christopher C Nicholls, Poonam Puri, & Caroline
Cakebread, *Back from the Brink: Lessons from the Canadian Asset-Backed
Commercial Paper Crisis* (Toronto: University of Toronto Press, 2016).

80 See *supra* note 4 for references on the global financial crisis. For the
    current crisis, see International Monetary Fund, "Policy Responses to
    Covid 19" entry on Canada, online: <https://www.imf.org/en/Topics
    /imf-and-covid19/Policy-Responses-to-COVID-19#C> [perma.cc/7JSM
    -QVAY]; Carolyn Wilkins, "Bridge to Recovery: The Bank's COVID-19
    Pandemic Response" (4 May 2020), online: *Bank of Canada* <https://
    www.bankofcanada.ca/2020/05/bridge-recovery-banks-covid-19
    -pandemic-response/> [perma.cc/5VVD-CEGF].
81 For a general discussion, Pablo Antolin, Sebastian Schich & Juan Yermo,
    "The Economic Impact of Protracted Low Interest Rates on Pension
    Funds and Insurance Companies" (2001) 1 OECD Journal: Financial
    Market Trends 15. The issue is discussed frequently in industry press. For
    a recent example, see Saheli Roy Choudhry, "Canada's Massive Pension
    Fund Is Reviewing Its Bond Holding in Light of Near Zero Interest
    Rates" (15 September 2020), online: *CNBC* <https://www.cnbc.com/2020
    /09/16/singapore-summit-cppib-ceo-on-zero-bound-interest-rates.html
    [perma.cc/9DTD-378T].
82 For example, see Amit Sinha, "Low Interest Rates Are Compounding
    the Big Problems Facing Pension Funds" (3 September 2019), online:
    Marketwatch, <https://www.marketwatch.com/story/low-interest-rates
    -are-compounding-the-big-problems-facing-pension-funds-2019-08-30>
    [perma.cc/CL6E-AMXS].
83 Rob Kozolski, "Funding Ratio for Canadian Funds Rises in Q3"
    (2 October 2020), online: *Pension and Investments* <https://www.pionline
    .com/pension-funds/funding-ratio-canadian-funds-rises-q3> [perma.cc
    /7NBG-Q7BJ].
84 See for example Kristin McKenna, "5 Explanations for the Disconnect
    between the Stock Market and the Economy," *Forbes* (3 May 2020), online:
    https://www.forbes.com/sites/kristinmckenna/2020/05/13/5
    -explanations-for-the-disconnect-between-the-stock-market-and-the
    -economy/?sh=2555315d5669 [perma.cc/P5LY-T5EH]; "The Market v the
    Real Economy", *The Economist* (7 May 2020), online: <https://www
    .economist.com/leaders/2020/05/07/the-market-v-the-real-economy>
    [perma.cc/L7V5-3K6M]; Deniz Igan, Divya Kirti & Soledad Martinez
    Peria, "The Disconnect between Financial Markets and the Real Economy",
    Special Research Notes (26 August 2020), online: *International Monetary
    Fund* <https://www.imf.org/~/media/Files/Publications/covid19
    -special-notes/en-special-series-on-covid-19-the-disconnect-between
    -financial-markets-and-the-real-economy.ashx> [perma.cc/29YD-U3MD].
85 "Despite Improvement in Q3, Major Risks Lie Ahead for Canadian
    Pension Plans" (1 October 2020), online: *Mercer* <https://www.mercer.ca
    /en/newsroom/defined-benefit-plans-improve-in-q3-with-major-risks
    -ahead.html [perma.cc/7Y4B-BTS2].

86 See, for example, *MacKinnon v Ontario (Municipal Employees Retirement Board)* (19 January 2011), Toronto, Ont SCJ 05-CL-06035 (motion). See also *MacKinnon v Ontario (Municipal Employees Retirement Board)*, 2007 ONCA 874. This case revolved around allegations that senior management of a pension fund were self-dealing with pension fund investment opportunities. The case settled.

3. Securities Regulators and Investor Education

1 Task Force on Financial Literacy, "Canadians and Their Money: Building a Brighter Financial Future" (2010) at 10, online (pdf): <http://www.edugains .ca/resourcesFL/Background/CanadiansAndTheirMoney-2011.pdf>.
2 Janet McFarland, Andrew Willis, Niall McGee, David Parkinson, Rita Trichur, Jacqueline Nelson, Christina Pellegrini, & James Bradshaw, "Mayday at Home Capital", *Globe and Mail* (13 May 2017); *Settlement Agreement in the Matter of Home Capital Group Inc, Gerald Soloway, Robert Morton and Martin Reid* (2017) at para 74, online (pdf): *OSC* <https://www .osc.gov.on.ca/documents/en/Proceedings-SET/set_20170614_home -capital.pdf> [Home Capital Settlement Agreement].
3 Jeffrey G MacIntosh, "Lessons of Bre-X (?) Some Comments" (1999) 32 Can Bus LJ 223 at 235.
4 Rob Carrick, "Home Capital Is a Reminder of the Risks of Reaching for Higher Interest Rates", *Globe and Mail* (27 April 2017).
5 See Home Capital Group Inc, "2018 Annual Report" (2019) at 9, online (pdf): *Home Capital Inc.* <https://s2.q4cdn.com/668293721/files/doc _financials/annual_meetings/2019/HomeCap_2018AR_posting.pdf>. ("In 2018 ... more Canadians turned to Home Capital when they no longer qualified for prime mortgages at the larger Canadian banks.").
6 See Lauren E Willis, "Against Financial-Literacy Education" (2008) 94 Iowa L Rev 197 at 282 (citing President George W. Bush).
7 See Carly Sawatzki, "Lessons in Financial Literacy Task Design: Authentic, Imaginable, Useful" (2017) 29 Mathematics Education Research J 25 at 25.
8 See Department of Finance Canada, News Release, 2009-067, "Minister of Finance Launches Task Force on Financial Literacy" (26 June 2009), online: *Department of Finance Canada* <https://www.canada.ca/en /news/archive/2009/06/minister-finance-launches-task-force-financial -literacy.html>. The National Strategy was launched in 2015. See generally Financial Consumer Agency of Canada, "National Strategy for Financial Literacy – Count Me In, Canada", (2015), online (pdf): *FCAC* https://www.canada.ca/en/financial-consumer-agency/programs /financial-literacy/financial-literacy-strategy.html [FCAC, "National Strategy"].

9   See Task Force on Financial Literacy, "Final Report of the Task Force on Financial Literacy, Canadians and Their Money: Building a Brighter Financial Future" (2010) at 21, online (pdf): *FCAC* <https://www.canada.ca/content/dam/fcac-acfc/documents/programs/financial-literacy/canadians-and-their-money.pdf>. [Task Force Report].

10 See *OSC Staff Notice 11-773 – The Investor Perspective* at 3 and 8–9, online (pdf): *OSC* <https://www.osc.gov.on.ca/documents/en/Securities-Category1/SecuritiesLaw_sn_20151030_11-773_investor-perspective.pdf> [OSC Staff Notice 11-773].

11 See generally Canadian Securities Administrators (CSA) Investor Education Committee (IEC), "Annual Activity Report 2018 (Apr 2017–Mar 2018)", online (pdf): *CSA* <https://www.securities-administrators.ca/uploadedFiles/General/pdfs/CSA_InvestorEd_AnnualReport_2018_EN_VF.pdf> [CSA IEC, "Annual Activity Report"].

12 See generally Toni Williams, "Empowerment of Whom and for What? Financial Literacy Education and the New Regulation of Consumer Financial Services" (2007) 29 Law & Pol'y 226; James A Fanto, "We're All Capitalists Now: The Importance, Nature, Provision and Regulation of Investor Education" (1998) 49 Case W Res L Rev 105.

13 Marie Drolet & René Morissette, "New Facts on Pension Coverage in Canada", Statistics Canada (18 December 2014), online: *Statistics Canada*, <https://www150.statcan.gc.ca/n1/en/pub/75-006-x/2014001/article/14120-eng.pdf?st=o9b88P6K>; Fanto, *supra* note 12 at 112 (rising cost of education) and 114–16 (on the shift from defined benefit to defined contribution workplace pensions); Gail E Henderson, "Group RESPs: The Intersection of Government Support for Education Savings and Securities Regulation" (2019) 69 UTLJ 44 at 50; International Organization of Securities Commissions (IOSCO), "Committee on Retail Investors (Committee 8)", online: *IOSCO* <https://www.iosco.org/about/?subsection=display_committee&cmtid=20> [IOSCO, "Committee 8"]; Williams, *supra* note 12 at 230.

14 See OSC, "2017–18 Annual Report" at 13, online (pdf): *OSC* <https://www.osc.gov.on.ca/documents/en/Publications/Publications_rpt_2018_osc-annual-rpt_en.pdf> [OSC, "Annual Report"].

15 Fanto, *supra* note 12 at 108, 156; Mark R Gillen, *Securities Regulation in Canada*, 3rd ed (Toronto: Thomson Canada Limited, 2007) at 94. The other is the registration of intermediaries.

16 See IOSCO, "Strategic Framework for Investor Education and Financial Literacy" (October 2014) at 6, online (pdf): *IOSCO* <https://www.iosco.org/library/pubdocs/pdf/IOSCOPD462.pdf> [IOSCO, "Strategic Framework"].

17 *Ibid* at 10.

18 Fanto, *supra* note 12 at 127–36.

19 I reviewed websites and reports for the British Columbia Securities Commission (BCSC), the Alberta Securities Commission (ASC), the Manitoba Securities Commission (MSC), the Ontario Securities Commission (OSC), Quebec's Autorité des marchés financiers (AMF) and the Nova Scotia Securities Commission (NSSC). I also reviewed the work and reporting of the Canadian Securities Administrators Investor Education Committee, which discusses the investor education work of all of the provincial and territorial securities commissions.

20 See Investment Industry Regulatory Organization of Canada (IIROC), "Investor Education", online: *IIROC* <https://www.iiroc.ca/investors/investoreducation/Pages/default.aspx>; Mutual Fund Dealers Association of Canada (MFDA), "Investor Education", online: *MFDA* <https://mfda.ca/investors/investor-education/> [MFDA].

21 See e.g. Fanto, *supra* note 12, who argues for a significant role for the private and non-profit sectors.

22 See generally BCSC, "InvestRight" (last visited 23 August 2019), online: *InvestRight* <https://www.investright.org/>; ASC, "CheckF1rst" (last visited 23 August 2019), online: *CheckF1rst* <http://www.checkfirst.ca/>; MSC, "Money Smart Manitoba" (last visited 23 August 2019), online: *Money Smart Manitoba* <https://www.moneysmartmanitoba.ca/>; OSC, "Get Smarter about Money" (last visited 23 August 2019), online: *Get Smarter about Money* <https://www.getsmarteraboutmoney.ca/>; AMF, "General Public" (last visited 23 August 2019), online: *AMF* <https://lautorite.qc.ca/en/general-public/>; NSSC, "For Investors" (last visited 23 August 2019), online: *NSSC* <https://nssc.novascotia.ca/for-investors>. The AMF and NSSC are web pages on the regulators' main website, rather than a separate website.

23 See e.g. BCSC, "Investing 101: Types of Investments" (last visited 23 August 2019), online: *InvestRight* <https://www.investright.org/investing-101/types-of-investments/>; MSC, "Mutual Funds, Fund Facts & Fees" (last visited 23 August 2019), online: *Money Smart Manitoba* <https://www.moneysmartmanitoba.ca/informed-investing/mutual-funds/>. See also IIROC, "Investment Basics" (last visited 23 August 2019), online: *IIROC* <https://www.iiroc.ca/investors/investoreducation/Pages/How-to-Invest.aspx>.

24 See generally BCSC, "Glossary" (last visited 23 August 2019), online: *InvestRight* <https://www.investright.org/resources/glossary/>; ASC, "Glossary" (last visited 23 August 2019), online: *CheckF1rst* <http://www.checkfirst.ca/financial-literacy/glossary/a/>; MSC, "Glossary" (last visited 23 August 2019), online: *MSC* <http://www.mbsecurities.ca/get-informed/learn_about/glossary.html>; AMF, "Financial Glossary" (last

visited 23 August 2019), online: *AMF* <https://lautorite.qc.ca/en
/general-public/financial-glossary/>.

25 See e.g. OSC, "Defining Your Financial Goals" (last visited 23 August 2019),
   online: *Get Smarter about Money* <https://www.getsmarteraboutmoney
   .ca/plan-manage/planning-basics/financial-planning/defining-your
   -financial-goals/>; AMF, "Reviewing Your Personal Finances?" (2019),
   online (pdf): *AMF* <https://lautorite.qc.ca/fileadmin/lautorite/grand
   _public/publications/consommateurs/finances-personnelles/comment
   -faire-point-finances-personnelles-an.pdf> [AMF, "Reviewing Your
   Personal Finances"].

26 See generally MSC, "Before You Invest" (last visited 23 August 2019),
   online: *MSC* <http://www.mbsecurities.ca/get-informed/learn_about
   /before-you-invest.html>; AMF, "Reviewing Your Personal Finances?",
   supra note 25 at 3; NSSC, "Working with an Adviser: Getting the Most Out
   of the Client–Adviser Relationship" (2019) online (pdf): *NSSC* <https://
   nssc.novascotia.ca/sites/default/files/Adviser%20booklet%20final.pdf>.

27 See *OSC Staff Notice 11-776 – Investor Office Activity Report 2015–16* at 45,
   online (pdf): *OSC* <https://www.osc.gov.on.ca/documents/en/Securities
   -Category1/SecuritiesLaw_sn_20161117_11-776_investor-office-activity
   -report.pdf> [OSC Staff Notice 11-776].

28 BCSC, "2018/19–2020/21 Service Plan" (February 2018) at 15, online
   (pdf): *BCSC* <https://www.bcsc.bc.ca/-/media/PWS/Resources/About
   _Us/Publications/BCSC_Service_Plan_20182021.pdf> [BCSC, "2018
   /19 Service Plan"]; BCSC, "2017/18 Annual Service Plan Report" (2018)
   at 15, online (pdf): *BCSC* <https://www.bcsc.bc.ca/-/media/PWS
   /Resources/About_Us/Publications/Annual-Report-201718.pdf> [BCSC,
   "Annual Service Plan Report"] at 15.

29 *OSC Staff Notice 11-773*, *supra* note 10 at 38.

30 *OSC Staff Notice 11-776*, *supra* note 27 at 50, 57.

31 *Ibid* at 50.

32 See BCSC, "2017/18 Annual Service Plan Report", *supra* note 28.

33 See NSSC, "Annual Accountability Report for the Fiscal Year 2018–2019"
   (2019) at 14, online (pdf): *NSSC* <https://nssc.novascotia.ca/sites/default
   /files/NSSC%20Accountability%20Report%202018-2019%20%28Final
   %29.pdf> [NSSC, "Annual Accountability Report"].

34 See ASC, "Classes" (last visited 23 August 2019), online: *CheckF1rst*
   <http://www.checkfirst.ca/go-beyond/classes/>.

35 See CSA, "Business Plan 2016–2019: Achievement Highlights" (2019) at
   6, online (pdf): *CSA* <https://www.securities-administrators.ca
   /uploadedFiles/General/pdfs/Achievements_CSA_Business_Plan_2016
   -2019.pdf>.

36 IOSCO, "Committee 8", *supra* note 13.

37 BCSC, "Annual Service Plan Report", *supra* note 28 at 13–15; ASC CheckF1rst, "Frequently Asked Questions – How Is Checkfirst Related to the ASC?" (last visited 23 August 2019), online: *CheckF1rst* <http://www .checkfirst.ca/financial-literacy/faqs/>; OSC Staff Notice 11-776, *supra* note 27 at 49; AMF, "Fraud Prevention" (last visited 23 August 2019), online: *AMF* <https://lautorite.qc.ca/en/general-public/fraud-prevention/>; NSSC, "Annual Accountability Report", *supra* note 33 at 14; FCAC, "National Strategy", *supra* note 8 at 8; Task Force Report, *supra* note 9 at 65.

38 See Innovative Research Group Inc, "2020 CSA Investor Index" (2020) at 10, 75, online (pdf): *CSA* <https://www.securities-administrators.ca /uploadedFiles/General/pdfs/CSA2020InvestorIndexSurveyReport.pdf> ["CSA Investor Index"].

39 See generally CSA IEC, "2017 Annual Activity Report: Apr. 2016–Mar. 2017" (2017) online (pdf): *CSA* <https://www.securities-administrators .ca/uploadedFiles/General/pdfs/CSA_InvestorEd_AnnualReport_2017 _FINAL_EN_96ppi_.pdf>. See also Manitoba Financial Services Agency, "2018 Annual Report" (2019) at 21, online (pdf): *MSC* <http://mbsecurities .ca/about-msc/pubs/2018_ar.pdf> [MSC, "Annual Report"].

40 See e.g. OSC, "4 Signs of Investment Fraud" (last visited 23 August 2019), online: *Get Smarter about Money* <https://www.getsmarteraboutmoney.ca /protect-your-money/fraud/protecting-against-fraud/4-signs-of -investment-fraud/>; AMF, "Red-Flagging Financial Fraud" (last visited 23 August 2019), online: <https://lautorite.qc.ca/fileadmin/lautorite /grand_public/publications/consommateurs/prevention-fraude/soyez -a-votre-affaire_an.pdf> [AMF, "Red-flagging"]; NSSC, "Safe Investing for Seniors" at 8, online (pdf): *NSSC* <https://nssc.novascotia.ca/sites /default/files/Seniors%20Guide.pdf>.

41 CSA IEC, "Annual Activity Report", *supra* note 11 at 15, 32, 34 (British Columbia, Nova Scotia, Northwest Territories); BCSC, "2018/19 Annual Service Plan Report", *supra* note 28 at 14; MSC, "Annual Report", *supra* note 39 at 21. See also *MFDA*, *supra* note 20.

42 See e.g. BCSC, "COVID-19 Information for BC Investors" (2021), online: *InvestRight* <https://www.investright.org/covid-19/>; New Brunswick Financial and Consumer Services Commission, "COVID-19 Fraud" (n.d.), online: *Financial and Consumer Services Commission* <https://fcnb .ca/en/frauds-and-scams/covid-19-fraud>; OSC, "Protecting Yourself from Scams during the COVID-19 Pandemic" (2020), online: GetSmart AboutMoney <https://www.getsmarteraboutmoney.ca/resources /covid-19-and-your-money/protecting-yourself-from-scams-during-the -covid-19-pandemic/>.

43 OSC, "Canadian Securities Regulators Warn Public of Coronavirus-Related Investment Scams" (19 March 2020), online: *OSC* <https://www

.osc.gov.on.ca/en/NewsEvents_nr_20200319_csa-warn-public
-coronavirus-related-investment-scams.htm>.

44 CSA, "COVID-19 & Investment Fraud" (n.d.), online: *CSA* <https://www
.securities-administrators.ca/investortools.aspx?id=1902>.

45 See e.g. ASC, "2019 Annual Report" (2019) at 17, online (pdf): *ASC*
<https://www.albertasecurities.com/-/media/ASC-Documents-part-1
/Publications/ASC_Annual_Report_2019_Digital.ashx> [ASC, "Annual
Report"]; OSC Staff Notice 11-779, *Seniors Strategy* [OSC, "Seniors
Strategy"]; AMF, "2017–2020 Strategic Plan" (2017) at 17, online (pdf): *AMF*
<https://lautorite.qc.ca/fileadmin/lautorite/grand_public/publications
/organisation/codes-politiques-plans-action/plan-strategique-AMF-2017
-2020_an.pdf> [AMF, "Strategic Plan"]. See also Jayne W Barnard,
"Deception, Decisions, and Investor Education" (2009) 17:2 Elder LJ 201 at
203 (discussing the U.S. Securities and Exchange Commission).

46 See e.g. CSA, "Financial Concerns Checklist" (n.d.), online (pdf): *CSA*
<https://www.securities-administrators.ca/uploadedFiles/General
/pdfs/FinancialConcernsChecklist_EN.pdf>.

47 OSC, "Seniors Strategy", *supra* note 45 at 48; AMF, "How to Plan for
Retirement" (last visited 23 August 2019), online: *AMF* <https://lautorite
.qc.ca/en/general-public/personal-finances/how-to-plan-for
-retirement/>.

48 Financial Consumer Agency of Canada, "Implementing the National
Strategy for Financial Literacy – Count Me In, Canada: Progress Report
2015–2019" (19 August 2019), online (pdf): FCAC, <https://www.canada
.ca/content/dam/fcac-acfc/documents/programs/financial-literacy
/progress-report-financial-literacy.pdf>.

49 McFarland, et al, *supra* note 2.

50 Jerry Buckland, Gail E Henderson, Kevin Schachter & Gaylen Eaton, with
Simon Chung, *The Regulation of Group Plan RESPs and the Experiences of Low
-Income Subscribers* (June 2018), online (pdf): *SEED* <http://seedwinnipeg
.ca/files/The_Regulation_of_Group_Plan_RESPs_and_the_Experiences_of
_Low-income_Subscribers.pdf>.

51 *OSC Staff Notice 11-776, supra* note 27 at 55; OSC, "Introduction to Investing:
A Primer for New Investors" (last visited 23 August 2019), online: *Investing
Introduction* <https://investingintroduction.ca/en/>.

52 *Supra* note 22.

53 See BCSC, News Release, "BC Securities Commission Releases Its
National Report Card on Youth Financial Literacy" (31 October 2011),
online: *BCSC* <https://www.bcsc.bc.ca/News/News_Releases/2011/82
_BC_Securities_Commission_releases_its_National_Report_Card_on
_Youth_Financial_Literacy_(ENG__and_FR_)/>. Although the program
has since ceased, the materials are still available at FCAC, "The City"

(last visited 23 August 2019), online: *Government of Canada* <https://www
.canada.ca/en/financial-consumer-agency/services/the-city.html>.

54 See MSC, "Make It Count: An Instructor's Resource for Youth Money
    Management" (last visited 23 August 2019), online: *Make It Count*
    <http://www.makeitcountonline.ca/msc/instructors/index_en.html>.

55 See ASC CheckF1rst, "Frequently Asked Questions: What's a Good Way
    to Teach Children About Money…?" (last visited 23 August 2019), online:
    CheckF1rst <http://www.checkfirst.ca/financial-literacy/faqs/>.

56 See AMF, "Teacher Zone" (last visited 23 August 2019), online: *AMF*
    <https://lautorite.qc.ca/en/general-public/tes-affaires/teacher-zone/>.

57 See Ontario, Department of Finance, *2019 Ontario Budget: Protecting What
    Matters Most* (Toronto: Department of Finance, 2019) at 229, online (pdf):
    Budget.Ontario.ca <http://budget.ontario.ca/pdf/2019/2019-ontario
    -budget-en.pdf> [Ontario Budget]; *OSC Notice 11-786, Notice of Statement
    of Priorities for Financial Year to End March 31, 2020,* (2019), 42 OSCB 5551
    (27 June 2019) at 9 [OSC, "Statement of Priorities"].

58 BCSC, "Annual Service Plan Report", *supra* note 28 at 22; ASC CheckF1rst,
    "Frequently Asked Questions: How Is the ASC Funded?" (2020), online:
    CheckF1rst <http://www.checkfirst.ca/financial-literacy/faqs/>; OSC,
    "Annual Report", *supra* note 14 at 50; AMF, "About the AMF" (2021),
    online: https://lautorite.qc.ca/en/general-public/about-the-amf/.

59 See *Securities Act*, RSBC 1996, c 418, s 15(3); BCSC, "Annual Service
    Plan Report", *supra* note 28 at 44; *Securities Act*, RSA 2000, c S-4, s 19(5);
    and *Securities Act*, RSO 1990, c S.5, s 3.4(2)(b)(ii) [Ontario *Securities Act*].
    This was previously the case for the AMF. See AMF, "Strategic Financial
    Education, Outreach and Research Partnerships Program" (last visited
    23 August 2019), note 1 (2021), online: *AMF* <https://lautorite.qc.ca/en
    /general-public/about-the-amf/amf-strategic-financial-education
    -outreach-and-research-partnerships-program/>.

60 See *Strong Action for Ontario Act (Budget Measures)*, SO 2012, c 8, Sched 55, s 2.

61 See Home Capital Settlement Agreement, *supra* note 2 at para 74. The
    other $1 million was allocated to HCG's investors.

62 OSC, "Annual Report", *supra* note 14 at 96.

63 BCSC, "Annual Service Plan Report", *supra* note 28 at 24–25.

64 ASC, "Annual Report", *supra* note 45 at 31.

65 *Ibid* at 33.

66 See Part IV, below, regarding the possible effect of the transition to the
    proposed Cooperative Capital Markets Regulatory System.

67 Ontario Budget, *supra* note 57 at 229; OSC, "Seniors Strategy", *supra* note
    45 at 48.

68 See ASC, "Three-Year Strategic Plan F2018–2020" (2018) at 1, online (pdf):
    ASC <https://www.albertasecurities.com/-/media/ASC-Documents

-part-2/About-the-ASC/ASC-3yr-strat-plan-summary.ashx?la=en&hash
=C8ABB687AF1C021BDA0EA5C7808C84B2> [ASC, "Strategic Plan"].

69 See NSSC, "Business Plan 2019–2020" (2018) at Appendix A (n.d.), online
(pdf): *NSSC* <https://nssc.novascotia.ca/sites/default/files/Final%20
NSSC%202019-20%20Business%20Plan%20%28Edit%202019-03-06%29
.pdf> [NSSC, "Business Plan"].

70 AMF, "Strategic Plan", *supra* note 45 at 10.

71 See MSC, "Strategic Plan 2015–2018" (2015) at 5, online (pdf): *MSC*
<http://www.mbsecurities.ca/about-msc/pubs/strategic_plan_2015.
pdf> [MSC, "Strategic Plan"]; CSA, "Business Plan 2019–2022" (2019) at
5 (n.d.), online (pdf): *CSA* <https://www.securities-administrators.ca
/uploadedFiles/General/pdfs/CSA_Business_Plan_2019-2022.pdf>;
OSC Staff Notice 11-776, *supra* note 27 at 3.

72 Ontario *Securities Act*, *supra* note 59, s 1.1. See also MSC, "About Us: Our
Mission and Mandate" (last visited 23 August 2019), online: *MSC* <http://
www.mbsecurities.ca/about-msc/our-mission-mandate.html> [MSC,
"About Us"]; AMF, "Mission" (last visited 23 August 2019), online: *AMF*
<https://lautorite.qc.ca/en/general-public/about-the-amf/mission/>.
See also *Securities Act*, RSNS 1989, c 418, s 1A; *Pezim v British Columbia
(Superintendent of Brokers)*, [1994] 2 SCR 557, 114 DLR (4th) 385; "Capital
Markets Act: A Revised Consultation Draft" (2015) s 1 (August 2015),
online (pdf): *CCMR* <http://ccmr-ocrmc.ca/wp-content/uploads/CMA
-Consultation-Draft-English-August-2015.pdf> [*Capital Markets Act*].

73 Ontario *Securities Act*, *supra* note 59, s 1.1; *Stronger, Fairer Ontario Act
(Budget Measures)*, 2017, SO 2017, c 34, Sched 37, s 2. See also "*Capital
Markets Stability Act (Canada)* – Draft for Consultation" (2016) s 4(b),
online (pdf): *CCMR* <http://ccmr-ocrmc.ca/wp-content/uploads/cmsa
-consultation-draft-revised-en.pdf>; *Capital Markets Act*, *supra* note 72.

74 CQLR c E-6.1, s 4(1) [emphasis added].

75 Task Force Report, *supra* note 9 at 10 (quoting then federal Minister of
Finance Jim Flaherty); Executive Order 13530: President's Advisory Council
on Financial Capability (29 January 2010); Williams, *supra* note 12 at 229.

76 See generally BCSC, "Mandate Letter from the Honourable Carole James
to Brenda Leong" (last visited 2019), online (pdf): *BCSC* <https://www
.bcsc.bc.ca/-/media/PWS/Resources/About_Us/Who_We_Are/Funding
/Mandate-Letter-of-Expectations-20192020.pdf>; MSC, "Strategic Plan",
supra note 71 at 2; OSC, "Statement of Priorities", *supra* note 57 at 5, 9;
NSSC, "Annual Accountability Report", *supra* note 33 at 14; IOSCO,
"Strategic Framework", *supra* note 16 at 4–5.

77 OSC, "Annual Report", *supra* note 14 at 29–31.

78 Fanto, *supra* note 12 at 156.

79 Williams, *supra* note 12 at 229.

80 See sources referenced at *supra* note 25.

81 See OSC Investor Office, "Summertime Savings" (26 June 2019), online: *OSC* <https://us11.campaign-archive.com/?u=b5a340c3888e873ca24e58c3b &id=e2a49ab8a0>.

82 ASC, "Calculators" (last visited 23 August 2019), online: *CheckF1rst* <http:// www.checkfirst.ca/tools-calculators/calculators/>.

83 AMF, "COVID-19 – Managing Your Personal Finances in Times of Crisis" (2021) online: *AMF* <https://lautorite.qc.ca/en/general-public/personal -finances/covid-19-managing-your-personal-finances-in-times-of-crisis>; OSC, "COVID-19 and Job Loss" (2021), online: *Get Smarter about Money*, <https://www.getsmarteraboutmoney.ca/resources/covid-19-and-your -money/covid-19-and-unemployment/>.

84 FCAC, "National Strategy", *supra* note 8.

85 Fanto, *supra* note 12 at 152.

86 *Registration Requirements, Exemptions and Ongoing Registrant Obligations*, OSC NI 31-103, (2019) s 13.2–13.3.

87 Gillen, *supra* note 15 at 92; Williams, *supra* note 12 at 232.

88 See e.g. MSC, "About Us," *supra* note 72.

89 See sources referenced at *supra* note 23.

90 Williams, *supra* note 12 at 232.

91 BCSC, "Guide to Investing: How to Be an Empowered Investor" (last visited 23 August 2019), online (pdf): *InvestRight* <https://www.investright. org/wp-content/uploads/2019/01/2019-Re-design_G2I_Empowered -Investor-IR.pdf> [BCSC, "Empowered Investor"].

92 Williams, *supra* note 12 at 233.

93 See, e.g., *supra* note 82.

94 ASC, "Welcome to Checkfirst" (last visited 23 August 2019), online: *Check-F1rst* <http://www.checkfirst.ca/> ("our goal is to…" [emphasis added].

95 See AMF, "Choosing an Investment Dealer or Representative" (2016) at 13, online (pdf): *AMF* <https://lautorite.qc.ca/fileadmin/lautorite /grand_public/publications/consommateurs/investissement/comment -choisir-avec-qui-investir-an.pdf> [AMF, "Choosing an Investment Dealer or Representative".

96 NSSC, "Annual Accountability Report", *supra* note 33 at 12.

97 Williams, *supra* note 12 at 233.

98 *Ibid.*

99 *Ibid* at 248.

100 See generally OSC, "Transcript, Roundtable on Reducing Regulatory Burden Related to Registration, Compliance and Investment Funds" (2019), online (pdf): *OSC* <https://www.osc.gov.on.ca/documents/en /Securities-Category1/sn_20190506_11-784_transcript-roundtable -burden-reduction.pdf>.

101   BCSC, "Empowered Investor", *supra* note 91 at 3. See also AMF, "Choosing an Investment Dealer or Representative", *supra* note 95 at 4.

102   OSC, "Seniors Strategy", *supra* note 45 at 14; *CSA Staff Notice 31-354 – Suggested Practices for Engaging with Older or Vulnerable Clients* (2019) [CSA Staff Notice 31-354]. See also *Guidance on Compliance and Supervisory Issues When Dealing with Senior Clients*, IIROC Notice 16-0114 (31 May 2016).

103   OSC, "Seniors Strategy", *supra* note 45 at 49.

104   *Ibid* at 8; CSA Staff Notice 31-354, *supra* note 102 at 1.

105   Williams, *supra* note 12 at 228.

106   OSC Staff Notice 11-776, *supra* note 27 at 45.

107   ASC, "Annual Report", *supra* note 45 at 7.

108   OSC Staff Notice 11-776, *supra* note 27 at 5, 50.

109   CSA Investor Index, *supra* note 38 at 119.

110   BCSC, "Annual Service Plan Report", *supra* note 32 at 14–15.

111   Innovative Research Group Inc., "2017 CSA Investor Index" (2017) at 89, online (pdf): *CSA*, <https://www.securities-administrators.ca/uploadedFiles/Investor_Tools/CSA07%20Investor%20Index%20Deck%20-%20Full%20Report%20-%2020171128.pdf>.

112   *Ibid* at 47 and 49.

113   *Ibid* at 65.

114   BCSC "Annual Service Plan Report", *supra* note 28 at 15.

115   BCSC, "2018/19–Service Plan", *supra* note 28; BCSC, "Annual Service Plan Report", *supra* note 28 at 15.

116   BCSC Invest Right, "Investment Fraud Explained: Recognize, Reject, and Report Investment Fraud" (24 March 2015), online: *YouTube* <https://www.youtube.com/watch?v=RIRARnWoEv4>.

117   BCSC, "2018/19 Service Plan", *supra* note 28 at 15.

118   BCSC, "2019/20–2021/22 Service Plan" (2019) at 14, online (pdf): *BCSC* <https://www.bcsc.bc.ca/-/media/PWS/Resources/About_Us/Publications/BCSC-Service-Plan-2019-2022.pdf>; BCSC, "2020/21–2022/23 Service Plan" (February 2020) at 12, online (pdf): *BCSC* <https://www.bcsc.bc.ca/-/media/PWS/Resources/About_Us/Publications/BCSC-Service-Plan-2020-2023.pdf>.

119   Andrew Parkin, "Family Savings for Post-Secondary Education: A Summary of Research on the Importance and Impact of Post-Secondary Education Savings Incentive Programs" (Toronto: Omega Foundation, November 2016) at 42–43 (discussing financial literacy education and low-income families).

120   BCSC, "2018/19 Service Plan", *supra* note 115 at 15.

121   See Jacob Ziegel, "Financial Literacy and Insolvent Consumers: It Takes Two to Tango" (2011) 51 Can Bus LJ 380 at 389; Willis, *supra* note 6 at 257.

122 See Ontario Lottery and Gaming Corporation, "2017–2018 Annual
     Report" (2018) at 43, online (pdf): *OLG* <https://about.olg.ca/wp-content
     /uploads/2018/11/OLGAnnualReport-2017-18-en.pdf>.
123 ASC, "Strategic Plan", *supra* note 68 at 6.
124 SEC, "Binary Options Fraud" (n.d.), online: *Investor.gov*, <https://www
     .investor.gov/protect-your-investments/fraud/types-fraud/binary
     -options-fraud> [SEC, "Binary Options Fraud"].
125 OSC, "Binary Options: Spot the Red Flags" (2021), online: *Get Smarter
     about Money* <https://www.getsmarteraboutmoney.ca/protect-your
     -money/fraud/protecting-against-fraud/binary-options-spot-red-flags/>.
     See also *Multilateral Instrument 91-102 Prohibition of Binary Options*, (2017),
     40 OSCB 7957, s 1 [MI 91-102].
126 CSA, "Binary Options Are NOT an Option for Canadians" (n.d.), online:
     CSA <http://www.binaryoptionsfraud.ca/>.
127 *Companion Policy 91-102 Prohibition of Binary Options*, (2017), 40 OSCB 7959
     [Companion Policy 91-102].
128 SEC, "Binary Options Fraud", *supra* note 124.
129 CSA, "Canadian Securities Regulators Announce Ban on Binary Options",
     News Release (28 September 2017), online: *OSC* <https://www.osc.gov
     .on.ca/en/NewsEvents_nr_20170928_canadian-regulators-announce-ban
     -on-binary-options.htm>.
130 *Companion Policy 91-102, supra* note 127.
131 CSA IEC, "Annual Activity Report", *supra* note 11 at 7; CSA IEC, "2017
     Annual Activity Report", online (pdf): *CSA* <https://www.securities
     -administrators.ca/uploadedFiles/General/pdfs/CSA_InvestorEd
     _AnnualReport_2017_FINAL_EN_96ppi_.pdf>.
132 MI 91-102, *supra* note 125.
133 CSA IEC, "Annual Activity Report", *supra* note 11 at 7. See also NSSC,
     "Annual Activity Report", *supra* note 33 at Supplemental Information
     and Appendices.
134 CSA Investor Index, *supra* note 38 at 75.
135 OSC, "Cryptoassets" (last visited 23 August 2019), online: *Get Smarter
     about Money* <https://www.getsmarteraboutmoney.ca/invest
     /investment-products/cryptoassets/>.
136 CSA, Multilateral Notice of Multilateral Instrument 91-102 Prohibition of
     Binary Options and Related Companion Policy (28 September 2017),
     online: *OSC* <https://www.osc.gov.on.ca/en/SecuritiesLaw_csa_20170927
     _91-102_binary-options.htm>.
137 *Supra* note 126.
138 Fanto, *supra* note 12 at 117–18.
139 BCSC, "Empowered Investor", *supra* note 91 at 3.

140 *Ibid.*
141 OSC, "Statement of Priorities", *supra* note 57 at 5551.
142 AMF, "Red-flagging", *supra* note 40 at 6.
143 OSC, "Statement of Priorities", *supra* note 57 at 9.
144 *Ibid* at 10; NSSC, "Business Plan", *supra* note 69 at 2.
145 MI 91-102, *supra* note 125.
146 Willis, *supra* note 6 at 267.
147 Elizabeth Warren, "Unsafe at Any Rate" (2007), online: *Democracy Journal* <https://democracyjournal.org/magazine/5/unsafe-at-any-rate/>.
148 *Supra* notes 66–71 and accompanying text.
149 See generally CCMR, "Memorandum of Agreement Regarding the Cooperative Capital Markets Regulatory System" (2016) online (pdf): *CCMR* <http://ccmr-ocrmc.ca/wp-content/uploads/moa-23092016-en .pdf> [Memorandum of Agreement]. In 2018, the Supreme Court of Canada held that the cooperative scheme as set out in the memorandum and draft legislation was constitutional. See *Reference re Pan-Canadian Securities Regulation*, 2018 SCC 48.
150 OSC, "Notice 11-789 Statement of Priorities for Financial Year to End March 31, 2021", online (pdf): *OSC* <https://www.osc.gov.on.ca/documents/en /Securities-Category1/sn_20200625_11-789_sop-end-2021.pdf>.
151 Memorandum of Agreement, *supra* note 149; Anita Anand, "What about the Investors? White Paper on the Proposed Cooperative Capital Markets Regulator" (1 July 2017) at 7, online (pdf): *FAIR Canada* <http://faircanada.ca /wp-content/uploads/2017/09/White-Paper-REVISED-Final-170811.pdf>.
152 Staff from the MSC Education & Communications division have attended the FCAC's annual conference, indicating some overlap and coordination. MSC, "Annual Report", *supra* note 39 at 21.
153 OSC, Staff Notice 11-773, *supra* note 10 at 32. See also IOSCO, "Strategic Framework", *supra* note 16 at 9.
154 OSC, *Staff Notice 11-778: Behavioural Insights: Key Concepts, Applications and Regulatory Considerations* (29 March 2017), online (pdf): *OSC* <https:// www.osc.gov.on.ca/documents/en/Securities-Category1/sn_20170329 _11-778_behavioural-insights.pdf> [OSC Staff Notice 11-778].
155 See Chris C Nicholls, *Securities Law*, 2nd ed (Toronto: Irwin Law, 2018) at 481; IOSCO, "Strategic Framework" *supra* note 16 at 22.
156 OSC Staff Notice 11-778, *supra* note 154; "OSC Staff Notice 11-783: Encouraging Retirement Planning through Behavioural Insights" (27 July 2018), online (pdf): *OSC* <https://www.osc.gov.on.ca/documents/en /Securities-Category1/sn_20180727_11-783_encouraging-retirement-plan .pdf>; OSC Staff Notice 11-782: Getting Started: Human-Centred Solutions to Engage Ontario Millennials in Investing" (12 July 2018), online (pdf): *Ontario Securities Commission* https://www.osc.gov.on.ca

/documents/en/Securities-Category1/sn_20180712_11-782_getting
-started.pdf>; OSC Staff Notice 11-787: Improving Fee Disclosure through
Behavioural Insights" (19 August 2019), online (pdf): *Ontario Securities
Commission* <https://www.osc.gov.on.ca/documents/en/Securities
-Category1/sn_20190819_11-787_improving-fee-disclosure-through
-behavioural-insights.pdf>.

4. Home Capital and Cross-Border Lessons in Mortgage Regulation

1 See Abacus Data, "Housing Affordability Is the Top Issue for Millennials
   Who Are Looking to Achieve the Dream of Homeownership" (1 October
   2018), online: *Abacus Data* <https://abacusdata.ca/housing-affordability
   -is-the-top-issue-for-millennials-who-are-looking-to-achieve-the-dream
   -of-homeownership/>.
2 See Canada Mortgage and Housing Corporation, "Household Debt-to
   -Income Ratio Near Record High" (13 December 2018), online: <https://
   www.cmhc-schl.gc.ca/en/housing-observer-online/2018-housing
   -observer/household-debt-income-ratio-near-record-high>
3 *Ibid*.
4 See Matt Schuffham, "Canada Watchdog Sets New Mortgage Rules,
   Acknowledges Risks" (17 October 2017), online: *Reuters* <https://www
   .reuters.com/article/canada-mortgages/update-3-canada-watchdog-sets
   -new-mortgage-rules-acknowledges-risks-idUSL2N1MS0HE>.
5 Armina Ligaya, "What Exactly Is Home Capital and Why Is It so
   Important to the Mortgage Industry?" (27 April 2017), online: *Financial
   Post* <https://business.financialpost.com/news/fp-street/what-exactly
   -is-home-capital-and-why-is-it-so-important-to-the-mortgage-industry>.
6 *Ibid*.
7 Homebuyers generally turn to alternative lenders when they are unable to
   obtain a mortgage from a traditional bank, often for lack of even income
   in the case of self-employment or their status as newcomers to Canada.
8 See Kareen Brown & Kevin Veenstra, "Home Capital Group – The High
   Cost of Dishonesty" (2018) 17:2 Accounting Perspectives 307 at 315.
9 See generally Office for the Superintendent of Financial Institutions
   Canada, "Guide to Intervention for Federally Regulated Deposit-Taking
   Institutions", online (pdf): *Office for the Superintendent of Financial Institutions Canada* <http://www.osfi-bsif.gc.ca/eng/docs/guide_int.pdf>.
10 See *Office of the Superintendent of Financial Institutions Act*, RSC 1985, c 18
   (3rd Supp) Part I, s 4(2).
11 Office of the Superintendent of Financial Institutions, "Residential Mortgage Underwriting Practices and Procedures – Effective January 1, 2018"
   (October 2017), online: *Government of Canada Office of the Superintendent of*

Financial Institutions <https://www.osfi-bsif.gc.ca/Eng/fi-if/rg-ro/gdn -ort/gl-ld/Pages/b20_dft.aspx#fnb1>.

12 See Office of the Superintendent of Financial Institutions, "Who We Regulate" (23 October 2014), online: <http://www.osfi-bsif.gc.ca/Eng /wt-ow/Pages/wwr-er.aspx>.

13 Office of the Superintendent of Financial Institutions, "Residential Mortgage Underwriting Practices and Procedures Guideline (B-20)" (28 January 2020), online: *Government of Canada Office of the Superintendent of Financial Institutions* <https://www.osfi-bsif.gc.ca/Eng/fi-if/rg-ro/gdn -ort/gl-ld/Pages/b20-nfo.aspx> [Guideline B-20].

14 *Office of the Superintendent of Financial Institutions Act, supra* note 11.

15 See Office of the Superintendent of Financial Institutions, "About Us" (4 February 2019), online: <http://www.osfi-bsif.gc.ca/Eng/osfi-bsif /Pages/default.aspx>.

16 See "Deposit Insurance" (last visited 20 November 2020), online: *Cambridge Dictionary* <https://dictionary.cambridge.org/dictionary/english /deposit-insurance>.

17 See *Canada Deposit Insurance Corporation*, RSC 1985, c C-3, s 7–9.

18 See Blair W Keefe & Wesley Isaacs, "CDIC Granted Extraordinary Powers over Troubled Institutions" (2009) 24:3 BFLR 539 at 540.

19 See Canada Deposit Insurance Corporation, "How Deposit Insurance Works" (last visited 11 September 2019), online: <http://www.cdic.ca/en /about-di/how-it-works/Pages/default.aspx>.

20 See Financial Services Regulatory Authority of Ontario, "Transition Updates" (1 April 2019), online: <https://www.fsrao.ca/en/transition-updates>.

21 See *Financial Consumer Agency of Canada Act*, SC 2001, c 9, s 3(2).

22 *Ibid.*

23 *Ibid.*

24 See Jacqueline J Williams, "Canadian Financial Services Ombudsmen: The Role of Reputational Persuasion" (2004) 20:1 BFLR 41 at 49.

25 See *National Housing Act*, RSC 1985, c N-11, ss 3, 75(j) (policy objectives and powers granted to the CMHC); *Canada Mortgage and Housing Corporation Act*, RSC 1985, s C-7 (statute incorporating the CMHC).

26 See Canada Mortgage and Housing Corporation, "What Are the General Requirements to Qualify for Homeowner Mortgage Loan Insurance?" (31 March 2018) online: <https://www.cmhc-schl.gc.ca/en/buying /mortgage-loan-insurance-for-consumers/what-are-the-general -requirements-to-qualify-for-homeowner-mortgage-loan-insurance>.

27 *National Housing Act, supra* note 25, Part I.

28 *Ibid*, Part X.

29 See Sierra Black, "Pros and Cons of Credit Unions – And There Aren't Many Cons" (1 June 2011), online: *Forbes* <https://www.forbes.com/sites

/moneybuilder/2011/06/01/pros-and-cons-of-credit-unions-and-there
-arent-many-cons/#41b8682a4bba>.

30 See Richard Woodbury, "Credit Unions Get OK from Feds to Offer
    'Banking' Services" (28 February 2018), online: *CBC News* <https://www
    .cbc.ca/news/canada/nova-scotia/credit-unions-canada-banking-terms
    -federal-budget-1.4555579>.

31 *Ibid*.

32 *Ibid*.

33 SC 1991, c 46.

34 SC 1991, c 48.

35 See e.g. *Credit Unions and Caisses Populaires Act*, SO 1994, c 11.

36 See Canadian Credit Union Association, "National System Results 2018
    4Q" online: <https://ccua.com/about-credit-unions/facts-and-figures
    /national-system-results/>.

37 See Canada Mortgage and Housing Corporation & Deloitte, "Impact
    of Credit Unions and Mortgage Finance Companies on the Canadian
    Mortgage Market" (June 2018) at 10, online (pdf): <https://eppdscrmssa01
    .blob.core.windows.net/cmhcprodcontainer/sf/project/archive/research
    _2/impact_of_credit_unions_w.pdf>.

38 See Nicholas Le Pan, "Opportunities for Better Systemic Risk Manage-
    ment in Canada" (2017) at 10, online (pdf): *C.D. Howe Institute* <https://
    www.cdhowe.org/sites/default/files/attachments/research_papers
    /mixed/Commentary_490%20%282%29%20revised.pdf>.

39 *Ibid* at 3.

40 See Koker Christensen, Craig Bellefontaine, & Tom Peters, "Current
    Trends in the Canadian Credit Union Sector" (4 September 2017), online:
    <https://www.mondaq.com/canada/financial-services/625964/current
    -trends-in-the-credit-union-sector>.

41 Le Pan, *supra* note 38 at 11.

42 *Ibid*.

43 See Federal Housing Finance Agency, "Fannie Mae and Freddie Mac"
    (last visited 11 September 2019), online: *Federal Housing Finance Authority*
    <https://www.fhfa.gov/SupervisionRegulation/FannieMaeandFreddie
    Mac/Pages/About-Fannie-Mae---Freddie-Mac.aspx>.

44 *Ibid*.

45 Congressional Budget Office, "Fannie Mae, Freddie Mac, and the Federal
    Role in the Secondary Mortgage Market" (last visited 13 October 2020), on-
    line: <https://www.cbo.gov/sites/default/files/111th-congress-2009-2010
    /reports/12-23-fanniefreddie.pdf>.

46 See GinnieMae, "Funding Government Lending" (14 November 2016),
    online: <https://www.ginniemae.gov/about_us/who_we_are/Pages
    /funding_government_lending.aspx>.

47 See U.S. Department of Housing and Urban Development, "The Federal Housing Administration (FHA)," online: <https://www.hud.gov /program_offices/housing/fhahistory>.

48 See Pete Evans, "Toronto, Vancouver among Biggest Property Bubbles in the World, UBS Says" (28 September 2018), online: *CBC News* <https://www .cbc.ca/news/business/toronto-vancouver-housing-bubble-1.4842272>.

49 See Canadian Bankers Association, "Focus: Changes to Canada's Mortgage Market" (3 October 2016), online: <https://cba.ca/Assets/CBA /Documents/Files/Article%20Category/PDF/bkg_canadamortgagemarket _en.pdf>.

50 *Ibid.*

51 See Canadian Real Estate Association, "Canadian Home Sales Improve in January 2019" (15 February 2019), online: <https://www.crea.ca/news /22182/>.

52 Canadian Bankers Association, *supra* note 49 (down-payment for non-owner occupied properties); *Vancouver Charter*, SBC 1953, c 55, Part XXX (restrictions on vacant homes in Vancouver); *Property Transfer Tax Act*, SBC 1996, c 378, s 2.02 (BC foreign buyer's tax); Ontario Ministry of Finance, News Release, "Ontario's Fair Housing Plan" (20 April 2017), online: <https://news.ontario.ca/mof/en/2017/04/ontarios-fair-housing-plan .html> (Ontario's foreign buyer's tax).

53 Canadian Bankers Association, *supra* note 49.

54 See Lawrence L Schembri, "Housing Finance in Canada: Looking Back to Move Forward" (2014) 230 National Institute Economic Rev R 45 at 52.

55 See Department of Finance Canada, News Release, "Technical Backgrounder: Mortgage Insurance Rules and Income Tax Proposals" (14 October 2016), online: <https://www.canada.ca/en/department -finance/news/2016/10/technical-backgrounder-mortgage-insurance -rules-income-proposals-revised-october-14-2016.html>.

56 *Ibid.*

57 *Ibid.*

58 *Ibid.*

59 *Ibid.*

60 *Ibid.*

61 See Office of the Superintendent of Financial Institutions (OSFI), News Release, "OSFI Is Reinforcing a Strong and Prudent Regulatory Regime for Residential Mortgage Underwriting" (17 October 2017) online: <http:// www.osfi-bsif.gc.ca/Eng/osfi-bsif/med/Pages/B20_dft_nr.aspx>.

62 *Ibid.*

63 See Pete Evans, "OSFI Sets New Mortgage Rules, Including Stress Test for Uninsured Borrowers" (17 October 2017), online: *CBC News* <https:// www.cbc.ca/news/business/osfi-mortgage-rules-1.4358048>.

64 See Robert Hogue, "As Expected, OSFI Tightens Rules for Non-Insured Mortgages" (2017) at 1, online (pdf): *RBC Economics* <http://www.rbc .com/economics/economic-reports/pdf/canadian-housing/housing _OSFI_Oct2017.pdf>.

65 *Ibid*.

66 See Robert McLister, "Why Ottawa Must Rethink the Stress Test on Mortgage Switches" (6 February 2019), online: *The Globe and Mail* <https://www.theglobeandmail.com/investing/personal-finance/article -why-ottawa-must-rethink-the-stress-test-on-mortgage-switches/>.

67 See Bank of Canada, "Policy Interest Rate: Recent Data", online: <https://www.bankofcanada.ca/core-functions/monetary-policy/key -interest-rate/>; Natalie Wong, "Time to Relax Mortgage Regulations, Canada Home Builders Say" (30 November 2018), online: *Bloomberg* <https://www.bloomberg.com/news/articles/2018-11-30/time-to-relax -mortgage-regulations-canada-home-builders-urge>.

68 Wong, *supra* note 67.

69 McLister, *supra* note 66.

70 *Ibid*.

71 *Ibid*.

72 Canada, Department of Finance Canada, *Investing in the Middle Class: Budget 2019*, (2019) at 26, online (pdf): *Department of Finance Canada* <https://www.budget.gc.ca/2019/docs/plan/budget-2019-en.pdf>.

73 *Ibid* at 24.

74 *Ibid*.

75 *Ibid* at 23.

76 *Ibid* at 24.

77 *Ibid*.

78 *Ibid*.

79 See Andrea Hopkins & Allison Lampert, "Quebec Seen as Tightening Mortgage Lending, Other Provinces Split" (30 January 2018), online: *Reuters* <https://ca.reuters.com/article/domesticNews/idCAKBN1FJ2QI -OCADN>.

80 *Ibid*.

81 Canada Mortgage and Housing Corporation & Deloitte, *supra* note 37.

82 See Evan Siddall, "In Conversation: Evan Siddall and Paul Taylor" (delivered at the Mortgage Professionals of Canada National Mortgage Conference, Montreal, 29 October 2018), online: *Canadian Mortgage Trends* <https://www.canadianmortgagetrends.com/2018/10/cmhc-evan -siddall-addresses-b-20-national-mortgage-conference/>.

83 *Ibid*.

84 See Jerome H Powell, "The Case for Housing Finance Reform" (delivered at the American Enterprise Institute, Washington DC, 6 July 2017), online:

Bank for International Settlements <https://www.bis.org/review/r170725a.htm>.

85 *Ibid*.

86 See Consumer Financial Protection Bureau (CFPB), "Creating the Consumer Bureau" (last visited 11 September 2019), online: <https://www.consumerfinance.gov/data-research/research-reports/building-the-cfpb/#:~:text=In%20July%202010%2C%20Congress%20passed, Protection%20Bureau%20(the%20CFPB)>.

87 See "Administrative Law – Agency Design – Dodd-Frank Act Creates the Consumer Financial Protection Bureau" (2011) 124:8 Harv L Rev 2123 at 2125.

88 See Jason Scott Johnston, "Do Product Bans Help Customers? Questioning the Economic Foundations of Dodd-Frank Mortgage Regulation" (2016) 23:3 Geo Mason L Rev 617 at 638.

89 *Ibid*.

90 *Ibid* at 639.

91 Harvard Law Review, *supra* note 87 at 2125.

92 See Diana Olick, "How Dodd-Frank Changed Housing, for Good and Bad" (16 July 2015), online: *CNBC* <https://www.cnbc.com/2015/07/16/how-dodd-frank-changed-housing-for-good-and-bad.html>.

93 CFPB, *supra* note 86.

94 *Ibid*.

95 See US, S.2155, *Economic Growth, Regulatory Relief, and Consumer Protection Act*, 115th Cong, 2017 (enacted); Sarah O'Brien, "How the Banking Rule Rollback Will Affect Your Mortgage, Credit and More" (24 May 2018), online: *CNBC* <https://www.cnbc.com/2018/05/23/how-the-just-passed-banking-overhaul-bill-affects-consumers.html>.

96 O'Brien, *supra* note 95.

97 See 15 U.S.C. § 1639c.

98 Johnston, *supra* note 88 at 634.

99 *Ibid*.

100 See Consumer Financial Protection Bureau, "What Is a Qualified Mortgage?" (1 August 2017), online: *Consumer Financial Protection Bureau* <https://www.consumerfinance.gov/ask-cfpb/what-is-a-qualified-mortgage-en-1789/>.

101 *Ibid*.

102 Johnston, *supra* note 88 at 648.

103 *Ibid* at 650.

104 *Ibid*.

105 CFPB, *supra* note 86.

106 See Consumer Financial Protection Bureau, "Ability-to-Repay and Qualified Mortgage Rule: Small Entity Compliance Guide" (17 October 2013) at 15–16, online (pdf): *Consumer Financial Protection Bureau* <https://

files.consumerfinance.gov/f/201310_cfpb_atr-qm-small-entity_compliance -guide.pdf>.

107 *Ibid.*

108 *Dodd-Frank Act, supra* note 95 at § 1026.43(e)(4)(ii); CFPB, "Basic Guide for Lenders: What Is a Qualified Mortgage?" (1 August 2017), online: *CFPB* https://files.consumerfinance.gov/f/201310_cfpb_qm-guide-for -lenders.pdf.

109 See Kate Barry, "GSE Reform, CFPB Underwriting Rule Are on Collision Course" (4 February 2019), online: *American Banker* <https://www .americanbanker.com/news/gse-reform-cfpb-underwriting-rule-are-on -collision-course>.

110 *Ibid.*

111 See Kenneth R Harney, "Fannie Mae Will Ease Financial Standards for Mortgage Applicants Next Month" (6 June 2017), online: *The Washington Post* <https://www.washingtonpost.com/realestate/fannie-mae-will -ease-financial-standards-for-mortgage-applicants-next-month/2017/06 /05/9b391866-4a0b-11e7-9669-250d0b15f83b_story.html?noredirect =on&utm_term=.2f505b51c283>.

112 Willis, *supra* note 108.

113 *Ibid.*

114 Ligaya, *supra* note 5.

115 Brown & Veenstra, *supra* note 8 at 316.

116 *Ibid.*

117 Ligaya, *supra* note 5.

118 *Ibid.*; The Canadian Press, "Warren Buffet's Company Buys into Troubled Home Capital Group" (22 June 2017), online: *CBC News* <https://www .cbc.ca/news/business/warren-buffet-home-capital-1.4172661>.

119 The Canadian Press, *ibid.*

120 OSFI, *supra* note 61.

121 See Armina Ligaya, "New Mortgage Stress Test Rules Have Borrowers Flocking to Alternative Lenders" (5 February 2018), online: *CBC News* <https://www.cbc.ca/news/business/mortgage-stress-test-1.4519972>.

122 See Jeremy Kronick, "Home Capital: How Did We Get Here?" (15 May 2017), online (blog): *C.D. Howe Institute* <https://www.cdhowe.org /intelligence-memos/jeremy-kronick-home-capital-how-did-we-get-here>.

123 Brown & Veenstra, *supra* note 8 at 321.

124 *Ibid* at 321–22.

125 *Ibid.*

126 See Evan Siddall, "Avoiding a Blind-Side Hit: Better Understanding Risk in the Credit Union Sector" (delivered at the National Conference for Canada's Credit Unions, Toronto, 30 April 2018), online: *Canada Mortgage and Housing Corporation* <https://www.cmhc-schl.gc.ca/en/media

-newsroom/speeches/2018/avoiding-blind-side-hit-better
-understanding-risk-credit-union-sector>.

5. Tax Reform: A Missing Piece in Canada's National Housing Policy

1 See Dan Andrews & Aida Caldera Sánchez, "Drivers of Homeownership Rates in Selected OECD Countries" (2011) at 8–11, online (pdf):
   Organisation for Economic Co-operation and Development <https://www.oecd
   .org/officialdocuments/publicdisplaydocumentpdf/?cote=ECO
   /WKP(2011)18&docLanguage=En>. See generally RBC Economic
   Research, "Focus on Canada's Housing Market" (2019), online (pdf):
   <http://www.rbc.com/economics/economic-reports/pdf/canadian
   -housing/Home_Ownership_Feb2019.pdf> [RBC Focus].
2 The principal residence was the largest asset, accounting for more than
   one-third of the total value of assets. See Statistics Canada, *Survey of
   Financial Security, 2016* (Ottawa: Statistics Canada, 7 December 2017)
   online: *Statistics Canada* <https://www150.statcan.gc.ca/n1/daily
   -quotidien/171207/dq171207b-eng.htm> [Financial Security Survey];
   Stephen S Poloz, "Canada's Economy and Household Debt: How Big Is
   the Problem?" (Address to the Yellowknife Chamber of Commerce delivered on 1 May 2018), online: *Bank of Canada* <https://www.bankofcanada
   .ca/2018/05/canada-economy-household-debt-how-big-the-problem/>.
3 See Evan Siddall, "Housing Should Be Affordable. Period," *The Globe and
   Mail* (29 June 2019) Opinion 05.
4 See Armina Ligaya & Barbara Shecter, "'Like the Perfect Storm': An FP
   Investigation into the Events That Took Home Capital to the Brink"
   (22 September 2017) online: *The Financial Post* <https://laptrinhx.com
   /like-the-perfect-storm-an-fp-investigation-into-the-events-that-took-home
   -capital-to-the-brink-294831992/>; Joe Castaldo, "What the Home Capital
   Crisis Reveals about the Housing Market" (5 May 2017) online: *Maclean's
   Magazine* <https://www.macleans.ca/economy/what-the-home-capital
   -crisis-reveals-about-the-housing-market/>; and James Saft, "Stay Tuned,
   Home Capital's Crisis May Puncture Canada's Housing Bubble Yet", *The
   Financial Post* (2 May 2017) <https://financialpost.com/news/economy
   /stay-tuned-home-capitals-crisis-may-puncture-canadas-housing-bubble>.
5 Making housing affordable to ordinary Canadians is a key objective of
   the National Housing Strategy. See Employment and Social Development
   Canada, "Canada's National Housing Strategy: A Place to Call Home" (2018),
   online (pdf): *Publications Canada* <http://publications.gc.ca/collections
   /collection_2018/edsc-esdc/Em12-54-2018-eng.pdf> [NHS Report].
6 See generally Robert G Dowler, *Housing-Related Tax Expenditures: An
   Overview and Evaluation* (Toronto: Centre for Urban and Community
   Studies, University of Toronto, 1983).

7 See generally George Fallis, "Tax Expenditures and Housing Policy in Canada" in Lisa Philipps, Neil Brooks & Jinyan Li, eds, *Tax Expenditures: State of the Art* (Toronto: Canadian Tax Foundation, 2011) at 10:1–26 [Fallis 2012]; George Fallis, "Stage Two Tax Reform and Housing" (1988) 26 Osgoode Hall LJ 603 at 603–28; George Fallis & Lawrence B Smith, "Tax Reform and Residential Real Estate" in Jack Mintz and John Whalley, eds, *The Economic Impacts of Tax Reform* (Toronto: Canadian Tax Foundation, 1989) 336; George Fallis, *Housing Programs and Income Distribution in Ontario* (Toronto: Ontario Economic Council, 1981); George Fallis, Arthur Hosios, Gregory Jump, James E Pedando, & Lawrence B Smith, *Final Report: The Economic Impact of Federal Rental Housing Program* (1989), online (pdf): *Publications Canada* <http://publications.gc.ca/collections /collection_2017/schl-cmhc/NH15-563-1989-eng.pdf>.

8 See generally Marion Steele, "The Canadian Home Buyers' Plan: Tax Benefit, Tax Expenditure, and Policy Assessment" (2007) 55:1 Can Tax J 1–30 at 1 [Steele 2007]; Marion Steele & Francois Des Rosiers, *Building Affordable Rental Housing in Unaffordable Cities: A Canadian Low-Income Housing Tax Credits* (Toronto: C.D. Howe Institute, 2009); Marion Steele & Peter Tomlinson, "Increasing the Affordability of Rental Housing in Canada: An Assessment of Alternative Supply-Side Measures" (2010) 3:2 *The School of Public Policy Publications* at 4.

9 See generally Richard M Bird, Enid Slack & Almos Tassonyi, *A Tale of Two Taxes: Property Tax Reform in Ontario* (Cambridge, MA: Lincoln Institute of Land Policy, 2012); Richard M Bird, "The Incidence of the Property Tax: Old Wine in New Bottles?" (1976) 2 Can Pub Pol'y 323–34; Enid Slack & Richard M Bird, "The Political Economy of Property Tax Reform" online (pdf): *OECD Library* <https://www.oecd-ilibrary.org/docserver /5jz5pzvzv6r7-en.pdf?expires=1567118051&id=id&accname=guest &checksum=3FF14082151C2B1567C9FE46B1B9CA32>.

10 See generally J David Hulchanski, "What Factors Shape Canadian Housing Policy?" in Robert Young and Christian Leuprecht, eds, *Canada: The State of the Federation: Municipal-Federal-Provincial Relations in Canada* (Montreal & Kingston: McGill-Queen's University Press, 2006) 221–47; J David Hulchanski & Michael Shapcott, eds, *Finding Room: Policy Options for a Canadian Rental Housing Strategy* (Toronto: CUCS Press, 2004); and J David Hulchanski, "Canada's Dual Housing Policy: Assisting Owners, Neglecting Renters" (2007) at 222, online (pdf): *Centre for Urban and Community Studies* <http://www.urbancentre.utoronto.ca/pdfs/researchbulletins /CUCSRB38Hulchanski.pdf> [Hulchanski -Dual Housing Policy].

11 United Nations Human Rights, Office of the High Commissioner, "Protecting the Right to Housing in the Context of the COVID-19 Outbreak" (29 October 2020), online: <https://www.ohchr.org/EN /Issues/Housing/Pages/COVID19RightToHousing.aspx>.

12 Stephanie Eliott & Scott Leon, "Crowded Housing and COVID-19: Impacts and Solutions" (24 July 24, 2020), online: <https://www .wellesleyinstitute.com/healthy-communities/crowded-housing-and -covid-19-impacts-and-solutions/>.

13 RSC 1985 (5th Supp), c 1 [*ITA*].

14 See Statistics Canada, "Housing in Canada: Key Results from the 2016 Census" (25 October 2017) online: <https://www150.statcan.gc.ca/n1 /daily-quotidien/171025/dq171025c-eng.htm>.

15 *Ibid*. The rate of homeownership rose from 62.6% in 1991 to 68.4% in 2006, to 69% in 2011. Homeownership was influenced by factors such as demographics, the size of the housing stock, availability, and cost of alternatives to homeownership, interest rates and access to financing, and the preferences and needs of Canadians. Canadians overwhelmingly prefer to live in a detached single-family home. See generally Mustel Group & Sotheby's International Realty Canada, "Modern Family Home Ownership Trends Report: The Evolution of the Canadian Dream" (2018), online (pdf): <https://sothebysrealty.ca/insightblog/2018/11/01/2018 -modern-family-home-ownership-trends-report/>; John R Miron, *Housing in Postwar Canada: Demographic Change, Household Formation, and Housing Demand* (Montreal & Kingston: McGill-Queen's University Press, 1988); Housing Services Corporation, "Canada's Social and Affordable Housing Landscape" (2014), online (pdf): *Homeless Hub* <https://www .homelesshub.ca/sites/default/files/attachments/531-Canada-Social -Housing-Landscape_2014.pdf>; NHS Report, *supra* note 5 at 3.

16 Ellen Bekkering, Jean-Philippe Deschamps-Laporte & Marina Smailes, "Housing Statistics in Canada: Residential Property Ownership: Real Estate Holdings by Multiple-Property Owners" (27 September 2019) <https://www150.statcan.gc.ca/n1/pub/46-28-0001/2019001/article /00001-eng.htm>.

17 *Ibid*.

18 See Statistics Canada, *Indebtedness and Wealth among Canadian Households*, by Guy Gellatly & Elizabeth Richards, online: <https://www150.statcan .gc.ca/n1/pub/11-626-x/11-626-x2019003-eng.htm>.

19 For those who owned their principal residence, the median reported value was $349,000 in 2016, up 10.3% from 2012 and double that of 1999. Home equity in 2016 was 115.2% higher compared with 1999. Financial Security Survey, *supra* note 2.

20 *Ibid*.

21 *Ibid*.

22 RBC Focus, *supra* note 1.

23 *Ibid*.

24 For the social impact of housing, see generally Matthew Desmond, *Evicted: Poverty and Profit in the American City* (New York: Crown

Publishing Group, 2016); Darcel Bullen, "A Road to Home: The Right
to Housing in Canada and around the World" (2015) 24 J L & Soc Pol'y
1–9: Matthew Desmond & Monica Bell, "Housing, Poverty, and the Law"
(2015) 11 Annual Rev L & Soc Science 15–35; Sarah Monk, Connie Tang &
Christine Whitehead, *What Does the Literature Tell Us about the Social and
Economic Impact of Housing? Report to the Scottish Government: Communities
Analytical Services* (Scottish Government, Social Research 2010) 24–33;
Siddall, *supra* note 3.

25 United Nations, Universal Declaration of Human Rights, art 25(1) –
"Everyone has the right to a standard of living adequate for the health
and well-being of himself and of his family." See also Office of the United
Nations High Commissioner for Human Rights, "The Right to Adequate
Housing" online: <https://www.ohchr.org/Documents/Publications
/FS21_rev_1_Housing_en.pdf>. This is iterated in the NHS Report, *supra*
note 5 at 8.

26 See Richard Eccleston, Kathleen Flanagan, Julia Verdouw, & Neil Warren,
Final Inquiry Report: Pathways to Housing Tax Reform (Melbourne: Australian
Housing and Urban Research Institute, 2018) at 7.

27 See generally CMHC, "Defining the Affordability of Housing in Canada"
(2019) online (pdf): *CMHC* <https://www.cmhc-schl.gc.ca/en/data-and
-research/publications-and-reports/research-insight-defining-affordability
-housing-canada> [CMHC Affordability].

28 *Ibid.* CMHC often uses this method. It is also widely used in other jurisdictions. Among its weaknesses is its failure to take into account the differences in household income, size, and composition. A residual income
method is an alternative, which looks at the amount of minimum income
that a household would need to pay for shelter costs, taxes, and basic
needs in their area. Another method is a basic needs (or residual income)
approach, which "subtracts from a household's disposable (that is, after-tax) income the cost of non-shelter necessities, based on the size and
composition of the household type. What is left after basic needs constitutes what is available, and therefore affordable, for shelter." CMHC,
"Housing Research Report: Defining the Affordability of Housing in
Canada" online: <https://eppdscrmssa01.blob.core.windows.net
/cmhcprodcontainer/sf/project/archive/research_2/defining
_affordability_of-housing-in-canada.pdf> at 10. This method considers
the types of households that are subject to affordability pressures and
the nature of those pressures. A challenge in applying this method is
the determination of the basket of goods and services that comprise
"necessities." The Bank of Canada's housing affordability index (a ratio)
estimates the share of disposable income that a representative household
would put toward housing-related expenses. The numerator of this ratio is the sum of housing-related costs (the average quarterly mortgage

payment plus utility fees), and the denominator is the average household disposable income. For details, see Bank of Canada, "Real Estate Market: Definitions, Graphs and Data" online: *Bank of Canada* <https://www .bankofcanada.ca/rates/indicators/capacity-and-inflation-pressures /real-estate-market-definitions/>.

29 CMHC Affordability, *supra* note 27.

30 See generally RBC Economic Research, "Housing Trends and Affordability: March 2019" (2019), online (pdf): *RBC* <http://www.rbc.com/economics /economic-reports/pdf/canadian-housing/house-mar2019.pdf> [RBC Housing Trends].

31 See Erica Alini, "Here's the Income You Need to Pass the Mortgage Stress Test across Canada" (14 April 2018), online: *Global News* <https:// globalnews.ca/news/4139837/heres-the-income-you-need-to-pass-the -mortgage-stress-test-across-canada/>.

32 See generally Matthieu Arseneau & Kyle Dahms, "Housing Affordability *Improves* in 2019Q1 amid Healthy Labour Market" (2019), online (pdf): *House Price Index* <https://housepriceindex.ca/wp-content/uploads/2019 /06/NBFM-Housing-Affordability-Monitor-Q1_2019-Eng.pdf>.

33 See e.g. Advocacy Centre for Tenants Ontario (ATCO), "Where Will We Live? Ontario's Affordable Rental Housing Crisis" (2018), online (pdf): <https://www.acto.ca/production/wp-content/uploads/2018/05 /wherewillwelive_may2018_acto_report.pdf>; York Region, "Bringing Affordable Rental Housing to York Region: Challenges and Recommen- dations for Markham, Ontario" (2014), online (pdf): <https://www .york.ca/wps/wcm/connect/yorkpublic/986e5820-fa49-4c5b-b49a -21c230d65e5d/the+housing+puzzlers.pdf?mod=ajperes> [Markham, Affordable Housing]; The Canadian Press, "Affordable Housing in Canada in Crisis as Rental Rates Climb, Supply Dwindles" (10 April 2018), online: *The Huffington Post* <https://www.huffingtonpost.ca/2018 /04/10/affordable-housing-crisis-canada_a_23407878/>.

34 See generally CMHC, "Housing Need Stable In Canada, 1.7 Million Cana- dian Households Affected" (14 November 2017), online: *Newswire* <https:// www.newswire.ca/news-releases/housing-need-stable-in-canada-17 -million-canadian-households-affected-657700653.html>. The CMHC uses core housing need as an indicator to identify households not living in, and not able to access, acceptable housing. Core housing need describes "house- holds living in dwellings considered inadequate in condition, not suitable in size, and unaffordable." Housing is deemed affordable when its shelter costs represent less than 30% of before-tax household income. Based on the 2016 census, the national rate of core housing need was 12.7% in 2016, rep- resenting 1.7 million households. The rate is 8.5% in Prince Edward Island, 15.3% in Ontario, 14.9% in British Columbia, and 36.5% in Nunavut.

35 *Ibid.*
36 For a recent study, see David Macdonald, *Unaccommodating: Rental Housing Wage in Canada* (Toronto: Canada Centre for Policy Alternatives, 2019).
37 *Ibid.*
38 See e.g. Michal Rozworski, "The Roots of Our Housing Crisis: Austerity, Debt and Extreme Speculation" (14 June 2019), online: *Policy Note* <https://www.policynote.ca/the-roots-of-our-housing-crisis-austerity -debt-and-extreme-speculation/>; Fatima Syed, "The Solution to Canada's Housing Crisis Is Right under Our Roofs", *The Toronto Star* (15 June 2019), online: <https://www.thestar.com/news/gta/2019/06/15/the-solution -to-canadas-housing-crisis-is-right-under-our-roofs.html>; Stuart Thomson, "Canada's Housing Crisis and Mortgage Stress Test Are Officially Election Issues" (31 January 2019), online: *The National Post* <https://nationalpost.com/news/politics/canadas-housing-crisis-and -mortgage-stress-test-are-officially-election-issues>.
39 See CMHC, "New Study Reveals Socio-Economic Housing Inequalities" (11 June 2019), online: *CMHC* <https://www.cmhc-schl.gc.ca/en/housing -observer-online/2019-housing-observer/new-study-reveals-socio -economic-housing-inequalities/>.
40 NHS Report, *supra* note 5 at 4.
41 See generally Paul Martin & Joe Fontana, "Finding Room: Housing Solutions for the Future: Report of the National Liberal Caucus Task Force on Housing" (1990), online (pdf): <http://www.urbancentre.utoronto .ca/pdfs/home/Finding_Room_1990_by_Paul_M.pdf>.
42 See CMHC, "Housing in Canada 1945 to 1986: An Overview and Lessons Learned" (1987) at 7, online (pdf): *Publications Canada* <http://publications .gc.ca/collections/collection_2017/schl-cmhc/NH15-518-1987-eng.pdf>; Fallis 2012, *supra* note 7.
43 Canada Mortgage and Housing Corporation, "History of CMHC" (2014), online: <https://web.archive.org/web/20140909232847/https://www .cmhc-schl.gc.ca/en/corp/about/hi/index.cfm>.
44 It provides mortgage loan insurance and engages in securitization of residential mortgages to make it easier for home buyers to obtain mortgages. It also provides funding for social housing (most of which is administered by provinces and territories, supporting low-cost loans to federally assisted social housing sponsors, providing funding to address housing needs in First Nation communities). See CMHC, "What Does CMHC Do?" (31 May 2018), online: <https://www.cmhc-schl.gc.ca/en/about-cmhc/cmhcs-story>.
45 See NHS Report, supra note 5.
46 *Ibid* at 5.
47 See Don Pittis, "Why the Canadian Economy Seems Divorced from Traditional Signs" (31 May 2019), online: *CBC* <https://www.cbc.ca/news

/business/bank-of-canada-economy-housing-1.5152705>; Darryl Dyck, "As Canada's Economic Engine Stalls, Can Other Industries Pick Up the Slack?" (8 January 2016), online: *The Globe and Mail* <https://www .theglobeandmail.com/real-estate/the-market/with-a-resource-slump-can -canadas-other-industries-power-the-economy/article28092680/>.

48 Siddall, *supra* note 3.

49 See Statistics Canada, "Gross Domestic Product, Income and Expendi- ture, Fourth Quarter 2017" (2018), online (pdf): *Statistics Canada* <https:// www150.statcan.gc.ca/n1/en/daily-quotidien/180302/dq180302a-eng .pdf?st=Ad0VEbe0>.

50 See generally Steve Pomeroy & Greg Lampert, "Examining the Dynamics of Canada's Housing Tenure System: Implications for a National Housing Strategy" (2017), online (pdf): *Canadian Housing and Renewal Association* <https://chra-achru.ca/examining-the-dynamics-of-canadas-housing -tenure-system-implications-for-a-national-housing-strategy/>.

51 See generally OECD, *Economic Policy Reforms 2011: Going for Growth* (Paris: OECD, 2011); Christophe Andre, *A Bird's Eye View of OECD Housing Markets*, OECD Economic Department Working Paper No. 736, ECO/WKP, 2010.

52 See Francis Fong, *The Real Story behind Housing and Household Debt in Canada: Is a Crisis Really Looming?* (Chartered Professional Accountants of Canada, 2018) at 2.

53 Evan Siddall, "Too Much of a Good Thing: On Housing, Wealth, and Intergenerational Inequality" (delivered at the Halifax Chamber of Commerce, 26 April 2018), online: *CMHC* <https://www.cmhc-schl .gc.ca/en/media-newsroom/speeches/2018/on-housing-wealth-and -intergenerational-inequity> [Siddall 2018].

54 See CMHC, "Household Debt-to-Income Ratio Near Record High" (13 December 2018), online: *CMHC* <https://www.cmhc-schl.gc.ca/en /housing-observer-online/2018-housing-observer/household-debt -income-ratio-near-record-high>.

55 See generally *RBC Housing Trends*, supra note 30. Spending by Canadians on real estate costs (broker fees, land-transfer taxes and legal costs) is 50% more than spending on research and development. Siddall, *supra* note 3. In contrast, Americans spent 25% more on research and develop- ment than they do on real estate costs.

56 Fong, *supra* note 52 at 2. See also Don Coletti, Marc-Andre Gosselin & Cameron MacDonald, "The Rise of Mortgage Finance Companies: Benefits and Vulnerabilities" (2016), online (pdf): *Bank of Canada* <https://www.bankofcanada.ca/wp-content/uploads/2016/12/fsr -december-2016-coletti.pdf>. It should be noted, however, that the level of household debt does not mean that Canadians are being irresponsible

with debt. In fact, the growth of such debt can be a rational response to falling interest rates and increasing housing prices. See generally Livio Di Matteo, *Household Debt and Government Debt in Canada* (Vancouver: Fraser Institute, 2017).

57 See RBC Report, "Seven Ways COVID-19 Is Affecting Canadian Housing" (October 2020), online: <https://thoughtleadership.rbc.com /seven-ways-covid-19-is-affecting-canadian-housing/>

58 Fong, *supra* note 52.

59 See generally Bank of Canada, "Financial System Review – 2019" (2019), online (pdf): <https://www.bankofcanada.ca/wp-content/uploads /2019/05/Financial-System-Review—2019-Bank-of-Canada.pdf>.

60 Siddall 2018, *supra* note 53.

61 See Ligaya & Shecter, "'Like the Perfect Storm'", *supra* note 4; Castaldo, "What the Home Capital Crisis Reveals about the Housing Market", *supra* note 4>.

62 Hulchanski, Canada's Dual Housing Policy, *supra* note 10 at 224.

63 See Part 3 below.

64 First introduced in Canada in 2018, the mortgage stress test for insured mortgages requires lenders to verify that mortgage applicants could still make payments based on the Bank of Canada's qualifying rate. To complete the test, mortgage lenders calculate the Gross Debt Service and Total Debt Service ratios to determine if applicants have sufficient income to make mortgage payments. In response to COVID-19, the CMHC, which is one of Canada's three insured mortgage providers, made changes to its underwriting criteria for new insured mortgage applications. For example, it requires that no more than 35% of a home-buyer's pre-tax income can go toward the mortgage costs; see CMHC, "CMHC Reviews Underwriting Criteria" (4 June 2020), online: <https://www.cmhc-schl.gc.ca/en/media-newsroom/news-releases /2020/cmhc-reviews-underwriting-criteria>.

65 *ITA*, *supra* note 13; *Excise Tax Act*, RSC, 1985, c E-15. General sales taxes are harmonized with the GST in many provinces.

66 For an overview, see Neil Brooks, Jinyan Li, & Lisa Philipps, "Tax Expenditure Analysis: State of the Art" in Lisa Philipps, Neil Brooks, & Jinyan Li, eds, *Tax Expenditures: State of the Art* (Toronto: Canadian Tax Foundation, 2011) at 1:1–1:25.

67 See e.g. *Property Transfer Tax Act*, RSBC 1996, c 378; *Land Transfer Tax Act*, RSO 1990, c L 6; *Assessment Act*, RSO 1990, c A31; *Municipal Act*, 2001, SO 2001, c 2; *Speculation and Vacancy Tax Act*, SBC 2018, c 46.

68 Until 2018, there was a tax subsidy to relocated employees under s 110(1)(j) of the *ITA*. Under this provision, benefits from employer-provided in-terest-free home relocation loans are not taxable. The amount of the

exemption is limited to the lesser of the amount of the taxable benefit and the deemed interest benefit on the first $25,000 of a five-year interest-free loan. This measure was repealed as of the 2018 taxation year.

69 In addition, the *ITA* provides for a Home Accessibility Tax Credit in respect of renovation or alteration expenses in order to improve assess for persons with disabilities. There was also a temporary home-renovation tax credit introduced in 2009 on eligible home renovation expenses in order to stimulate spending following the 2008 global financial crisis. For a discussion of earlier housing-related tax expenditures, see Dowler, *supra* note 6.

70 See e.g. *ITA, supra* note 13, ss 12(4), 12(11), 91, 95.

71 *Ibid*, ss 3(b), 38(a).

72 *Ibid*, s 54, "principal residence".

73 For further discussion, see Edwin C Harris, "A Case Study in Tax Reform: The Principal Residence," (1983) 7 Dalhousie LJ 169 at 193. The taxation of capital gains was introduced as part of the 1972 tax reforms. The provision was amended in Budget 1981 so that, for years after 1981, a family may treat only one property as its principal residence for a taxation year. It was amended again in 2016 to require the reporting of dispositions, introduce an indefinite reassessment period for unreported dispositions, and limit the types of trusts that are eligible to designate a property as a principal residence for a taxation year beginning after 2016.

74 See Department of Finance, *Proposals for Tax Reform: White Paper on Taxation* (Ottawa: Department of Finance, 1969) at 33, online (pdf): *Publications Canada* <http://publications.gc.ca/collections/collection_2016/fin/F32 -169-1969-eng.pdf> [Taxation White Paper].

75 See generally Department of Finance, *Summary of 1971 Tax Reform Legislation* (Ottawa: Department of Finance, 1971), online (pdf): *Publications Canada* <http://publications.gc.ca/collections/collection_2016/fin /F2-241-1971-eng.pdf>; Department of Finance, "Report on Federal Tax Expenditures: Concepts, Estimates and Evaluations 2020" (28 February 2020), online: *Department of Finance* <https://www.canada.ca/en /department-finance/services/publications/federal-tax-expenditures /2020/part-1.html> [Tax Expenditure Report].

76 Taxation White Paper, *supra* note 74 at 31.

77 Tax Expenditure Report, *supra* note 75; see generally David Macdonald, *Out of the Shadows: Shining a Light on Canada's Unequal Distribution of Federal Tax Expenditures* (2016) at 6, online (pdf): *Canadian Centre for Policy Alternatives* <https://www.policyalternatives.ca/sites/default/files/uploads /publications/National%20Office/2016/11/Out_of_the_Shadows.pdf> [Macdonald 2016]; Neil Brooks, "Policy Forum: The Case against Boutique Tax Credits and Similar Tax Expenditures" (2016), 64 Can Tax J 65–133.

78 Tax Expenditure Report, *supra* note 75. In terms of revenue cost, the Principal Residence Exemption is second only to the tax subsidy to registered pension plans and RRSPs. See Macdonald 2016, *supra* note 77.

79 See Office of the Parliamentary Budget Officer, *Federal Program Spending on Housing Affordability* (Ottawa: Office of the Parliamentary Budget Officer, 2019) at 3, online (pdf): *Office of the Parliamentary Budget Officer* <https://www.pbo-dpb.gc.ca/web/default/files/Documents/Reports /2019/Housing_Affordability/Federal%20Spending%20on%20Housing %20Affordability%20EN.pdf>.

80 Macdonald 2016, *supra* note 77; Dowler, *supra* note 6 at 18.

81 Siddall 2018, supra note 53.

82 The Home Buyers' Plan is similar to an earlier Canadian homeownership stimulation program (CHOSP) that provided grants to first-time homeowners buying newly built homes. It was in effect from June 1982 to May 1983. It was administered by the CMHC.

83 *ITA, supra* note 13, s 118.05.

84 Tax Expenditure Report, *supra* note 75.

85 *ITA, supra* note 13, ss 56, 60, 146.

86 See "What Is the Home Buyers' Plan?" (28 March 2019), online: *Government of Canada* <https://www.canada.ca/en/revenue-agency /services/tax/individuals/topics/rrsps-related-plans/what-home -buyers-plan.html>.

87 *Ibid.*

88 Most other OECD countries, including the United States, include this item as a tax expenditure, and some countries, such as the Netherlands, tax imputed rent as income. See Fallis 2012, *supra* note 7 at 10:9.

89 Jinyan Li, Joanne E Magee & J Scott Wilkie, *Principles of Canadian Income Tax Law*, 9th ed (Toronto: Thomson Reuters, 2017) at 119–20.

90 Dowler, *supra* note 6 at 64; Patricia Fulton, "Tax Preferences for Housing: Is There a Case for Reform?" in Wayne R Thirsk & John Whalley, eds, *Tax Policies and Options in the 1980s* (Toronto: Canadian Tax Foundation, 1981).

91 For further discussion of the MURB program, see generally Alex MacNevin, *Research Report: Federal Tax Regimes and Rental Housing* (Ottawa: CMHC, 1993), online (pdf): *Publications Canada* <http://publications .gc.ca/collections/collection_2018/schl-cmhc/nh18-1/NH18-1-441-1993 -eng.pdf>; Clayton Research Associates, *Tax Expenditures: Housing* (Ottawa: CMHC, 1981), online (pdf): <http://publications.gc.ca/collections /collection_2017/schl-cmhc/NH15-514-1981-eng.pdf>.

92 MacNevin, *supra* note 91; Robert D Brown, "A Critical Review of Tax Shelters", in Thirsk & Whalley, *supra* note 90.

93 See generally Brown, *supra* note 92.

94 For an explanation of the CCA regime, see Li, Magee & Wilkie, *supra* note 89 at 270–82.

95 In comparison, if an individual invests her capital on purchasing shares, she cannot deduct any portion of the investment cost (even if the share's value went down), as the CCA deduction does not apply to shares.

96 *ITA*, *supra* note 13, s 3(d).

97 2002 SCC 46 [*Stewart*].

98 *Stewart v R*, [2000] 2 CTC 244, 2000 DTC 6163 (Fed CA) at para 10, citing the Tax Court judge's finding.

99 *Stewart*, supra note 97 at para 68.

100 See generally Li, Magee & Wilkie, *supra* note 89 at 528–39.

101 The GST is defined in Part IX of the *Excise Tax Act*, *supra* note 8. In addition to the GST, every province (except Alberta) levies a provincial sales tax. The provincial sales tax is harmonized with the GST in New Brunswick, Newfoundland and Labrador, Nova Scotia, Ontario, and Prince Edward Island.

102 For purposes of GST, housing includes shares in a co-operative housing, mobile homes and floating homes. See Canada Revenue Agency, Guide RC4028, "GST/HST New Housing Rebate" (4 October 2016), online (pdf): <https://www.canada.ca/content/dam/cra-arc/formspubs/pub/rc4028/rc4028-10-16e.pdf>.

103 Excise Tax Act, *supra* note 65, ss 254, 256. The rebate is available to builders or purchasers of newly constructed and substantially renovated residential housing as long as the housing is for use as a primary place of residence. The rebate is 36% of the total GST paid to a maximum of $6,300 for houses valued at or below $350,000. The rebate is gradually phased out for houses valued between $350,000 and $450,000.

104 Tax Expenditure Report, *supra* note 75 at 33.

105 *Excise Tax Act*, *supra* note 65, Schedule V, Part I, s 6.

106 Tax Expenditure Report, *supra* note 75 at 122.

107 *Ibid*.

108 *Excise Tax Act*, *supra* note 65, Schedule V, Part 1, s 6(b).

109 *Excise Tax Act*, *supra* note 8, s 256.1.

110 For more discussion, see generally Altus Group Economic Consulting, "Economic Implications of the Municipal Land Transfer Tax in Toronto" (Toronto: 2014) at 6; Christian AL Hilber & Teemu Lyytikainen, "Transfer Taxes and Household Mobility: Distortion on the Housing or Labour Market?" (London: Spatial Economics Research, 2015) at 23; Ben Dachis, "Stuck in Place: The Effect of Land Transfer Taxes on Housing Transactions" (Toronto: C.D. Howe Institute, 2012) at 11; Ben Dachis, Gilles Duranton & Matthew A Turner, "Sand in the Gears: Evaluating the Effects of Toronto's Land Transfer Tax" (Toronto: C.D. Howe Institute, 2008) at 3.

For an assessment of the recent BC and Ontario taxes on foreign buyers and owners of vacant homes, see generally Noah Sarna & Zheting Su, "Policy Forum: Taxing Non-Residents' Residences – A Critical View of the Law behind the New Realty Taxes in British Columbia and Ontario" (2018) 66:3 Can Tax J 553; Thomas Davidoff, "Policy Forum: Vancouver's Property Taxes in Perspective," (2018) 66:3 Can Tax J 573; Paul Kershaw, "Policy Forum: A Tax Shift – The Case for Rebalancing the Tax Treatment of Earnings and Housing Wealth" (2018) 66:3 Can Tax J 585; Kevin Milligan, "Policy Forum: Editor's Introduction – New Approaches to Property Taxation" (2018) 66:3 Can Tax J 549.

111 Alberta charges a registration fee and a mortgage registration fee. Title registration fee includes a base fee of $50 plus an additional $1 charge for every $5,000 of the fair market value of the property (rounded up to the nearest $5,000). Mortgage registration fee includes a base fee of $50 plus $1 for every $5,000 of the mortgage loan.

112 The same rates apply under the Toronto land transfer tax.

113 See City of Toronto, "Municipal Land Transfer Tax (MLTT) Rates and Fees" (March 2017), online: *Toronto* <https://www.toronto.ca/services -payments/property-taxes-utilities/municipal-land-transfer-tax-mltt /municipal-land-transfer-tax-mltt-rebate-opportunities/>.

114 In British Columbia, Bill 28, the *Miscellaneous Statutes (Housing Priority Initiatives) Amendment Act, 2016*, came into force on 2 August 2016. In Ontario, a Non-Resident Speculation Tax was introduced on 21 April 2017 as an additional tax levied under s 2(2.1) of the *Land Transfer Tax Act*, RSO 1990, c L6.

115 Office of the Premier, Ontario, News Release, "Making Housing More Affordable" (20 April 2017).

116 In Ontario, a rebate of the tax may be available if the foreign buyer subsequently became a permanent resident of Canada (four years following the purchase), is an international student enrolled full-time for a continuous period of at least two years, or has legally worked full-time under a valid work permit in Ontario for a continuous period of at least one year since the date of purchase or acquisition.

117 For example, assessment value of residential housing in Ontario is established by the Municipal Property Assessment Corporation by using a direct comparison approach (that is, using recent sales of comparable properties as indication of value of the assessed property) and assessment is done every four years. See MPAC, "How Your Property Tax Is Calculated", online: <https://www.mpac.ca/en/UnderstandingYourAssessment /PropertyValueandPropertyTaxes>.

118 Local governments are creatures of the provinces. As such, local governments have no independent taxing powers. Although the property

tax is largely a local tax, most provinces in Canada also levy a property tax. For further discussion on Ontario's property tax, see Bird, Slack & Tassonyi, *supra* note 9; Hemson Consulting Ltd, "Property Taxation in Ontario: A Guide for Municipalities" (2012), online (pdf): <https://www .mfoa.on.ca/MFOA/WebDocs/HEMSON%20-%20Property%20Tax %20Guide%20May%2012%202012.pdf>.

119 See City of Toronto, "2018 Property Tax Rates & Fees" (2018), online: <https://www.toronto.ca/services-payments/property-taxes-utilities /property-tax/property-tax-rates-and-fees/2018-property-tax-rates-fees/>.

120 See generally Budget 2018, *Working for You: Budget and Fiscal Plan 2018/19– 2020/21* (Victoria, BC: Ministry of Finance, 2018), online (pdf): <https:// bcbudget.gov.bc.ca/2018/bfp/2018_Budget_and_Fiscal_Plan.pdf>.

121 *Ibid* at 7.

122 *Ibid* at 72.

123 See generally City of Vancouver, by-law no 11674, *Vacancy Tax Bylaw* (11 January 2017).

124 See City of Vancouver, "Empty Homes Tax" (last visited 30 August 2019), online: <https://vancouver.ca/home-property-development/empty -homes-tax.aspx>.

125 See Li, Magee & Wilkie, *supra* note 89 at 40–2.

126 A draft of section 3.1 of the *ITA* was released by the Department of Finance on 31 October 2003. It was to deal with the deductibility of interest and other expenses for income tax purposes. The intent of the proposed legislation was to address concerns resulting from adverse court decisions that departed significantly from what the government had considered to be the law regarding interest deductibility.

127 See generally Paul Kershaw & Eric Swanson, "A Housing Policy Frame- work and Policy Options for the 2019 Federal Election" (2019), online (pdf): *Generation Squeeze* <https://d3n8a8pro7vhmx.cloudfront.net/gensqueeze /pages/5290/attachments/original/1559941195/Federal-housing -framework_2019-05-29.pdf?1559941195>.

128 Andrews & Sánchez, *supra* note 1 at 17–18 shows that the homeowner- ship rate is influenced by two main factors: (1) a household's preference for home ownership relative to renting, which, in turn, is influenced by policies, including taxation; and (2) purely demographic and socioeco- nomic developments, such as population aging. Academic literature em- phasizes one of three sets of factors assumed to influence decisions about owning and renting housing: economic and financial considerations, socio-demographic characteristics, and psychological and behavioral drivers. See generally K Fu, "A Review of Housing Tenure Choice," in Jiayuan Wang, Zhikun Ding, Liang Zou, & Jian Zuo, eds, *Proceedings of the 17th International Symposium on Advancement of Construction Management*

and Real Estate (Berlin: Springer, 2013) 351–60. Beliefs about the benefits of homeownership are strong indicators of expectations to own, more so than even some economic and socio-demographic characteristics that are commonly assumed to drive tenure preferences, such as family composition and income. See generally Rachel Bogardus Drew, "Believing in Homeownership: Behavioral Drivers of Housing Tenure Decisions," (2014), online (pdf): *Harvard University* <https://www.jchs.harvard.edu/sites/default/files/w14-3_drew.pdf>.

129 Research shows the mortgage interest deduction (MID) in the United States "has little if any positive effect on homeownership". See generally William G Gale, Jonathan Gruber & Seth Stephens-Davidowitz, "Encouraging Homeownership through the Tax Code" (2007) at 1179, online (pdf): *The Brookings Institute* <https://www.brookings.edu/wp-content/uploads/2016/06/20070618.pdf>.

130 There are similar tax preferences for housing in the United States, such as non-taxation of imputed rent and tax exemption of capital gains. The United States also allows mortgage interest to be deducted in computing income – a measure that is not available in Canada. See generally Edward L Glaeser & Jesse M Shapiro, "The Benefits of the Home Mortgage Interest Deduction" (2003) 17 Tax Policy & Economy 37–82; and Gale, Gruber & Stephens-Davidowitz, *ibid*; Eccleston et al, *supra* note 26.

131 Gale, Gruber & Stephens-Davidowitz, *ibid*.

132 See Eccleston et al, *supra* note 26.

133 *Ibid* at 8.

134 See J Bossons, "The Effect of Inflation-Reduced Hidden Wealth Taxes" (Toronto: Canadian Tax Foundation, 1981) at 16.

135 Dowler, *supra* note 6 at 61.

136 RBC Housing Trends, *supra* note 30.

137 The Ontario Energy and Property Tax Credit is available to low- to middle-income taxpayers on the basis of the amount of rent, property taxes, or long-term housing costs; see Ontario Trillium Benefit (2021), online: <https://www.ontario.ca/page/ontario-trillium-benefit#section-2>.

138 For example, CMHC is leading and delivering the National Housing Strategy. Initiatives on creating new housing supply include providing low-cost repayable loans and forgivable loans for building new affordable housing shelters, transitional and supportive housing; and providing low-cost loans to encourage the construction of sustainable rental apartment projects across Canada. See CMHC, "National Housing Strategy" (2 May 2018), online: <https://www.cmhc-schl.gc.ca/en/nhs/guidepage-strategy/about-the-initiatives?guide=CREATE%20NEW%20HOUSING%20SUPPLY>.

139 NHS Report, *supra* note 5 at 5.

140   Harris, *supra* note 73 at 172.
141   *Ibid.* Even then, however, the Principal Residence Exemption was criticized for compromising the basic tax policy goals of equity and neutrality.
142   Kershaw & Swanson, *supra* note 127 at 4.
143   For instance, the Liberal government introduced the National Housing Strategy. See also Progressive Conservative Party of Ontario, "For the People: A
Plan for Ontario" (2018), online (pdf): *PCPO* <https://www.ontariopc.ca
/plan_for_the_people>; "Federal Conservative Leader Andrew Scheer on
GO Trains, Affordable Housing, and Election" (20 August 2019), online: *CBC*
< https://www.cbc.ca/news/canada/kitchener-waterloo/conservative
-leader-andrew-scheer-waterloo-region-1.5252441>; NDP, "Making Life
More Affordable for Everyday People" (2021), online: <https://www.ndp
.ca/affordability>; and Green Part of Canada, "Green Party of Canada Housing Policies: A Closer Look" (2018), online: <https://www.greenparty.ca
/en/blog/2019-10-08/green-party-canada-housing-policies-closer-look>.
144   See Macdonald 2016, *supra* note 77.
145   Department of Finance, *Report on Federal Tax Expenditures – Concepts,
Estimates and Evaluations 2020* (2 February 2020), online: <https://www
.canada.ca/en/department-finance/services/publications/federal-tax
-expenditures/2020.html> shows at page 35 that the estimated cost of the
Principal Residence Exemption is: $5,045 million (2014), $6,135 million
(2015), $7,960 million (2016), and $7,520 million (2017), and the projected
cost is $5,315 million in 2018, $4,870 million in 2019, $5,870 million in
2020, and $7,070 million in 2021.
146   Macdonald 2016, *supra* note 77 at 13.
147   Kershaw & Swanson, *supra* note 127 at 588.
148   Martin & Fontana, *supra* note 41. Recommendation 25 states that "the
Task Force recommends that the Conservative government begin con-
sultations with Canadians and provincial governments on the creation
of a fair and integrated reform of the entire tax system. The present
Manufacturers Sales Tax ... must not be replaced with a tax that creates
more inequities and deepens the affordability crisis faced by hundreds of
thousands of Canadian households."
149   NHS Report, *supra* note 5 calls for more research on housing. It is hoped
that more national data are available to inform the design of this limit.
150   *ITA, supra* note 13, s 110.6.
151   See Canada, *Report of Royal Commission on Taxation*, Vol 3 (Ottawa: Queen's
Printer, 1966) at 353, online (pdf): *Publications Canada* <http://publications
.gc.ca/site/eng/9.699804/publication.html>.
152   See Internal Revenue Service, "Publication 523 (2018), Selling Your Home"
(10 January 2019), online: *Internal Revenue Service* <https://www.irs.gov
/publications/p523>.

153 Since health care is funded by federal general tax revenues, the foregone tax revenue under the Principal Residence Exemption could be used to defray the increasing health-care cost of caring for older Canadians instead of working younger taxpayers who may struggle with housing.

154 *ITA, supra* note 13, ss 63, 146(1).

155 See generally Wendell Cox & Ailin He, "Canada's Middle-Income Housing Affordability Crisis", (2016) online (pdf): *Frontier Centre for Public Policy* <https://fcpp.org/wp-content/uploads/2016/06/Cox-He -Middle-Income-Housing-Crisis.pdf>. Since 2002, the federal and provincial governments have jointly funded initiatives to increase social housing for low-income households through social housing. Current programs include grants for the construction of new rental units; rent subsidies for low-income households; renovation grants; and down-payment assistance for home purchases by low-income households. See generally Auditor General of Ontario, "Annual Reports – Social and Affordable Housing", online: *Auditor General of Ontario* <www.auditor.on.ca/en /content/annualreports/arreports/en17/v1_314en17.pdf>.

156 Among the non-tax instruments suggested by researchers are reducing restrictions on land use, removing "barriers (regulatory, administrative or otherwise) inhibiting home developers and builders to respond quickly to the demand for new housing – especially when that demand is rising rapidly," or exempting new secure purpose-built rental housing from rent controls. See Cox & He, *supra* note 155; RBC Focus, *supra* note 1; LandlordBC, "Understanding BC's History of Rent Control and Tax Policy to Improve Today's Rental Housing Crisis" (8 April 2019), online: *LandlordBC* <https://landlordbc.ca/understanding-bcs-history-of-rent -control-and-taxy-policy-to-improve-todays-rental-housing-crisis/>.

157 See supra notes 91–2 and the accompanying text.

158 Steele & Tomlinson, *supra* note 8.

159 See *Internal Revenue Code*, 26 USC § 42. It was introduced in the U.S. Tax Reform Act of 1986. See Steele & Des Rosiers, *supra* note 8 suggesting that this tax credit is a better way for CMHC to disburse money to lower levels of government for building social housing and that such credit is "an ideal way to leverage some of the $2 billion in short-term stimulus funding for the construction of social housing into a sustainable long-term investment."

160 See Congressional Research Service, "An Introduction to the Low-Income Housing Tax Credit" (27 February 2019), online (pdf): <https://fas.org /sgp/crs/misc/RS22389.pdf>.

161 See generally Joint Committee on Taxation, *Present Law and Data Relating to Tax Incentives for Rental Housing*, JCX-40-17 (Washington, DC: Joint Committee on Taxation, 2017); Mark P Keightley, *An Introduction to the*

Low-Income Housing Tax Credit, RS22389 (Washington, DC: Congressional Research Service, 2018); Corianne Payton Scally, Amanda Gold & Nicole DuBois, *The Low-Income Housing Tax Credit: How It Works and Who It Serves* (Washington, DC: Urban Institute, 2018).

162 *ITA*, supra note 13, s 125.

163 *Ibid*, s 127.

164 See Statistics Canada, *Incomes from Owner-Occupied Housing for Working-Age and Retirement-Age Canadians, 1969 to 2006* by W Mark Brown & Amelie Lafrance (Ottawa: Statistics Canada, 2010). The study finds that the increase in implicit returns helped reduce the income gap between retirement-age and working-age households over the period. For example, before accounting for home equity, from 1969 to 2006 the relative income ratio of households aged 70 and older to the 40–49 age class and the 50–59 age class increased by 15 and 8 percentage points, respectively.

165 See generally AF Sheppard, "The Taxation of Imputed Income and the Rule in Sharkey v. Wernher" (1973) 11 Can Bar Rev 617–41; Li, Magee & Wilkie, *supra* note 89 at 96–100 (an overview of the comprehensive tax base) and at 119–21 (imputed income).

166 *ITA, supra* note 13, s 15.

167 *Ibid*, ss 12(4), 12(11).

168 *Ibid*, ss 91, 95.

169 Andrews & Sánchez, *supra* note 1.

170 See generally Statistics Canada, *User Guide: Canadian System of Macroeconomic Accounts: Chapter 5 Income and Expenditure Accounts*, catalogue no 13-606-G (Ottawa: Statistics Canada, 2016), online (pdf): *Statistics Canada* <https://www150.statcan.gc.ca/n1/en/pub/13-606-g/2016001/article/14620-eng.pdf?st=MeZmrw_B>.

Contributors

ABOUT THE EDITOR

Stephanie Ben-Ishai, a Distinguished Research Professor at Osgoode Hall Law School, is an internationally recognized expert on insolvency, corporate governance, and commercial law. Professor Ben-Ishai is the director and founder of the LLM in Finance Law at Osgoode Professional Development and the director of the Osgoode Business Clinic.

ABOUT THE CONTRIBUTORS

Simon Archer is a partner at Goldblatt Partners, co-director of the Comparative Research in Law and Political Economy Forum at Osgoode Hall Law School, and a fellow at King's College London. Mr. Archer has published and advises clients in the areas of pension funds, trust administration, labour law, insolvency, and corporate governance.

Gail Henderson is an associate professor and associate dean at Queen's University Faculty of Law, where she researches and teaches in the areas of corporate law, contracts, corporate governance, the regulation of financial institutions, and securities regulation. Professor Henderson is well known for her expertise in the areas of financial literacy education, protection of vulnerable financial consumers and low-income retail investors, and community economic development.

Jinyan Li is a professor at Osgoode Hall Law School, co-director of the Tax LLM program, and former interim dean of Osgoode Hall Law School. Professor Li is an internationally recognized expert in the areas of taxation of e-commerce, Canadian income tax law, and international taxation, among others.

Poonam Puri is internationally recognized as one of Canada's leading experts in corporate governance, corporate law, and securities law. She is a full professor at Osgoode Hall Law School and founder and director of the Osgoode Investor Protection Clinic as well as the Business Law LLM.

Lightning Source UK Ltd.
Milton Keynes UK
UKHW010740120921
390399UK00004B/91/J